P9-CEN-361

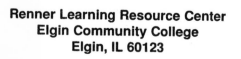

Renner Learning Resource Center
Elgin Community College
Elgin, IL 60123

Busting the Mob

Busting the Mob

United States v. Cosa Nostra

James B. Jacobs

with Christopher Panarella
and Jay Worthington

New York University Press

New York and London

RENNER LEARNING RESOURCE CENTER
ELGIN COMMUNITY COLLEGE
ELGIN, ILLINOIS 60123

NEW YORK UNIVERSITY PRESS
New York and London

© 1994 by New York University Press

All rights reserved

Library of Congress Cataloging-in-Publication Data

Jacobs, James B.
Busting the Mob : United States v. Cosa Nostra / James B. Jacobs,
with Christopher Panarella and Jay Worthington.
p.   cm.
Includes bibliographical references and index.
ISBN 0–8147–4195–9
1. Mafia trials—United States.   2. International Brotherhood of
Teamsters, Chauffeurs, Warehousemen, and Helpers of America—Trials,
litigation, etc.   3. Racketeering—United States.   4. Organized
crime—United States—Bibliography.   I. Panarella, Christopher.
II. Worthington, Jay.   III. Title.
KF224.M2J33   1994
345.73'02—dc20
[347.3052]   94–27470
                       CIP

345. 02
J 17

Book design by Kathleen Szawiola

New York University Press books are printed on acid-free paper, and their
binding materials are chosen for strength and durability.

Manufactured in the United States of America

10 9 8 7 6 5 4 3 2 1

From JBJ to Jan, Tom, and Sophi

From CP to Mom, Dad, Karen Ann, and Nick

From JW to my Mom and Dad

I'm not in the mood for the toys or games or kidding, no time. I'm not in the mood for clans. I'm not in the mood for gangs, I'm not in the mood for none of that stuff there. And this is gonna be a Cosa Nostra till I die. Be it an hour from now or be it tonight or a hundred years from now when I'm in jail. It's gonna be a Cosa Nostra.

—John Gotti
(intercepted conversation)

With instability at all levels and with continuing sociological change inevitable, if current law enforcement efforts are maintained in the next five to ten years, the mob is likely to be rendered totally unrecognizable from what it has been for the last sixty years.

—Ronald Goldstock, Director,
New York State Organized Crime Task Force

Contents

PART III

Preface

The purpose of this book is to put the extraordinary law enforcement attack on Cosa Nostra since the late 1970s "on the record" for present and future generations of students, scholars, and others interested in organized crime in America. Despite, or perhaps because of, the magnitude of this attack, few scholars have immersed themselves in the most important period of organized crime control in the history of the United States. Mining the trial transcripts, affidavits, depositions, legal briefs, and court opinions generated in the hundreds of mob trials that have taken place in the past fifteen years could consume the full-time energies of a platoon of researchers for years. This massive data base has a potential to reveal the history, structure, social organization, operations, conflicts, norms, economics, and politics of the mob. Moreover, it contains rich material on the organization and operation of federal law enforcement.

We intend this book to be a contribution to the contemporary history of organized-crime control in the late twentieth century.* We hope that it will

---

*The leading text on organized crime is Howard Abadinsky, *Organized Crime*, 2d ed. (Nelson-Hall, 1985). For the history of organized crime see Joseph Landesco, *Organized Crime in Chicago* (University of Chicago Press, 1968; originally published in 1929); Frederic Sondern, Jr., *Brotherhood of Evil: The Mafia* (Farrar, Straus, and Cudahy, 1959); Humbert Nelli, *The Business of Crime* (Oxford University Press, 1976); and Donald Cressey, *Theft of the Nation* (Harper and Row, 1969).

stimulate others to take advantage of the tremendous opportunities for research in this area. There are hundreds of cases and major investigations that have escaped the attention of scholars. Historians, sociologists, criminologists, lawyers, political scientists, and economists ought to bring their respective disciplines to bear on these data.

A word of caution—a history based upon court documents, even depositions and trial testimony, is a story written from "above." "The record" is constructed by the government through its witnesses, experts, and physical evidence. To be sure, some of the most important government witnesses are mobsters who chose to testify for the government in exchange for promises of protection and/or leniency. Their descriptions of Cosa Nostra's organization and operations provide the best "data" we have ever had on the secret society of organized crime. Nevertheless, their testimonies have been extracted through direct questioning by government prosecutors bent on persuading juries of a definite reality. We do not mean to imply that the prosecutors' view is false or inaccurate, only that it is constructed from a perspective that emphasizes Cosa Nostra's strength, power, wealth, ruthlessness, and organizational efficiency.

Part 1 provides a general overview of the law enforcement attack on Cosa Nostra since the late 1970s. It aims to provide the reader with a picture of what took place during the past fifteen years (1978–1993). It documents the number of investigations, prosecutions, and convictions, explains the legal tools and organizational strategies that the FBI and federal prosecutors used, and speculates on why the government's efforts came together at this point in history. This chapter does not purport to provide a comprehensive history of the massive law enforcement effort during the contemporary period; such a history would require a multivolume work. In our view, this book will have achieved its purpose if it makes a significant start on the formidable task of documenting what happened, how it happened, and why it happened. We do not attempt to *answer*, although we do address, the question of whether this unprecedented law enforcement attack on Cosa Nostra was "successful"—it is too soon to tell.

Part 2 consists of five chapters, each devoted to one of the following notorious organized crime cases—the Teamsters Local 560 case, the Pizza Connection case, the Commission case, the Teamsters International case, and the John Gotti case. Each of these cases was based upon months or years of investigation. Each has generated a mass of legal materials, including pretrial motions, affidavits, depositions, trial transcripts, appeals, and remedial-phase litigation. Each would justify a book-long case study in its own right; all except the Local 560 case have generated journalistic or true-crime type books.

Each chapter consists of an introductory essay and original source materials drawn from the indictment, trial, appeal, or other stages of the litigation. These primary source documents are included not only to provide information about the case but also to acquaint the reader with the diverse documents that constitute the public record. Such materials offer a wealth of opportunities for researchers at all levels. (In presenting these primary documents, we have taken the liberty of deleting nonessential material. Only where substantial portions of the original document have been deleted is the deletion indicated by asterisks.)

Admittedly, there is an element of arbitrariness in our selection of five cases. We could have selected many others that were extremely important for what they reveal about Cosa Nostra and the government's ability to investigate and prosecute organized crime. Nevertheless, while some people might have different nominees for inclusion in the "top five," we think anyone knowledgeable about organized crime would agree that our choices are reasonable.

Teamsters Local 560 for decades had been one of the most, if not the most, notoriously mob-controlled major union local in the United States. *United States v. Local 560*, a civil racketeering suit, marked the government's first effort to place a mobbed-up union under court-imposed trusteeship. The litigation has lasted a decade and, at the time of this writing, is still not complete. *United States v. Badalamenti* ("The Pizza Connection") deserves its place in our book and in American history, if for no other reason than that it was based on a massive worldwide investigation and involved a seventeen-month-long megatrial of twenty-two defendants. *United States v. Salerno* ("The Commission case") is extraordinary for its creativity and audacity in jointly prosecuting four Cosa Nostra crime-family bosses for conducting the affairs of "the commission," a kind of board of directors for the mob. The case demonstrated once and for all that the Cosa Nostra organized-crime families have for decades been joined together in a kind of loose federation that relegates to a commission of family bosses certain (if vague) authority to deal with interfamily disputes and other matters of common concern. *United States v. International Brotherhood of Teamsters* is the most ambitious labor racketeering suit ever filed. It charged Cosa Nostra members and Teamster officials with having entered into a "devil's pact" whereby organized crime would support the union's leadership in exchange for the leadership's grant of benefits and favors to organized crime. We chose *United States v. Gotti* for inclusion because the charismatic Gotti is the most notorious American mafioso of this generation. His success in defeating three previous prosecutions had created an aura of invincibility that was magnified by the publicity he attracted in the national newspapers and news magazines.

Part 3 consists of a post-1980 bibliography of organized-crime books, articles, and prosecutions. We hope that the availability of this bibliography, especially the case citations, will encourage future research. It is surprising and unfortunate that so few criminologists and criminal law scholars are significantly involved in studying organized crime. If this bibliography and this book encourage just a few more, our efforts will have been rewarded.

Acknowledgments

The roots of this book lie in my mid-1980s collaboration with the New York State Organized Crime Task Force (OCTF) on an investigation of corruption and racketeering in the New York City construction industry (see *Corruption and Racketeering in the New York City Construction Industry,* New York University Press, 1990). I owe a great debt of gratitude to my colleagues on that project for educating me concerning organized crime; thus, I wish to acknowledge Joe DeLuca, Ron Goldstock, Wilda Hess, Marty Marcus, Robbie Mass, and Toby Thacher.

Originally, my colleague, Ronald Noble, was to have joined me on this book. Indeed, he did a good deal of spade work on the Gotti chapter and was ably assisted by Alex Gendzier. But his participation ended when he became assistant secretary of the treasury in charge of law enforcement. The Clinton administration's gain was my loss.

I have been extremely fortunate to have had the assistance of Christopher Panarella and Jay Worthington. Over seventeen years as a faculty member at Cornell and New York University, I have had many outstanding research assistants. However, none of them was more talented or hard working than were Chris and Jay. They have functioned as my colleagues on this project and I'm proud to recognize them as coauthors.

The three of us are grateful to Steve Bennett, John Gleeson, Ron Goldstock, Susan Jennick, Marty Marcus, John Savarese, Edward Stier, and Robert Stewart for interviews and for reading parts of the (and, in Stewart's case, the entire) manuscript. We are indebted to John Sexton, dean of the New York University Law School, and to the Law School's Max and Filomen D'Agostino Greenberg Research Fund for encouraging and supporting the research. We also want to thank my secretary, Elizabeth Reece, who has been an enormous help all along the way.

James B. Jacobs
New York University

PART I

1

Introduction

For most of the twentieth century, what has been called the "Mafia," "Cosa Nostra," or simply "organized crime" seemed as inevitable as increased taxes. Some Mafia chieftains even attained widespread public notoriety and were treated like folk heroes in their neighborhoods, cities, and beyond. People who understood power and "the way things worked" in New York and other large cities recognized organized crime as a key player in politics, vice, and legitimate industry ranging from shipping and trucking to garbage disposal and the garment trade.

Despite, or perhaps because of, its power and pervasiveness, with a few notable exceptions Cosa Nostra faced relatively little opposition from law enforcement. Local police forces did not have the resources, strategies, or tools to engage in long-term investigations of secret societies that carefully covered their tracks and insulated their leaders from scrutiny through hierarchical organization and a code of silence. Sometimes local law enforcement personnel, as well as prosecutors and judges, were dissuaded from organized-crime control initiatives by potentially adverse political or even professional consequences; sometimes they were just bribed. Remarkably, until well into the 1960s the FBI, under the leadership of J. Edgar Hoover, disputed the very existence of an American Mafia.[1]

Congressional attention to organized crime dates back to the Kefauver

Committee hearings in 1951 and the McClellan Committee hearings in 1957. The Department of Justice began to focus on organized crime during Robert Kennedy's tenure as attorney general in the early 1960s. He sponsored antiracketeering legislation in the early 1960s. By the end of the decade Congress had passed the Organized Crime Control Act; Title III provided a comprehensive regimen for electronic surveillance by federal, state, and local police. After Hoover's departure from the FBI in 1972, that agency began to devote significant resources to organized-crime control. Various successes can be identified throughout the 1960s and 1970s,[2] but there can be no mistaking the proliferation of achievements beginning in the late 1970s.

From approximately 1978, the federal government mounted an extraordinary effort to eradicate Cosa Nostra. Utilizing extensive electronic surveillance, undercover government agents, and mob turncoats, the FBI, the federal Organized Crime Strike Forces, and the United States attorneys' offices initiated a steady stream of intensive investigations and produced a regular flow of Cosa Nostra prosecutions throughout the country. The federal effort was supplemented by more limited, but not inconsequential, efforts by state and local investigative and prosecutorial agencies. Joint task forces involving federal, state, and local agencies became routine. No other period in American history comes close in terms of the number of investigations and prosecutions. Ultimately, whether this effort will prove sufficient to destroy Cosa Nostra or whether, phoenixlike, organized crime will rise from the ashes, remains to be seen. This introductory chapter seeks to place the government's organized-crime control efforts in perspective by examining what was accomplished, how, and why, and with what likely consequences for the future.

The Scope of the Government's Attack on Cosa Nostra

There is no exact figure on how many criminal and civil cases were brought by the federal government (much less state and local prosecutors) against organized crime in the 1980s. However, in 1988, FBI Director William Sessions reported to the Senate Subcommittee on Investigations that since 1981 nineteen bosses, thirteen underbosses, and forty-three capos (crew chiefs) had been convicted.[3] Another witness, David Williams, director of the GAO's Office of Special Investigations, stated that between 1983 and 1986, there had been twenty-five hundred indictments of Cosa Nostra members and associates.[4]

The magnitude of the government's attack on Cosa Nostra is nothing short of incredible. There were major prosecutions in every city where organized-crime families have been identified. The following is a list of Cosa Nostra bosses who were convicted between 1981 and 1992. (The list shows that several Cosa Nostra families have had more than one boss convicted during this period.)

1. Funzi Tieri—Genovese family in New York City
2. Anthony Salerno—Genovese family
3. Anthony Corallo—Lucchese family in New York City
4. Carmine Persico—Colombo family in New York City
5. Philip Rastelli—Bonanno family in New York City
6. Carlos Marcello—New Orleans family
7. Eugene Smaldone—Denver family
8. Joseph Aiuppa—Chicago family
9. Nick Civella—Kansas City family
10. Carl Civella—Kansas City family
11. Dominick Brooklier—Los Angeles family
12. Frank Balistrieri—Boston family
13. Gennaro Anguilo—Boston family
14. Russel Buffalino—Pittston, Pa., family
15. Nicodemo Scarfo—Philadelphia family
16. James Licavoli—Cleveland family
17. Michael Trupiano—St. Louis family
18. Sam Russotti—Buffalo crime family
19. John Gotti—Gambino family in New York City
20. Raymond Patriarca—Patriarca family in Providence, R.I.
21. Vittorio Amuso—Lucchese family
22. Vicorio Orena—Colombo family
23. John Riggi—DeCavalcante family in New Jersey

These federal cases, supplemented by some state and local prosecutions, systematically decimated whole organized-crime families. In New York City, the leadership and many soldiers of each of the five Cosa Nostra crime families (Bonanno, Colombo, Gambino, Genovese, Lucchese) were prosecuted in separate RICO suits on the theory that the defendants conducted the affairs of an "enterprise" (their respective crime families) through a pattern of racketeering activity (their many rackets, extortions, and crimes of violence). In *United States v. Salerno*, the heads of four of the five families, and several other key figures, were prosecuted together for constituting and operating a "commission," in effect a regional and perhaps national board of directors for the mob.[5]

Some of the investigations and prosecutions had international dimensions, especially linking the investigatory agencies and efforts of the United States and Italy. The most famous of these cases was *United States v. Badalamenti*, in which a cooperative effort of American, Italian, Swiss, Brazilian, and Spanish law enforcement agencies closed down a massive international drug trafficking and money laundering conspiracy involving American Cosa Nostra and Sicilian Mafia groups.

The government not only put Cosa Nostra bosses, capos, soldiers, and associates in prison, but it also attacked mob-controlled enterprises, such as labor unions, construction companies, restaurants, and mobbed-up industries. Perhaps the modern era in the government's anti-organized-crime war dates to the FBI's massive UNIRAC investigation of the International Longshoremen's Association in the late 1970s. This labor racketeering investigation, the subject of special Senate hearings in 1981, resulted in the conviction of 130 businessmen, union officials, and Cosa Nostra members, including Anthony Scotto.[6]

In 1982, the Newark Strike Force made history by filing the first civil RICO suit against a labor union, Local 560, the largest Teamsters local in the state and a union that had been dominated by organized crime through the Provenzano brothers and the Genovese crime family since the 1950s; the suit resulted in a court-imposed trusteeship, which gave the trustee extensive powers to run the union until the racketeering element could be purged and fair elections held. Six years later, the United States Attorney's Office in the Southern District of New York filed a civil RICO suit against the International Brotherhood of Teamsters (IBT), its general executive board, and the board's incumbents; under a consent decree that settled the case, the IBT agreed to a three-person trusteeship whose goals were to purge corruption and racketeering and to supervise a direct election of the president and general executive board. In New York City, as a result of civil RICO suits, court-appointed trustees and monitors were appointed in a half-dozen RICO cases involving historically mobbed-up unions.[7]

The government also moved against mob-dominated businesses. New York City's largest concrete contractor, jointly owned and operated by several organized-crime families, was put out of business. As part of a consent decree between the United States Department of Justice and the Genovese crime family, the Fulton Fish Market was placed under the supervision of a court-appointed trustee.[8] Similarly, mob control of the garment industry was addressed by a plea bargain between the Manhattan District Attorney's Office and the Gambino brothers, whereby they promised to sell off a substantial portion of their garment-industry trucking interests and pay a $12 million fine; their trucking companies (which were also defendants) agreed to withdraw from an industry they had dominated for decades.[9] The Brooklyn Strike Force's investigation of the Bonanno family's 25-year domination of New York City's moving and storage industry led to convictions of the family's boss, Phillip Rastelli, and fourteen other defendants, including the entire leadership of Teamster Local 814, and a number of executives of moving and storage firms.[10]

There were similar victories over mob-controlled enterprises outside of the New York City metropolitan area. In 1981, Eugene Boffa, owner of a nationwide labor leasing business, was convicted and sentenced to twenty years' imprisonment and ordered to forfeit assets worth $250,000 as well as his interest in the leasing corporations.[11] The "roofers" case in Philadelphia resulted in a notoriously mobbed-up union being placed in trusteeship.[12]

The prosecutorial attack on Cosa Nostra was supplemented and supported by high-visibility government hearings and inquiries that kept the spotlight on organized crime throughout the decade. From 1983 to 1987, the President's Commission on Organized Crime held public hearings and issued twelve reports; among other things, it laid out the structure of the organized-crime families, documented their extensive involvement in drug trafficking and labor racketeering, and recommended that the Department of Justice bring a civil RICO suit against the International Brotherhood of Teamsters. The United States Senate's Permanent Subcommittee on Investigations, under the leadership of Senator Sam Nunn, held dramatic hearings on the role of Cosa Nostra in legitimate industry and illicit rackets.[13] The committee called hundreds of witnesses, including former Sicilian Mafia boss Tomasso Buscetta and ex–Cosa Nostra members Vincent Cafaro and Angelo Lonardo. They provided testimony on the history, customs, and operations of Cosa Nostra.

The unprecedented law enforcement attack and the intensive government attention paid to Cosa Nostra generated serious instability within the families. By the end of the decade, the inconceivable had become commonplace: Cosa Nostra members, even leaders, were agreeing to become cooperating government witnesses in exchange for leniency and admission into the Witness Security Program. A mob defector of the stature of Salvatore ("Sammy the Bull") Gravano, underboss of the Gambino crime family, would have seemed unimaginable just a decade earlier. Defections added to problems of leadership succession and led to many intra- and interfamily assassinations. By the early 1990s, the accumulated prosecutions had been so extensive and the internal deterioration of the families so severe that some law enforcement experts began to predict the end of Cosa Nostra.

How the Government Succeeded

The government's success can be attributed to powerful legal tools, personnel and structural changes in the Department of Justice and the FBI, the initiative of presidents and attorney generals during the 1980s, and the internal deterioration of Cosa Nostra itself.

Legal Weaponry

The most important legal weapons deployed in the government's attack on organized crime have been electronic surveillance authority, the Racketeer Influenced and Corrupt Organizations Act (RICO), and the Witness Security Program.

Electronic Surveillance

Title III of the Omnibus Crime Control and Safe Streets Act of 1968 provided comprehensive authority for electronic surveillance by federal, state, and local law enforcement agencies.[14] The two main justifications for the act, according to its proponents, were the necessity for electronic surveillance in national security and in organized-crime investigations.[15] Title III brought federal, state, and local wire tapping within the framework of a comprehensive statute. It permits electronic eavesdropping only with a judicial warrant issued upon a showing of probable cause and of necessity due to the absence of alternative means. The interception is limited to thirty days, although extensions can be obtained. The law requires "minimization"; the eavesdropping device must be turned off if, after a brief period of listening, it is apparent that the intercepted conversation is not relevant to the subject of the warrant. Amendments in 1986 strengthened the law and, for the first time, authorized "roving surveillance" to cover sophisticated criminals who use a number of different phones or sites to conduct business.[16]

The sheer number of federal electronic eavesdropping orders increased over the course of the 1980s, peaking in 1984 and then jumping to an apparently new plateau in the 1990s.[17] The absolute number of authorizations, however, is only a rough indicator of surveillance activity, because some of the interceptions lasted many months, covered multiple phones and locations, and resulted in the seizure of thousands of conversations.

Year	Number of Court Authorized Electronic Surveillance Orders
1978	570
1979	553
1980	564
1981	589
1982	578
1983	648
1984	801
1985	784
1986	754
1987	673
1988	749
1989	763
1990	897
1991	823
1992	991

Electronic eavesdropping figured prominently in almost every organized-crime prosecution of the modern period; some prosecutions were based almost entirely on intercepted conversations. The FBI and state and local agencies utilized both telephone intercepts and hidden microphones in cars, homes, restaurants, and social clubs. In some cases, the FBI was able to pick up conversations on the streets with high-power surveillance microphones. By the end of the decade, there was no place where Cosa Nostra members could converse without concern for government eavesdroppers.

Some of the major organized-crime investigations involved thousands of conversations intercepted over months. In the Pizza Connection case, actors were hired to read to the jury from hundreds of transcripts of intercepted conversations. Likewise in *United States v. Gotti*, the government introduced extremely inculpatory conversations between Gotti and his subordinates that had taken place in the Ravenite Social Club and in an apartment above the club.

RICO

The Racketeer Influenced and Corrupt Organizations (RICO) Act, part of the 1970 Organized Crime Control Act, created the most important substantive and procedural law tool in the history of organized-crime control. A brainchild of Professor G. Robert Blakey (who worked on Senator McClellan's organized-crime hearings in the late 1950s and later with the Organized Crime and Racketeering Section of the Department of Justice when Robert F. Kennedy was attorney general) brought into existence a new kind of law punishing "enterprise criminality." RICO was explicitly aimed at organized crime, especially its infiltration of legitimate business.[18] It took investigators and prosecutors some years to become fully familiar and comfortable with the new law; after 1980, almost every major organized-crime case was brought as a RICO prosecution.[19] Moreover, the concept of enterprise racketeering changed the way organized-crime investigations were conceived and executed. The FBI began to think in terms of gathering evidence and obtaining indictments against entire "enterprises" like each organized crime family and the Cosa Nostra commission.

RICO makes it a crime to infiltrate, participate in, or conduct the affairs of an enterprise through a pattern of racketeering activity. An enterprise is defined as any "association in fact" comprised of two or more people. In *United States v. Turkette*,[20] the United States Supreme Court held that an enterprise could be a wholly illegitimate group. This provided a green light for prosecuting individuals for participating in criminal syndicates like Cosa Nostra crews, families, and the commission.

Having to prove an "association in fact" in an organized-crime case provides prosecutors with an excellent opportunity to introduce extensive evidence, complete with charts and tables of organization, depicting the structure of an organized-crime family. In the Commission case and other organized-crime prosecutions, the government has been able to introduce testimony about the history of organized crime in order to establish the enterprise's existence over time. Angelo Lonardo's (former underboss of the Cleveland crime family) lengthy account of the history of the Cosa Nostra commission provided some of the most valuable evidence in the Commission case.[21] In the Pizza Connection case, the prosecution used Tomasso Buscetta, a former leader of the Sicilian Mafia, to lay out the history and structure of both the Sicilian Mafia and the American Cosa Nostra.

RICO requires the government to prove that a defendant conducted or participated in the affairs of an enterprise through "a pattern of racketeering activity," defined as at least two racketeering acts committed within ten years of one another. A racketeering act (also called a "RICO predicate") is defined as virtually any serious federal felony and most state felonies. Thus, in a RICO trial, the defendant may find himself charged with all sorts of different crimes, allegedly committed at different times and places. The prosecution need only prove that the defendant committed all these crimes in furtherance of the defendant's participation in conducting the affairs of the same enterprise. Critics complain that this puts a defendant at an enormous disadvantage because the judge or jury can hardly help concluding that he must be guilty of at least some of the diverse offenses being alleged, especially given his connection to a racketeering enterprise like Cosa Nostra. Proponents of RICO argue that it simply allows the government to present a complete picture of what the defendant was doing and why—instead of the artificially fragmented picture that traditional criminal law demands.

From the prosecutor's standpoint, another of RICO's advantageous procedural features is its ability to join all the members of a criminal enterprise in a single trial, even though they are not all charged with the same predicate offenses. For example, in a single trial some defendants may be charged with participating in the affairs of the enterprise (e.g., a Cosa Nostra crime family) through murders and loansharking, while others are charged with participating in the affairs of the same enterprise through drug trafficking. Moreover, where two or more defendants are charged with racketeering related to the same enterprise, a RICO conspiracy count can also be brought. The consequence is the potential for "megatrials" (like the Pizza Connection case) in which all the members and associates of a crime syndicate are tried together because two predicate offenses are alleged against each one of them. The advantages to the government are obvious; it can pour into the trial masses of evidence about murders, drug deals, extortions, labor racketeering, and so forth, allegedly committed by each defendant. The prosecution can present a complete picture of a large-scale, ongoing, organized-crime group engaged in diverse rackets and episodic explosions of violence. At the end of the trial, the jurors will be admonished not to allow evidence against one defendant to affect their judgment about the guilt of the others, but it is hard to believe that "guilt by association" is not a danger in such megatrials.

RICO also provides for very severe sentences: twenty years on each RICO violation and twenty years more for a RICO conspiracy. The defendant can also be sentenced for each of the predicate offenses. This sentencing structure made Cosa Nostra bosses in *United States v. Salerno*, the Commission case, liable to three hundred years' imprisonment for taking kickbacks from concrete contractors, although their actual sentences were a mere one hundred years each. In addition, RICO provides for severe fines ($250,000, or twice the loss/gain) and for the forfeiture of property (broadly defined to include businesses, offices, jobs, personal property, cars, boats, planes, and real estate) that has been acquired with the proceeds of racketeering activity. While it is by no means clear that Cosa Nostra bosses or families can actually be "bankrupted," the combination of forfeitures, fines and million-dollar lawyers' fees must cause problems for organized crime's financial base and cash flow.

In addition to its criminal provisions, RICO contains powerful civil provisions. One of them allows RICO victims to sue for treble damages but, for obvious reasons, private parties have not opted to sue the mob. However, another provision has proven extremely important: it gives the federal government the right to sue civilly for wide-ranging injunctive remedies in order to prevent a RICO offense from continuing.[22] In some labor racketeering cases, like the Teamsters Local 560 case and the Teamsters International case, government prosecutors elected to use civil rather than criminal RICO. Proceeding civilly, the government first has to prove that the defendant union officials and mob figures have been participating in the affairs of the union enterprise. Then it must show the pattern of racketeering activity by entering into evidence the defendants' past criminal convictions (if related to labor racketeering), or by proving that the defendants had committed or conspired to commit various labor racketeering offenses, including soliciting bribes, extortion, embezzlement of pension and welfare funds, and multifarious frauds. In some cases, the defendants' liability has been predicated on their aiding and abetting labor racketeering and other crimes by failing to take any action against officials whom they knew to be victimizing their unions.

Civil RICO suits are governed by civil procedure, which includes the opportunity for wide-ranging pretrial discovery. The government has the right to take affidavits from key defendants and defense witnesses and to look through masses of union or company books and records. Perhaps to avoid being exposed in this way, or simply to minimize their exposure at and after trial, union leaders have settled a number of civil RICO labor racketeering cases, like the Teamsters International case, resulting in complex court-approved consent agreements.

Civil RICO's focus is future oriented and preventative, not punitive. In effect, the judge can issue whatever injunction or other remedial orders are necessary to prevent further racketeering by the defendants. In the RICO labor racketeering cases, the government has sought to have courts appoint trustees to purge mobbed-up unions of the essential conditions that caused the racketeering problem and, in furtherance of that end, to help affected unions make the transition from a mob-dominated dictatorship to a democratic organization.

The RICO union trusteeships represent an evolutionary step in society's ability to cope with organized crime. In contrast to a successful prosecution that ends when the defendant is sent to prison, the court can put a trustee in place for months or years to purge mob influence, root and branch. During the remedial phase, some trustees have vigorously continued to investigate mob influence in the unions that they supervise and have removed business agents and other officials tainted by organized-crime ties (even though they haven't been convicted of a crime). Other trustees have been less aggressive.

The success of court-appointed or court-approved trustees in purging organized crime from traditionally mob-dominated unions is mixed. In these cases, the trustee faces enormous problems in dealing with a deeply entrenched power structure that yields its power and privileges reluctantly, if at all. Typically, and the Teamsters Local 560 case is an excellent example, the government and the trustee find themselves repeatedly back in court seeking further relief against obstructionist union tactics or defending themselves against harassing litigation brought by the racketeer element within the union. The results are not yet in on whether the trusteeships can break organized crime's hold on mobbed-up unions, but they are the best mechanism yet devised.

The Witness Security Program

Historically, the unwillingness of victims and other witnesses to testify posed a major impediment to successful organized-crime prosecutions. Fear of retribution was well founded since there were many examples of potential witnesses' having been murdered or beaten. The Witness Security Program, authorized in the Organized Crime Control Act of 1970, sought to guarantee the safety of witnesses who agreed to testify for the government in organized-crime cases.[23]

Run by the United States Marshalls Service, the Witness Security Program applies to witnesses before, during, and after trial. It protects them during their prison terms and, if they are released provides them with new identities, jobs, and homes in new locations. This protection makes it feasible to testify against Cosa Nostra and survive.

The Witness Security Program has encouraged, or at least facilitated, a number of major defections from organized crime. Up until the trials of the 1980s, no member of organized crime, with the single exception of Joseph Valachi in 1963, had ever broken the code of *"omerta"* and gone public, much less testified at a criminal trial against fellow Cosa Nostra members. In the 1980s, facing the prospect of long prison terms, a number of mob figures "flipped," agreeing to testify for the government in exchange for concessions in the charges against them and admission into the Witness Security Program.[24]

One of the first Cosa Nostra members to flip was Aladema ("Jimmy the

Weasel") Fratianno, acting boss of the Los Angeles crime family; he testified for the government in the first RICO prosecution against a Cosa Nostra boss *(United States v. Tieri)* and later in the Commission case.[25] Shortly thereafter, Angelo Lonardo, the one-time underboss of the Cleveland crime family, became a government witness, and also provided important testimony in the Commission case. The prosecution in the Pizza Connection case was assisted by the testimony of Tomasso Buscetta, a former high-ranking member of the Sicilian Mafia who agreed to testify for the Italian and American governments after his two sons and son-in-law were murdered by a rival Sicilian Mafia faction. Probably the most notorious Cosa Nostra member turned government witness is Sammy Gravano, Gambino crime family underboss and John Gotti's long-time comrade. As part of his plea agreement with the government, Gravano admitted to having carried out nineteen gangland murders on orders from Gotti and other superiors.

Structural Changes in the Department of Justice

The Organized Crime and Racketeering section of the Department of Justice was formed in 1954–55. Robert Kennedy (who had been counsel to the McClellan Committee in the late 1950s) reactivated this unit when he became attorney general in 1961, making organized crime a top priority. In 1967, the Justice Department formed the Organized Crime Strike Forces, comprised of prosecutors and representatives of the federal investigative agencies in fourteen cities. Over the years they came to be led by seasoned federal prosecutors. The strike forces were separate and distinct from the United States attorneys; their attorneys in charge of each field unit reported to the head of the Organized Crime and Racketeering Section of the Justice Department. They concentrated more attention and resources on organized crime than ever before. According to their supporters, the strike force lawyers stayed in their jobs longer than the typical United States attorneys and assistant United States attorneys, developed more specialized expertise in organized-crime control, and were more successful in gaining the confidence of the FBI and other law enforcement agencies.

Nevertheless, up to the late 1970s and early 1980s, the strike forces were criticized for their inability to define organized crime, for pursuing low-priority targets, and for lacking the authority to control the activities of the investigative agencies upon which they depended.[26] Soon, however, the strike forces began functioning more effectively, and the FBI significantly elevated its commitment to organized-crime control.[27] The payoff soon became evident as success followed success. For example, UNIRAC (the investigation of racketeering in the Longshoremen's Association) started as a Miami Strike Force project and spread to New York City and ultimately up and down the East Coast. Operation BRILAB was directed by the New Orleans Strike Force and involved strike force attorneys in New Orleans, Los Angeles, and Washington, D.C. It resulted in the conviction of Cosa Nostra boss Carlos Marcello and numerous other organized-crime members and associates.[28]

From the outset, the strike forces were anathema to many of the United States attorneys in whose jurisdictions they operated. Historically, the United States attorneys decided how prosecutorial resources were deployed and who would prosecute what cases. Many United States attorneys, therefore, objected to the strike forces' independence. When Richard Thornburgh, a former United States attorney in Pittsburgh and a strike force opponent, became attorney general in 1988, he moved immediately to disband the strike forces and transfer their mission and personnel back to the United States attorneys. Although there was some opposition in Congress, which held hearings on the issue, the strike forces were disbanded in 1989.[29] Many experienced strike force prosecutors resigned from the Justice Department. Whether this will mean a diminution of effort against Cosa Nostra or a more efficient deployment of resources remains to be seen.

Developments in the FBI

One reason for the success of the FBI's organized-crime program was its ability to develop an intelligence base on the structure, makeup, and activities of Cosa Nostra over many years and to disseminate intelligence from one field division to another. This was facilitated by the development and implementation of the Organized Crime Information System (OCIS), a computer network (initiated in 1980) designed to collect, evaluate, store, and disseminate organized-crime intelligence information.

Given the concentration of Cosa Nostra families and members in New York City, the New York City FBI office was, not surprisingly, the Bureau office most involved in organized-crime investigations throughout the 1980s. In 1979, that office's coordinator of organized-crime investigations, James Kossler attended G. Robert Blakey's summer institute on organized crime at Cornell University. Blakey explained how RICO could be used to attack Cosa Nostra and argued for the targeting of organized criminal *enterprises.* Kossler, maintaining close touch with Blakey, redeployed resources on New York City's five Cosa Nostra crime families. Under operation GENUS teams of FBI agents were assigned to develop intelligence on each family. Each team's job was to develop a table of organization for each family, identify all the members and their status in the organization, and then determine which rackets and industries the family was involved in. After that, the prosecutions would fall into place.[30] By the mid-1980s, the New York FBI office had 165 agents assigned to the organized-crime division.

FBI agent Joseph Pistone's penetration of the Bonanno family in New York City from 1976 to 1982 constitutes one of the most extraordinary chapters in the modern history of law enforcement's attack on Cosa Nostra. No law enforcement agent had ever before been able, through disguise and guile, to get so deeply inside a Cosa Nostra family. Indeed, that the FBI would even attempt to place a secret agent in the ranks of organized crime reveals how commited, confident, and creative the agency had become.[31] Pistone hung out at the bars and restaurants frequented by organized-crime members and associates. Eventually, he was noticed by organized-crime figures, whom he cut in on a number of phony schemes. In the course of some of these "crimes," he was able to bring other agents into contact with members of Cosa Nostra. Pistone's undercover operation lasted six years; just before he had to surface and break his cover, he was promised induction into the Bonanno family. Pistone provided a mountain of intelligence material and served as a witness at a number of key Cosa Nostra trials, especially the Commission case.[32] No doubt, this infiltration was a blow to Cosa Nostra morale, raising doubts about how many of its secrets had been revealed.

Cooperation among Federal, State, and Local Law Enforcement Agencies

Historically, effective organized-crime control was severely hampered by bitter rivalry among the federal, state, and local law enforcement agencies. Each agency distrusted the others, even to the point of charging that rival agencies were neither secure nor trustworthy; frequently, each felt that the others were trying to seize credit unfairly for successes. The history of American law enforcement, especially in combatting organized crime, is replete with lost opportunities due to inability or unwillingness to reach interagency agreements.

Beginning in the 1970s, joint federal, state, and local task forces began to make significant headway in overcoming agency parochialism. In 1970, the National Council on Organized Crime was established to formulate a strategy to eliminate organized crime. While the council failed to formulate a national strategy, it mobilized attention to the problem of interagency relations. The federal strike forces made major strides in coordinating the efforts of federal prosecutorial and investigative agencies and also, by promising to cover costs of joint investigations, were very successful in involving state and local agencies in their operations. In 1976 the National Organized Crime Planning Council was formed to facilitate planning and coordination between the strike forces and the federal law enforcement agencies. In 1980, the Executive Working Group for Federal-State-Local Prosecutorial Relations was initiated. It provided the first formal liaison between the Department of Justice, the National District Attorneys Association, and the National Association of Attorneys General for the purpose of improving relations between the federal, state, and local prosecutors.

These formal institutional mechanisms of cooperation were supplemented and reinforced by many informal multiagency working arrangements. In New York City, FBI Agent-in-Charge James Kossler worked out an immensely valuable agreement with Deputy New York City Police Commissioner Patrick Murphy whereby the Bureau and the New York Police Department agreed to share resources, intelligence, and coordinate their investigations. The agreement married the Bureau's substantial budgetary resources and sophisticated intelligence apparatus with the NYPD's street-level intelligence and highly developed informant system. NYPD detectives were able to confirm FBI intelligence hypotheses and provide leads for identifying crime family members, their roles, and criminal activities.

The organized-crime squad in the New York City Police Department began to cooperate much more harmoniously and effectively with its FBI counterparts and with state agencies like the New York State Organized Crime Task Force. This kind of interagency cooperation was instrumental in initiatives like the investigation of the Fulton Fish Market, the massive investigation of the Pizza Connection, and the preparation of the Gotti prosecution.

The practice of "cross-designating" prosecutors from one agency to prosecute on behalf of another agency also proved to be a major breakthrough in interagency cooperation. This practice allows state and local prosecutors who have worked on an investigation to follow the case if it becomes federal and vice versa. For example, after Paul Castellano was assassinated, Pat Ryan of the Manhattan District Attorney's Office was cross-designated as an assistant United States attorney in the Southern District and Walter Mack from the Southern District United States attorney's office was cross-designated as an assistant district attorney in the Manhattan District Attorney's Office. This proved to be an enormously valuable mechanism for investigating the Gotti case that was eventually turned over to the United States attorney for the Eastern District of New York.

Why the 1980s?

Why did the government's attack on Cosa Nostra reach its zenith in the 1980s? Perhaps the 1980s' successes were simply the culmination of an organized-crime control process that began in the 1950s and steadily gained strength and momentum thereafter. Perhaps the 1951 Senate hearings organized by Senator Kefauver, the 1957 revelation of a secret meeting of organized-crime bosses from all over the country at Apalachin, New York, Kennedy's tenure as attorney general, the Valachi revelations, and the passage of organized-crime control legislation provided the foundation for a gradual, sometimes halting, process that led to the investigations and prosecutions of the 1980s. This "explanation," however, does not focus on key decisions or decisionmakers or major shifts in formal policy. It interprets organized-crime control initiatives as having "evolved" or "matured," perhaps following their own internal logic or time clock. Those who favor such an interpretation tend to speak in terms like the following: "It took ten years for federal prosecutors to learn to use RICO."

We believe that the evidence will ultimately support a different hypothesis, albeit one that could be reconciled with the evolutionary hypothesis. While maturation, evolution, and internal logic are certainly part of the story, there were also key decisions and decisionmakers who consciously chose to make organized-crime control an important priority despite relentless pressure to accord preference to other crime problems.

The attitude, politics, priorities, and policies of presidents and the attorneys general have surely had an impact on federal organized crime-control initiatives. The president can have a positive impact via his choice of attorney general and FBI director, his support for enhanced crime-control budgets, and his "jawboning" on organized-crime themes. On the other hand, a president can have a negative impact if, for political or other reasons, he chooses an attorney general disinclined to pursue organized crime or makes it clear to the attorney general and other subordinates either that attacking organized crime is not a priority or that some other goals are higher priorities.

Likewise, the attorney general can have great impact on organized-crime control by lobbying or not lobbying for legislation (e.g., RICO, electronic eavesdropping, Witness Security Program) and by allocating or not allocating substantial resources to the Organized Crime and Racketeering Section. While the United States attorneys have some independence from the central Justice Department, there is little doubt that the attorney general has the power to establish priorities through persuasion and manipulation of resources.

Robert F. Kennedy, for example, was highly committed to a full-scale attack on organized crime. He had played a key role during the McClellan hearings and was extremely well informed about the Mafia, especially its role in the Teamsters and other labor unions. Prosecuting Jimmy Hoffa was a top priority of his administration. Furthermore, Kennedy quadrupled the Organized Crime Section and encouraged it to move aggressively against organized crime.[33] By contrast his successor, Ramsey Clark, had little interest in organized-crime control and opposed electronic surveillance.

The Reagan administration seems to have been the most aggressively anti–organized crime since the Kennedy administration. In one speech on the subject, Reagan announced his commitment to attacking organized crime and described a special cabinet session he called to address the problem on September 30, 1982.

Attorney General William French Smith . . . talked not only about the steady rise in street crime over two decades but the growth and increasing sophistication of regional and national networks of professional criminals. He described the alarmingly success-ful attempts of these networks to corrupt legitimate business, unions, political figures and members of law enforcement and government agencies. He made it clear that career criminals had not only grown bolder in their activities but were continuing to extend their reach ever deeper into law-abiding sectors of our society, buying and bribing their way to the kind of official protection and respectability that would permit them to operate their criminal undergrounds with impunity.[34]

According to Reagan, this special cabinet decided that the Justice Department would "more vigorously prosecut[e] the mob, including use of the RICO statute to confiscate more of its financial assets . . . and [forge] closer co-operation with state and local law enforcement agencies, including new training programs at a federal facility in Glynco, Georgia, that would focus on the mob's new and more sophisticated tactics." Moreover, Reagan appointed a presidential commission to determine what else might be done to further the anti–organized-crime effort.

Two General Accounting Office (GAO) reports, in 1976 and 1981, criticized the Ford and Carter administrations' Justice Departments' organized-crime control effort for failing to concentrate on Cosa Nostra and for failing to engage in strategic planning and cooperative ventures with other agencies.[35] There were no similar GAO criticisms thereafter, which lends support to the hypothesis that after 1981, the Justice Department got its organized-crime-control program on track.

Policy is also made by each of the ninety-two United States attorneys, who have historically enjoyed a great deal of independence in running their offices. In 1983, Rudolph Giuliani left a top position in the Department of Justice to become United States attorney for the Southern District of New York.[36] Ultimately, it was the Southern District United States Attorney's Office, under Giuliani, that brought the Commission case, four family RICO cases, the Pizza Connection case, and the Teamsters International case as well as many others. Whatever debate there might be about the impact of presidents and attorneys general in making organized crime a higher priority, there is no doubt about Giuliani's importance.

The FBI's priorities were also crucial to the history of organized-crime control. Clearly, Hoover was not interested in taking on Cosa Nostra. However, at least one, perhaps all, of his successors must have seen an attack on organized crime as consistent with and even central to the agency's mission.[37] The investigations that took place from the late 1970s onward could not have occurred without the strong support of the FBI directors. Moreover, the priorities and decisions of other FBI officials, especially in New York City, are sure to figure prominently when the full history of this law enforcement effort is finally written.

Internal Weakening of Cosa Nostra

Ronald Goldstock, long-time director of the New York State Organized Crime Task Force, echoing the thesis of mob-boss-turned-author Joe Bonanno,[38] has argued that Cosa Nostra has been weakened as much by internal forces as by external forces.[39] In Goldstock's opinion, the modern generation of Cosa Nostra leaders has different values from its predecessors. Honor, respect, and family have given way to greed and the fast buck. Moreover, Goldstock argues that with the demise of "Little Italies" around the United States, the mob lost its recruitment base and did not, perhaps could not, adequately replenish itself with young members. He concludes that Cosa Nostra became less competent at the very time when law enforcement was becoming more competent.

Goldstock's thesis deserves serious consideration because of its plausibility and the author's expertise. All organizations experience change resulting from leadership transitions, alterations in environment, and oscillations in the economy. Some changes are merely deviations from long-term patterns and others permanent changes in goals, priorities, strategies, and culture. Goldstock believes cultural change has diminished organized crime's capacity to carry out its goals and strategies effectively. The strongest evidence in favor of Goldstock's thesis is the apparent breakdown of *omerta*, the code of silence, and the willingness of scores of mobsters to cooperate with the government. This certainly reflects some sort of change, either much more powerful and effective law enforcement than ever before (including especially the draconian RICO sentences) and the possibility of defecting without being killed (thanks to the Witness Security Program) or a different attitude among Cosa Nostra members about the importance of loyalty to their organization.

While plausible, Goldstock's thesis is difficult to evaluate because it is hard to compare the "values" of yesterday's organized-crime leaders, middle managers, and soldiers with today's. There is a tendency in many contexts to romanticize the values and accomplishments of past generations. Just as many of us do not believe that this generation's political leaders or college presidents measure up to their counterparts of the past, so it is not surprising that Joe Bonanno believes that today's mob leaders are less capable and worthy than he.[40]

This romanticizing tendency is compounded by the methodological error of comparing all (or the average) of today's leaders with only the best of yesterday's leaders. Not all of yesterday's mob members and bosses were like Marlon Brando's depiction of a man of honor in *The Godfather*. The Goldstock thesis is intriguing, but it needs to be carefully and critically examined.

Organized-Crime Control and Civil Liberties

Whatever one thinks of the events examined in this book, *United States v. Cosa Nostra* is not a case of law enforcement agencies' ignoring or taking the law into their own hands; rather it is an example of how substantive and procedural criminal laws have been expansively amended and recast in order to provide law enforcement agencies powerful means for defeating Cosa Nostra and other organized-crime groups. While some observers may applaud the government's attack on Cosa Nostra as an impressive example of how a democratic government can defeat an immensely powerful crime syndicate while respecting the rule of law and due process of law, other observers may conclude that the rule of law and important principles of fairness, due process, and substantive justice have been stretched too far in the relentless effort to put the leaders of Cosa Nostra behind bars. Such critics would point to the expansion of accessorial and conspiratorial liability under RICO, electronic eavesdropping, grand jury supoenas, making deals with dangerous and reprehensible criminals, mass trials, and draconian punishments as too great a price to pay, even for the dismantling of Cosa Nostra.

Politicians have shown no concern for the privacy of or justice for organized-crime figures. Senators and representatives have competed with one another to be toughest on organized crime. The only doubts raised in congressional debates over organized-crime legislation have involved the possibility that organized-crime-control tactics would be used against people other than organized-crime members, especially unpopular political groups.

Cosa Nostra members have been demonized in Congress and defined as social pariahs against whom extraordinary rules ought to apply. Thus, a system of substantive and procedural law has evolved so that once a person is identified as head of an organized-crime family, there is usually probable cause to bug his home and car and tap his phones. Under RICO the crime boss can practically be automatically charged with participating in an enterprise (his crime family) through racketeering activity (the crimes committed by his underlings). No matter what the underlying crimes proved against him, the sentencing law is structured so that the boss can be imprisoned for a very long time, probably for life.

For the most part, the appellate courts have not rejected the government's aggressive use of RICO and other anti-organized-crime tactics. The appellate courts are loathe to reverse a conviction resulting from many months of trial against a defendant whom "everybody knows" is a major organized-crime figure. Even when they are obviously troubled by such things as megatrials and status crimes, the appellate judges have upheld organized-crime convictions, while expressing their "doubts" and "concerns."

Civil libertarians have rarely chosen organized-crime cases to challenge government over-reaching and abuse of authority. Indeed, from a civil liberties standpoint, major organized-crime cases provide the worst set of facts on which to test the propriety and constitutionality of new law enforcement and crime control tactics. Perhaps there is an implicit assumption that the rules are different in organized-crime cases. Perhaps it is generally accepted that Cosa Nostra bosses and members assume the risk of (and have no justifiable complaint about) whatever law enforcement tactics the legislative and the executive branches come up with.

Rather than defend the rights of organized-crime figures, civil liberties groups have often warned against and opposed the tactics designed for the "war on organized crime" on the ground that they would inevitably be used in other contexts, especially to chill bona fide political expression. In fact, organized-crime-control devices, from conspiracy law to RICO, and from electronic eavesdropping to criminal and civil forfeitures, have inexorably seeped into other contexts. One reason for this is the plasticity of the term "organized crime." Many kinds of criminality can plausibly be labeled organized crime. The RICO statute, for example, has frequently been used against non–Cosa Nostra defendants who, under even the broadest definition, could not be linked to an organized-crime group. Furthermore, the use of civil RICO provisions in disputes among corporations has triggered repeated, albeit unsuccessful, efforts to reign in the reach of the statute. If anything, however, the tactics that have proven so successful against Cosa Nostra are being transplanted to the war against drugs, and even to "wars" against official corruption, violent crime, and pornography.

The Future of Organized Crime

After each of the major organized-crime cases presented in this book, some law enforcement officials and academic observers predicted that America was on the threshold of defeating Cosa Nostra.[41] While one cannot help being impressed by the government's overwhelming successes in organized-crime prosecutions across the United States since 1980, one must also be impressed by Cosa Nostra's power and expansive reach as evidenced in the testimony, wiretaps, and physical evidence that have been adduced in these same trials. It is sobering to consider that, at least until recently, Cosa Nostra exerted powerful influence over the nation's largest union (the Teamsters), several other important national unions (Longshoreman's Association, Hotel Employees and Restaurant Employees International Union, and the Laborers International Union of North America), the New York City/New Jersey waterfront, the Fulton Fish Market, the New York City construction industry, garment industry, and trash-hauling industry, and numerous other businesses throughout the country. Over the last several decades, Cosa Nostra leaders have stood at the side of mayors, governors, and even presidents. The sum total of this much influence and power makes organized crime a significant part of the political economy of the United States.

Unfortunately, there is no systematic way to determine how successful the government's organized-crime-control campaign has been, much less *will be*, in weakening or eliminating Cosa Nostra or in reducing the amount of racketeering and harm associated with Cosa Nostra.[42] There are no systematic and reliable data on the health, wealth, and power of Cosa Nostra as a whole or of its individual crime families. Hundreds of Cosa Nostra members have been sentenced to long prison terms, but we do not know whether replacements have or will move into their vacated roles. Many law enforcement professionals see the Cosa Nostra families as being in disarray and in permanent decline. But these observations are generally ad hoc and not part of systematic nationwide intelligence gathering and analysis effort. Electronic monitoring, computer systems, and the emergence of well-trained organized-crime-control units and specialists make conceivable the implementation of an extensive intelligence operation. But resources and technology have to be supported by political will and organizational commitment. The danger is that attention will be drawn away from organized-crime control to other pressing law enforcement priorities and that, while the law enforcement machinery sleeps, Cosa Nostra will reconstitute itself. Finally, even if Cosa Nostra as an organization has been substantially weakened, we obviously cannot be sure that Cosa Nostra's racketeering activities have not been (or will not be) taken over by newly emerging crime groups, thereby negating any reduction in racketeering or societal harm.

Many of the economic and social forces that allowed organized crime to achieve such immense power are still operative. The citizenry's demand for illicit goods and services remains strong. Many unions remain vulnerable to labor racketeering, and those that have been "liberated" from organized crime have been very slow to repudiate their mob ties, if they have done so at all. Thus, it may be premature to predict that the investigations and trials of the 1980s constitute the beginning of the last chapter in the history of Cosa Nostra. Whatever the future may hold, the period from the late 1970s to the early 1990s has been marked by the most concerted and sophisticated attack on organized crime in the history of the United States. The goal of this book is to begin the herculean task of documenting, explaining, and critiquing this recent history so that it will be available to this and future generations of students, scholars, and members of the public who are interested in organized crime in American society.

Notes

1. Hoover's resistance to investigating or even recognizing the existence of organized crime has been very well documented. See, e.g., J. R. Nash, *Citizen Hoover*, chapter 6, "The Organization That Didn't Exist" (Hall, 1972); Arthur M. Schlesinger, Jr., *Robert Kennedy and His Times* (Ballantine, 1978).

2. A useful, if somewhat abbreviated, chronology of milestones and major prosecutions is Department of Justice, Criminal Investigation Division, Organized Crime Section, *Chronological History of la Cosa Nostra in the United States: January 1920–August 1987* (Washington, D.C., October 1987).

3. The fact that these FBI statistics did not include *consiglieri*, advisors or counselors to the bosses, is indicative of the lack of a systematic and comprehensive official reporting system for organized-crime prosecutions.

4. This could mean twenty-five hundred separate "counts" charged against a much smaller number of individuals (although some individuals were charged in several different indictments). It seems implausible that twenty-five hundred different organized-crime members were charged in criminal cases, since this would constitute

most of the members. However, twenty-five hundred might be a plausible number if mob "associates" are counted, since the number of associates far exceeds the number of "made" members.

5. For a description of Cosa Nostra and its crime families, see President's Commission on Organized Crime, Report to the President and Attorney General, *The Impact: Organized Crime Today* (Washington, D.C., April 1986).

6. Other major labor racketeering investigations of the late 1970s were (1) "PENDORF," which focused on Cosa Nostra control of the Teamster Central States Pension Fund and which resulted in the conviction of the Teamsters' president, Roy Williams; (2) "STRAWMAN," which focused on a conspiracy by four Cosa Nostra families to utilize the Central States Pension Fund to secure interests in Las Vegas casinos and to skim profits from those businesses; (3) "LILREX," which focused on racketeering in the New York City construction industry; and (4) "LIUNA," which focused on Cosa Nostra racketeering in the Laborers International Union of North America.

7. See Randy Mastro, Steven C. Bennett, and Mary P. Donlevy, *Private Plaintiffs' Use of Equitable Remedies under the RICO Statute: A Means to Reform Corrupted Labor Unions,* 24 University of Michigan Journal of Law Reform 571 (1991).

The local unions placed under trusteeships are Local 6A of the Cement and Concrete Workers of the Laborers International Union of America; District Council of Carpenters; Teamsters Local 814; United Seafood Workers Local 359; (Philadelphia) Roofers Union Local 30-30B, and Local 1814 of the International Longshoreman's Association. Local 100 of the Restaurant Workers Union, charged with being dominated by the Gambino family, was spared a court-appointed trustee when the judge permitted the union voluntarily to install a union international vice-president as trustee.

8. See *United States v Local 359, United Seafood Workers,* 87 Civ 7351 (SDNY filed October 15, 1987); for a discussion of the case, see Brian Carroll, *Combatting Racketeering in the Fulton Fish Market,* in Cyrille Fijnaut and James Jacobs, *Organized Crime and Its Containment: A Transatlantic Initiative* (Kluwer, 1991).

9. For a discussion of the case, see Robert Maas, *Organized Crime Infiltration of Legitimate Industry in New York,* in Cyrille Fijnaut and James Jacobs, *Organized Crime and Its Containment: A Transatlantic Initiative* (Kluwer, 1991).

10. *United States v Rastelli,* 85 CR 345 (EDNY filed June 10, 1985).

11. *United States v Boffa,* 688 F2d 919 (3d Cir 1982).

12. *United States v Local 30, United States Tile and Slate Roofers,* 686 F Supp 1139 (ED Pa 1988). See Randy Mastro, Steven C. Bennett, and Mary P. Donlevy, *Private Plaintiffs' Use of Equitable Remedies under the RICO Statute: A Means to Reform Corrupted Labor Unions,"* 24 *University of Michigan Journal of Law Reform* 571 (1991).

13. Permanent Subcommittee on Investigations of the Committee on Govern-

RENNER LEARNING RESOURCE CENTER
ELGIN COMMUNITY COLLEGE
ELGIN, ILLINOIS 60123

mental Affairs, *Twenty-Five Years after Valachi,* 100th Cong., 2d sess., 11, 15, 21, 22, 29 April 1988.

14. United States Code, vol. 18, secs. 2510–20 (1982).

15. See Michael Goldsmith, *The Supreme Court and Title III: Rewriting the Law of Electronic Surveillance,* 74 Journal of Criminal Law and Criminology 1 (1983).

16. *Electronic Communications Privacy Act,* Public Law 99-508, *United States Statutes at Large* 100 (1986): 1848. New technologies brought within Title III include electronic mail, computer transmissions, video teleconferencing, cellular telephones, some telephonic pagers, and certain types of radio transmissions. See Michael Goldsmith, *Eavesdropping Reform: The Legality of Roving Surveillance,* University of Illinois Law Review 401 (1987).

17. Statistical Analysis and Reports, Administrative Office of the United States Courts, *Reports on Applications for Orders Authorizing or Approving the Interception of Wire, Oral, or Electric Communications.*

18. See Gerald Lynch, *RICO: The Crime of Being a Criminal,* 87 Columbia Law Review 661 (parts 1, 2) (1987); 87 Columbia Law Review 920 (parts 3, 4) (1987).

19. The first RICO conviction of a Cosa Nostra family boss was *United States v Frank (Funzi) Tieri* in 1981.

20. 452 United States 576 (1981). Prior to *Turkette,* it was plausible to argue that RICO required proof of racketeer infiltration of a legitimate business, union, or governmental organization. After *Turkette,* RICO could be used to prosecute any ongoing criminal group.

21. This history had been previously and remarkably revealed in mob boss Joseph Bonanno's memoir, *A Man of Honor* (Simon and Schuster, 1983).

22. United States Code, vol. 18, sec. 1964.

23. See *Organized Crime Control Act of 1970.* Public Law 91-452, *United Statutes at Large* 84, secs. 922, 922–23 (1970) (Statement of Findings and Purpose).

24. See Nicholas Pileggi and Henry Hill, *Wiseguy* (Simon and Schuster, 1985).

25. See Ovid Demaris, *The Last Mafioso: The Treacherous World of Jimmy Fratianno* (Fitzhenry and Whiteside, 1981).

26. Comptroller General of the United States, *War on Organized Crime Faltering: Federal Strike Forces Not Getting the Job Done* (United States Government Accounting Office, 1976); Comptroller General of the United States, *Stronger Effort Needed in Fight against Organized Crime* (United States Government Accounting Office, 1981).

27. See *Proposed Merger of the Organized Crime Strike Forces into the Various United States Attorneys Offices: Hearings before the Subcommittee on Criminal Justice of the Judiciary Committee of the House of Representatives* 101st Cong., 1st Sess., June 1989; *Status of the Department of Justice Organized Crime Strike Forces: Joint Hearings before the Senate Committee on the Judiciary and the Senate Committee on Government Affairs* 101st Cong., 1st Sess., September 1989.

See also General Accounting Office, *Report on Organized Crime: Issues Concerning Strike Forces*, report prepared for the Permanent Subcommittee on Investigations, Senate Committee on Government Affairs, 101st Cong., 1st Sess., April 1989.

28. Concerning Marcello, see Donald W. Cox, *Kingfish: Carlos Marcello and the Assassination of John F. Kennedy* (McGraw Hill, 1989). Another major investigation of the late 1970s/early 1980s period was operation PENDORF. It resulted in the conviction of top organized-crime figures in Chicago, Milwaukee, Cleveland, Las Vegas, and Kansas City.

29. Attorney General Order No. 136-89, 26 December 1989 ("Order Directing Realignment of Organized Crime Program Resources").

30. For an excellent example of how tenacious attention to Paul Castellano, because he was boss of one of the crime families, contributed to the Gambino and Commission RICO prosecutions, see Joseph O'Brien and Andris Kurins, *Boss of Bosses* (Simon and Schuster, 1991).

31. See J. R. Nash, *Citizen Hoover*, chapter 6, "The Organization That Didn't Exist" (Hall, 1972).

32. See Pistone's account of his undercover experience in Joseph Pistone with Richard Woodley, *My Undercover Life in the Mafia: Donnie Brasco* (New American Library, 1987).

33. See Arthur M. Schlesinger, *Robert Kennedy and His Times*, at 287 (Ballantine, 1979).

34. See Ronald Reagan, *Declaring War on Organized Crime*, New York Times Magazine, sec. 6, p. 26, col. 1, 12 January 1986.

35. Comptroller General of the United States, *War on Organized Crime Faltering: Federal Strike Forces Not Getting the Job Done* (United States Government Accounting Office, 1976). Comptroller General of the United States, *Stronger Federal Effort Needed in Fight against Organized Crime* (United States Government Accounting Office, 1981).

36. In 1968, a strike force had been created for the Southern District of New York, but in 1976 it was merged into the United States Attorney's office by then Assistant Attorney General Richard Thornburgh.

37. After Hoover, the succession at the FBI has been as follows: Patrick Gray (acting director 1972–73); William Ruckelshaus (acting director 1973); Clarence Kelley (director 1973–78); William Webster (director 1978–87); William Sessions (director 1987–93); Louis Freeh (director 1993–).

38. Joe Bonanno, *Man of Honor* (Simon and Schuster, 1983).

39. Ronald Goldstock, Some Ruminations on the Current and Future Status of Organized Crime in the United States and on Efforts to Control Illicit Syndicates and Enterprises, unpublished report for the New York State Organized Crime Task Force, n.d.

40. According to Jimmy Fratianno, Bonanno was made persona non grata by the commission some time in the 1970s. According to his account, any Costra Nostra

member who had contact with Bonanno was subject to capital punishment. Fratianno does not say why Bonanno had this falling out with the commission.

41. See, e.g., Sellwyn Raab, *The Mob in Decline—A Special Report: An Ailing and Battered Mob Is Losing Its Grip on America, New York Times,* 22 October 1990, A1.

42. See Michael D. Maltz, *Measuring the Effectiveness of Organized Crime Control Efforts* (Office of International Criminal Justice, 1990); Herbert Edelhatz, Roland J. Cole, and Bonnie Berle, *The Containment of Organized Crime* (Lexington Books, 1984).

PART II

2

Teamsters Local 560: *United States v. Local 560 (IBT)*

(Filed March 1982; Decided February 1984)

Introduction

United States v. Local 560 (IBT) is the most important civil labor racketeering case ever brought by the Justice Department against a union local.[1] *Local 560* broke new ground because it was the first time the Department of Justice brought a civil RICO action against a labor union. Unlike a traditional organized-crime criminal prosecution, this suit did not aim for a criminal conviction. Instead, the Justice Department sought to free Local 560 from the influence of organized crime by means of a wide-ranging civil injunction. The litigation that began in the early 1980s and continues into the early 1990s reveals the pervasiveness of organized crime's role in a "captive labor union," demonstrates the value of civil RICO as an anti–labor-racketeering tool, and highlights the problems a court-appointed trustee faces in returning a mob-dominated union to the rank and file.

Local 560, an unincorporated labor association chartered by the International Brotherhood of Teamsters (IBT), is one of the largest Teamster Union locals in New Jersey. It was once one of the most powerful IBT locals in the United States, but years of mob exploitation drained its resources and pressured honest members to seek work elsewhere. In May 1982, it had approximately ten thousand members employed by about 425 companies located in the metropolitan New Jersey-New York area.

Background

From the early 1950s, Local 560 has been controlled or influenced by Genovese crime family capo Anthony ("Tony Pro") Provenzano, his two brothers, and their hand-picked successors. Provenzano joined Local 560 in the late 1940s, became a business agent in 1952, and muscled his way to the presidency in 1960. As president, he appointed his brothers and enforcers to key positions as trustees, business agents, and shop stewards. He also placed family members and friends in well-paid positions as administrators of the welfare and benefit funds and on the payrolls of businesses that employed Local 560 members. The Provenzanos silenced dissidents and rivals who dared to challenge their rule by having them fired and blacklisted by Local 560 employers (who were dependent upon the union's cooperation and goodwill). Two union members who opposed Provenzano were murdered.

Provenzano's career in organized crime prospered along with his fortunes in Local 560. At some point in the early 1960s he became a made member of the Genovese crime family and turned Local 560 into a cash cow subsidiary of Cosa Nostra. Provenzano began by organizing thievery at the New Jersey docks. Over the next decade, he and his associates extorted labor peace payoffs from employers, sold out the rank-and-file members through sweetheart contracts with trucking firms, forced employers to put no-show employees on the payroll, and defrauded the union's benefit funds through phony loans and worthless or highly overpaid contracts with various service providers.

Criminal convictions did not hamper a member's advancement in the union. For example, after Nunzio Provenzano was convicted in a labor peace extortion scheme in 1963, his brother Tony appointed him as a business agent. In 1966, Tony and Nunzio Provenzano were imprisoned on separate convictions and Sam Provenzano assumed the union's presidency. While he awaited trial, the union paid all of Tony Pro's legal fees and voted him a lucrative five-fold salary increase that enabled him to amass some $240,000 while he served his prison term.

After release from prison, members of the Provenzano clique routinely returned to positions in Local 560 (in violation of federal labor law). Indeed, after he served five years in prison, Tony Pro was appointed secretary-treasurer. However, in 1978, the Manhattan district attorney successfully prosecuted him for murder of a union rival, which led to a sentence of life imprisonment. In 1979, at a federal trial, he and Gabe Briguglio, his long-time associate, were convicted of accepting payoffs from a major shipping firm in exchange for sweetheart contracts. After his murder conviction,

Provenzano's daughter assumed his position on Local 560's executive board and his brother Sam became president. In 1981, Nunzio was convicted federally on a similar sweetheart scheme involving four interstate trucking companies, and in 1983, Sam was convicted federally of dental-benefit-fund kickbacks. In 1984, the Provenzanos designated long-time associate Michael Sciarra as their successor. Thus, despite Tony Pro's and his two brothers' convictions and incarceration, organized crime's grip on Local 560 remained firm.

The Civil RICO Suit

March 1982 marked the beginning of the government's protracted attack on organized crime's labor racketeering in Local 560. The Newark Strike Force, in conjunction with the United States attorney for New Jersey, filed a 35-page civil complaint with a 300-page appendix documenting a quarter-century of racketeering domination and exploitation. The named defendants included Local 560, its pension and welfare funds, each current member of its executive board, and former executive board members Anthony and Nunzio Provenzano, Stephen and Thomas Andretta, and Gabriel Briguglio, all of whom had been convicted in individual racketeering cases. The government announced that it had targeted Local 560 because of its "lurid history of criminal activity."

The civil complaint charged two substantive violations of RICO and a RICO conspiracy. First, the complaint alleged that the individual convicted racketeers, aided and abetted by members of the executive board, had acquired and maintained an interest in Local 560 and its pension and welfare funds through a pattern of racketeering activity, including murder and extortion. In support of the allegation, the government included a long list of the previous criminal convictions of Local 560 officers and members.[2] Second, the complaint charged the defendants with operating Local 560 and its benefit plans through a pattern of racketeering activity. It alleged numerous predicate offenses: mail and wire fraud, extortion, embezzlement from the union, hijacking cargo, and accepting kickbacks. Third, the government alleged a conspiracy among the defendants to acquire and maintain control of Local 560 through a pattern of racketeering activity.

According to the government, wide-ranging equitable relief was necessary because decades of organized-crime domination had created an environment of intimidation and terror. Purging the racketeers through criminal prosecution had proven ineffective against the Provenzanos' revolving-door policy. The government therefore sought appointment of a trustee to run the union until organized crime and the conditions fostering it could be eliminated and the union returned to its members.

Several important consequences flowed from the decision to use civil RICO. Pursuant to the rules of civil procedure, the United States attorney obtained a good deal of information about Local 560's operations through civil discovery. The threat of being deposed by government counsel may have convinced several defendants to settle by agreeing to be forever barred from participating in Local 560 affairs. In addition, a single federal judge tried the case, as defendants have no right to a jury trial in civil suits asking for injunctive and other equitable relief. Furthermore, the government only had to meet the lesser burden of proof (preponderance of the evidence) that applies to civil cases rather than the beyond-a-reasonable-doubt standard that applies in criminal cases.

During the five-month trial, which took place in 1983, Judge Harold Ackerman heard from a number of different witnesses who occupied key positions within the union. For example, he listened to testimony from Sam Provenzano, the president of Local 560; Joseph Sheridan, the vice-president of Local 560; Josephine Provenzano, Tony Pro's daughter and the secretary-treasurer of Local 560 since 1978 when she was elected to that position at the age of twenty-three; Michael Sciarra; and J. W. Dildine, the recording secretary of Local 560 since 1968. Judge Ackerman listened as the witnesses expressed their loyalties to Tony Pro and the other union leaders. Some steadfastly refused to concede that Tony or Nunzio Provenzano was guilty of the charges for which he had been convicted.[3] Other witnesses testified that, if it were possible, they would return Tony or Nunzio Provenzano to his old position.

Salvatore Sinno, a member of the Provenzano clique since the 1940s, became a government witness and provided invaluable testimony. He linked Anthony and Nunzio Provenzano to the Genovese crime family and described the criminal activity and intimidation that assured the Provenzano group's dominance of Local 560.

The trial resulted in a spectacular victory for the government. Judge Ackerman found in the government's favor on all three RICO charges. All members of the executive board were held to be accomplices on the grounds that they had appointed known labor racketeers to union positions and had failed to take any action to attack racketeering in Local 560 or to dispel the aura of fear permeating the union. Specifically, Judge Ackerman held;

Local 560 has been since 1961, and continues to be a captive labor organization, which the Provenzano Group has dominated through fear and intimidation and has exploited through fear and corruption. . . . This victimization [of individual union members and segments of the trucking industry] [is] likely to recur as long as Local 560 remains a captive labor organization.

In support of his finding that the union had been captured by organized crime, Judge Ackerman pointed to the murders of Anthony Castellitto, a popular member of Local 560 during the late 1950s, and Walter Glockner, a vocal critic of the Provenzano group in the early 1960s; the extraction of labor peace payoffs by members of the Provenzano group; and the appointments to union office of former members who had been either indicted or convicted.[4]

The court stayed its remedial plan pending appeal. In December 1985, the United States Court of Appeals for the Third Circuit affirmed the district court's judgment. The litigation entered its remedial phase, which has continued until the present time.

The Remedial Phase

Judge Ackerman temporarily suspended the executive board members of their offices during the active phase of the trusteeship. His remedial order provided for a court-appointed trustee with powers including, but not limited to, (a) all powers exercised by the executive board [of the union] under the constitution and by-laws; (b) all powers of those removed from office; (c) the power to negotiate and enter into contracts and to engage in collective bargaining; (d) the power to institute and settle litigation; and (e) the power to hire and discharge union employees and to set wages, conditions, and terms of employment for union employees.

Judge Ackerman did not place any limitation on the duration of the trusteeship; he provided for the trustee to serve "for a curative period of sufficient length . . . to effectively dispel the existing atmosphere of intimidation within Local 560, to restore union democracy, and to ensure (to the extent possible) that racketeers do not obtain positions of trust within the local."[5]

In January 1986, Judge Ackerman appointed Joel Jacobson, an experienced union leader, as the court-appointed trustee. Upon assuming responsibility for the union, Jacobson immediately noted three major problems with Local 560: the lack of union solidarity (i.e., it was not uncommon for a shop steward to testify *against* a union member in a grievance hearing, an unheard-of practice in other American unions), the disarray of the records of the pension and welfare funds, and the lack of education and training programs for the members. Thus, Jacobson decided that his main responsibility was to run the union competently and openly. However, he did not seem to draw a connection between reforming the union and rooting out the union's organized-crime elements; most of the business agents were left in place and the union continued to run much as it always had. Judge Ackerman did not agree with this strategy and ultimately replaced Jacobson in May 1987.[6]

Edwin Stier, a former federal and state prosecutor, succeeded Jacobson.[7] Stier was dismayed to find that Tony Pro's picture still hung on the wall of the Local 560 union hall, symbolizing the pervasive racketeering atmosphere. He immediately ordered its removal. Stier and his associate trustee assumed the day-to-day managerial functions of the union's executive board, investigating suspicious collective bargaining agreements and the operations of the pension and welfare funds, and nurturing union democracy by encouraging membership interest and participation.

Stier believed that ultimately union democracy was the antidote for labor racketeering. Only when the rank and file became committed to taking control over their destiny would the yoke of organized-crime dominance be broken. The challenge, in Stier's view, was to convince the members that they could participate in the union without fear of retaliation.

A free election, eventually scheduled for 1988, was the critical plank in his reform agenda. He had four goals for the election. First, he sought to encourage the formation of party tickets and the nomination of candidates. Second, he sought to assure that the members would vote, so he encouraged them to take an interest in and become involved in union affairs and politics. Third, he aimed to guarantee both the perception and the reality of a secret-ballot election. Fourth, he endeavored to assure that the election procedures (voter eligibility, ballot protection, tallying votes) guaranteed a fair process.[8]

However, the Provenzano forces threw themselves into the electoral fray, organizing a ticket called "Teamsters for Liberty" (TFL), and long-time Provenzano henchman and former 560 president, Michael Sciarra, announced his candidacy for the presidency. (The other two tickets were the United Ticket and Wise Choice.)

The government, represented by the same indefatigable assistant United States attorney who had filed the initial suit, Robert Stewart, returned to court to disqualify Sciarra from running for office. In the course of two preliminary injunction hearings (1988 and 1990) and a civil RICO trial (1990), Stewart presented testimony and tape recordings to show that Sciarra maintained regular contacts with Genovese crime-family members and that the Genovese family chose him to control the union. Sciarra's association with the Provenzano group dated back at least as far as the early 1960s. He served the union as business agent (1972–86), as an executive board trustee (1981–1984), as president of the Local (1984–86), and as a trustee of the benefit-plan system (1983–86). According to Stier, the membership universally regarded Sciarra as the Provenzanos' hand-picked successor.

Judge Dickinson Debevoise, who handled the Sciarra litigation, agreed with the government that Sciarra had to be disqualified:

The [Ianniello-Andretta] tapes constitute strong evidence that the Genovese Crime Family intended to maintain its control over Local 560 during the pendency of the appeal from Judge Ackerman's March 16, 1984 Judgement Order, during any pendency of trusteeship, and thereafter. The tapes constitute strong evidence that this control was to be exercised through Anthony Salerno's *caporegime* Mathew Ianniello, and that Ianniello, upon the advice of Stephen Andretta, selected Michael Sciarra to be the man on the scene at Local 560 to whom orders and instructions could be given.[9]

Judge Debevoise concluded that "if Sciarra . . . were to become President . . . there would be a very real danger that all the efforts expended during the trusteeship to free the union from racketeering control would be undone." Thereupon, the TFL substituted Michael Sciarra's brother Daniel as its candidate for the Local 560 presidency, presumably confident that Daniel would ensure the continuity of the Provenzano legacy in the union.

The election, held in December 1988, resulted in a resounding two-to-one victory for Daniel Sciarra and the TFL slate of executive board nominees (62 percent to 38 percent). The board immediately appointed Michael Sciarra as business agent; the Provenzano group seemed to have triumphed despite all the government's effort to remove them from the union.

According to a study by Linda Kaboolian of Harvard's Kennedy School, the TFL prevailed for a number of reasons. First, the membership viewed the former leadership of the union as the best-qualified and most experienced candidates—not surprising given that for decades members of the Provenzano group were the only union members allowed to participate in union management. Second, many members opposed the trusteeship and voted for continuity with the old regime. Third, the TFL was better organized and ran a stronger campaign than the opposition.

After the election, Stier turned over day-to-day management to the newly elected executive board and assumed the role of monitoring any renewed racketeering. Stier immediately determined that Daniel Sciarra, the new executive board, and much of the rank and file regarded Michael Sciarra as the de facto boss of the union. Indeed, the board proposed to appoint

Michael Sciarra to the additional position of trustee of the benefit plans. After thirteen months, the government again went to court, charging that Michael Sciarra continued to dominate the union despite the district court's injunction, and alleging that as long as he continued to have any role in the union's governance, by virtue of his charismatic personality and ties to the Genovese crime family, he would continue to exercise a dominant role. The evidence persuaded Judge Debevoise to expand the preliminary injunction and remove Sciarra from his position as business agent. A year later, after trial, Judge Debevoise issued a permanent injunction barring Michael Sciarra from holding any office or position of trust within Local 560 or from endeavoring to influence its affairs.

As long as Michael Sciarra holds any position within Local 560 he will be able through his forceful personality and through his hold on a large and vocal segment of the membership to dominate and control the Local and its pension and welfare funds. If he assumes power within the Union, it is highly likely that upon termination of the court-appointed trustee's oversight the Genovese Family would reassert control over Local 560, undoing all the efforts of the past eight years. . . . The return of Sciarra and, through him, Genovese Family influence, would crush the movement towards membership control and bring back the dark night of the strong arm and repression. [10]

Thus, for the first time in the history of the American labor movement, an individual was enjoined from holding any union position based upon a civil adjudication that his continued involvement with a Cosa Nostra family posed a danger to the welfare of the union.

In September 1991, the union's executive board petitioned the district court for an early termination of the trusteeship on the grounds that its remedial objectives had been achieved with the issuance of the permanent injunction against Michael Sciarra six months earlier. The government argued that the board had acted irresponsibly in allowing Michael Sciarra to usurp its powers and in seeking to appoint Michael Sciarra as a benefit-fund trustee. According to the government, the board remained a tool of the Provenzano group and the union could not become free and independent while the executive board officers remained in office.

In February 1992, after hearing evidence for over seven days, the government and the executive board reached an interim settlement. Under the terms of this agreement, Daniel Sciarra resigned from the presidency but remained eligible to serve as shop steward. The office of president would remain vacant until the court called for a new election. Two other Sciarra loyalists on the executive board resigned and Stier named their replacements. The agreement also provided for an executive board comprised of three TFL members and three independent union members, with the powers of the union presidency shared between one member from each group.

This settlement had to be revised when a TFL board member resigned. Under the new agreement, the executive board was comprised of four independent members and two TFL members (the seventh position on the board remained vacant). As of February 1994, Al Vallee, a union member not connected with the Provenzano-Sciarra legacy, served as the president. Vallee had been the independent union member who previously shared presidential powers. Ed Stier remained the trustee and also retained his position as chairman of the Welfare and Pension Funds. While he no longer exercised day-to-day managerial authority, he continued to monitor the union and worked closely with the executive board to investigate any wrongdoing.

Conclusion

United States v. Local 560 is a highly visible test case of the power and ability of federal prosecutors and courts to wrest control of captive labor unions away from Cosa Nostra and return them to their rank and file. Ten years of litigation and court-ordered change have not yet guaranteed that the future of Local 560 will be free of organized-crime racketeering. While some opposition to the Provenzano group has surfaced, it is still not clear that a solid majority of union members is in favor of ousting the racketeer element.[11] The case demonstrates just how difficult it is to defeat Cosa Nostra once it is well entrenched in a labor union and has enjoyed the advantages of incumbency for decades, doling out favors to friends and imposing punishments on dissidents.

United States v. Local 560 provides a valuable case study for determining the usefulness of civil RICO in the labor racketeering context. Criminal prosecutions alone, which only result in the replacement of one racketeer by another, cannot liberate a captive labor local such as Local 560. Civil RICO gives the court authority to issue wide-ranging equitable relief, including the appointment of a trustee who can remain on the job as long as it takes to transform the corrupted organization. Whether even this extraordinary relief will succeed in achieving its objectives remains to be determined.

In his testimony before the Senate Permanent Subcommittee on Investigations, Ed Stier stated that a trusteeship such as the one established for Local 560 aims to effect structural and cultural change within the union. Stier testified that in future trusteeships, success may hinge on three improvements: funding trusteeships from other than union treasuries in order not to make the membership resentful of government intervention, providing a stronger and larger investigative team, and, perhaps most importantly, including organized labor in any solution to the problems of corruption and racketeering.

Finally, *United States v. Local 560* demonstrates the important roles individuals play in the war against Cosa Nostra. Assistant United States Attorney Robert Stewart has been the driving force behind the government's efforts for almost a decade. He has authored or coauthored almost all the government briefs, coordinated communication with the court-appointed trustee, and given the case top priority. Without this kind of continuity and commitment it is unlikely that such a suit and remedial effort could be sustained. However, because of the typical tenure among federal prosecutors (who usually serve three to four years), this type of continuity is unusual. Moreover, Judge Ackerman and Judge Debevoise have been steadfast in their determination that the rule of law ultimately prevail in Local 560. Other judges, who might have been more wary of involving the courts so actively in "running a union," might have moved more cautiously and thereby doomed whatever chances of success inhere in the civil racketeering strategy.

The court-appointed trustee, Ed Stier, has borne the brunt of the day-to-day work of reconstructing the union and standing up to countless threats and intimidations. Without his courage and steadfastness, his vision in developing a remedial strategy, and his energy, real change would not even be a possibility. It is a major challenge to find committed and competent trustees who have the mix of experience and skills necessary to attack corruption, promote union democracy, and administer labor unions.

The court's effort to purge racketeering and to restore union democracy in Local 560 might be likened to previous efforts in court-ordered institutional reform in the school-desegregation and prison-conditions contexts. There is no reason to believe that changing corrupt unions will be easier than changing segregated schools or improving jail and prison conditions. The unions are large and their memberships and activities decentralized and far flung. The leaders of unions like Local 560 are even more defiant of the rule of law and judicial authority than the most recalcitrant school, mental hospital, and prison personnel who were found to be operating their organizations unconstitutionally. Labor unions are not public institutions. Their leaders, being elected by the membership, are under no external pressure to abide by and facilitate court orders. Indeed, the labor movement has staunchly opposed the idea of RICO union trusteeships. In a recent poll, the majority of Local 560's members unfavorably compared the government to the former leadership. Until the time comes when a clear majority of union members desires *and can freely and openly support* clean candidates, the struggle to purge unions of mob influence will continue to be exceedingly difficult.

The *Local 560* case also requires one to ask whether there are any limits on the scope of government intervention into the affairs of a union in the name of corruption control. The trustee of Local 560 was empowered to *run* the union; he had complete control over all union functions, including negotiating collective bargaining agreements, taking the union members out on strike, and handling grievances. Can a court-appointed trustee, no matter how well meaning, adequately represent the interests of the union members? Even if he can, is this consistent with the nation's commitment to a free and autonomous labor movement? If court-appointed trusteeships become a regular tool of government crime-control policy, how do we develop measures of "success" that require their terminations? If success cannot be achieved, does the trusteeship remain indefinitely?

Chronology of the United States v. Local 560 (IBT) *Litigation: Partial List of Most Important Reported Decisions*

United States v Local 560, 581 F Supp 279 (DNJ 1984) (Judge Ackerman's opinion reviewing racketeering in Local 560 and granting the government wide-ranging injunctive relief).

United States v Local 560, 780 F2d 267 (3d Cir 1985) (criticizing the logic in part of the district court's legal theory on the RICO counts, but affirming in all respects the district court judgment and remedy).

United States v Local 560, 694 F Supp 1158 (DNJ 1988) (Judge Debevoise's opinion disqualifying Michael Sciarra from running for the presidency of Local 560).

United States v Local 560, 865 F2d 252 (3d Cir 1988) (affirming Judge Debevoise's disqualification of Sciarra).

United States v Local 560, 731 F Supp 1206 (DNJ 1990) (approving payment of fees from union treasury to the court-appointed trustee, Ed Stier).

United States v Local 560, 736 F Supp 601 (DNJ 1990) (Judge Debevoise's opinion granting temporary injunction against Michael Sciarra's holding any position within Local 560).

United States v Local 560, 754 F Supp 395 (DNJ 1991) (Judge Debevoise's opinion granting permanent injunction against Michael Sciarra's participation in union affairs).

Notes

1. Organized crime's labor racketeering has been the subject of several major congressional investigations and national commissions. The most recent is President's Commission on Organized Crime, *The Edge: Organized Crime, Business, and Labor Unions* (Washington, D.C., 1986).

2. Even during the pendency of the civil RICO trial, Local 560–related criminal cases continued to be prosecuted. For example, in December 1983 president Sam Provenzano and long-time fund administrator Marvin Zalk were convicted in a fraud involving the union's dental benefit plan.

In mid-1984 a law firm was retained by the new Local 560 president, Michael Sciarra, to provide prepaid legal services despite the conviction of an attorney from the firm for fraud and failure to account for five hundred thousand dollars from the 1-84 (IBT) "direct payment" plan.

3. *United States v Local 560*, 581 F Supp 279, 295 (1984).

4. Id. at 311.

5. Id. at 326.

6. See Linda Kaboolian, Teamsters Local 560: A Case Study of a Court-Imposed RICO Trusteeship (hereinafter Kaboolian Report), unpublished report, John F. Kennedy School of Public Affairs, Harvard University, June 1992, 19. Mr. Jacobson did not leave quietly. He remained an outspoken critic of Judge Ackerman's approach until his death in 1989.

7. Also at this time, Judge Ackerman provided for appointment of an associate trustee with the authority "to promote and enhance the spirit of participation in trade union affairs among the entire membership of Local 560 and to provide effective trade union representation in all areas of the Local's activities."

8. Kaboolian Report, 25.

9. *United States v Local 560*, 694 F Supp 1158, 1178 (DNJ 1988).

10. *United States v Local 560*, 754 F Supp 395, 407 (DNJ 1991).

11. See generally Kaboolian Report

United States v. Local 560, Opinion of Judge Harold A. Ackerman

(February 8, 1984)

HAROLD A. ACKERMAN, District Judge.

John L. Lewis, former president of the Congress of Industrial Organizations and the United Mine Workers once said that "Labor, like Israel, has many sorrows."

A careful review of the evidence in this unprecedented case reveals the verity of that observation.

It is not a pretty story. Beneath the relatively sterile language of a dry legal opinion is a harrowing tale of how evil men, sponsored by and part of organized criminal elements, infiltrated and ultimately captured Local 560 of the International Brotherhood of Teamsters, one of the largest local unions in the largest union in this country.

This group of gangsters, aided and abetted by their relatives and sycophants, engaged in a multifaceted orgy of criminal activity. For those that enthusiastically followed these arrogant mobsters in their morally debased activity there were material rewards. For those who accepted the side benefits of this perverted interpretation of business unionism, *see* J. Hutchinson, *The Imperfect Union*, p. 371, (1970), there was presumably the rationalization of "I've got mine, why shouldn't he get his." For those who attempted to fight, the message was clear. Murder and other forms of intimidation would be utilized to insure silence. To get along, one had to go along, or else.

It is important to state what the evidence in this case does and does not show.

It shows that a trade union which is by origin and nature a voluntary organization is susceptible to the malicious machinations of others, as Congress perceived in enacting the Landrum-Griffin and RICO Acts.

It does not demonstrate that unions or union officials in general are riddled with racketeering or corruption. Most authorities are convinced that the overwhelming number of unions and union officials are "untroubled by the problem of corruption." *Id*. Crooks and racketeers are anathema to a significant portion of the trade union movement.

* * *

I. The Parties

Defendant Local 560 is an unincorporated labor association which was originally chartered on May 11, 1911 by the International Brotherhood of Teamsters. As of May, 1982, it had approximately 10,000 members employed by approximately 425 companies in the metropolitan New Jersey-New York area. As such it is a labor organization engaged in an industry affecting interstate commerce within the meaning of Section 402 of Title 29 of the United States Code.

Under its constitution, seven elective officers are charged with managing the day to day affairs of Local 560. These officers are: a president, a vice-president; recording secretary; secretary-treasurer; and three trustees. These seven officers together constitute Local 560's Executive Board. This Executive Board is generally authorized and empowered to conduct and manage the affairs of the organization between membership meetings.

Defendant Trucking Employees of North Jersey Welfare Fund, Inc. and its Pension Account are located in Local 560's building in Union City. The funds were and are today welfare and pension benefit plans within the meaning of Section 1002 of Title 29 of the United States Code.

The Funds are controlled by a governing body which is composed of four trustees appointed by the Executive Board of Local 560 and four trustees appointed by two employer associations whose member companies have collective bargaining agreements with Local 560. The current employee trustees include defendant Salvatore Provenzano, defendant Stanley Jaronko, and defendant Joseph Sheridan.[10]

The Local 560 Officers and Employees Severance Pay Plan is also operated out of Local 560's offices. It is an employee benefit plan within the meaning of Section 1002 of Title 29 of the United States Code in that it provides severance pay benefits to the employees of Local 560. The current trustees of the Plan are Salvatore Provenzano and Josephine Provenzano.

A brief description of each of the remaining nine individual defendants may be useful at this point. First, Salvatore "Sam" Provenzano has been the President of Local 560 since approximately July of 1981, when the Executive Board appointed him to that position.[11] Prior to that time he had been employed by Local 560 as a Business Agent between approximately November 10, 1959 and August 8, 1961; as a Trustee between approximately August 8, 1961 and November of 1965, and again between approximately January and May of 1966; as President between approximately May of 1966 and November of 1975; and as the Vice-President between approximately December of 1975 and July of 1981.

Joseph Sheridan has been the Vice-President of Local 560 since approximately

---

10. Thomas Reynolds, Sr. was a trustee of the Fund as of the time this litigation commenced and for a period after the trial began, but has since resigned. [Footnote numbering retained from original].

11. This appointment was presumably made pursuant to the Executive Board's authority to fill officer vacancies which occur during the term of an office.

July of 1981, when the Executive Board appointed him to that position. Prior to that time he had been a Business Agent between approximately July 7, 1972 and September 1, 1978, and thereafter a Trustee between approximately September 1, 1978 and July of 1981.

Josephine Provenzano has been the Secretary-Treasurer of Local 560 since approximately June of 1978, when the Executive Board appointed her to that position. Prior to that time, she had been employed by Local 560 as an office worker from 1976 until the time of her appointment. Josephine Provenzano is the daughter of defendant Anthony Provenzano and the niece of defendants Salvatore and Nunzio Provenzano.

J. W. Dildine has been the Recording Secretary of Local 560 since approximately 1968, when the Executive Board appointed him to that position. Prior to that time he had been employed by Local 560 as a Business Agent between approximately 1963 and 1968.

Thomas Reynolds, Sr. has been a Trustee of Local 560 since February 9, 1977. Before that time, he was employed by Local 560 as a Business Agent between September 24, 1970 and February 9, 1977. He is the brother-in-law of defendant Nunzio Provenzano and the father of former Business Agent Andrew Reynolds.

Michael Sciarra has been a Trustee of Local 560 since May 28, 1981. Prior to that time he was employed by Local 560 as a Business Agent between July 7, 1972 and September 30, 1976, and again between December of 1977 and May 28, 1981. Sciarra has been a member of Local 560 since approximately 1954.

Stanley Jaronko has been a Trustee of Local 560 since July 13, 1981. Before that time, he served Local 560 in the capacity of Business Agent between December 12, 1977 and February 19, 1981, and as a Trustee between February 19 and May 28, 1981.

Stephen Andretta, who testified at trial pursuant to a grant of use immunity, was a Business Agent for Local 560 between approximately August of 1973 and October of 1976. His membership in Local 560 dates from the early 1950's, and he held the position of shop steward for Local 560 at Eazor Express Co. between the mid-1960's and August of 1973, and again between approximately October of 1976 and 1980.

The evidence at trial indicated that Stephen Andretta had known Salvatore Briuglio for over twenty years as of the early 1970's. Either through Salvatore Briuglio or his brother Thomas, Stephen Andretta met Armand Faugno sometime during the latter 1960's. Around 1971, notwithstanding his position as a shop steward with Local 560, Stephen Andretta had an ownership interest in West End Trucking Company, which was controlled at least in part by Armand Faugno. Further, during the period between approximately 1971 and late 1972, Stephen Andretta and Salvatore Briuglio would not infrequently visit Armand Faugno at the latter's place of business in Jersey City, New Jersey. During the early 1970's, Stephen Andretta also knew Frederick Salvatore Furino, and was friendly with Ralph Pellechia and Ralph Michael Picardo.

On February 22, 1979, Stephen Andretta was indicted in the District of New Jersey, along with Anthony Provenzano, Thomas Andretta, Gabriel Briuglio and Ralph Pelleccia, on RICO charges (specifically 18 U.S.C. § 1962(c) and (d)) stemming *inter alia* from the demand for and receipt of "labor peace" payments from trucking companies which serviced Seatrain Lines between 1969 and 1977 (Seatrain Labor Peace Payoffs). On July 10, 1979, following his conviction, Stephen Andretta was sentenced to a ten-year term of imprisonment, which he is currently serving. *See United States v. Provenzano*, 620 F.2d 985, 989 (3d Cir. 1980).

Gabriel Briguglio was a member and officer of Local 84 of the International Brotherhood of Teamsters until March 31, 1980. Local 84 merged with Local 560 in May of 1980.[12]

Gabriel Briguglio was indicted on February 22, 1979, in the District of New Jersey, along with Anthony Provenzano and others, in the Seatrain Labor Peace Payoffs case. On May 25, 1979, he was convicted of those charges, and on July 10, 1979 he was sentenced to seven years of imprisonment. *United States v. Provenzano*, 620 F.2d 985, 989 (3d Cir. 1980).

As to the three individual defendants who have entered into consent judgments in this matter, Anthony Provenzano was employed by Local 560 as a Business Agent between approximately 1948 and 1958, as the President between approximately 1958 and May of 1966, and as Secretary-Treasurer between November 24, 1975 and June of 1978.

Anthony "Tony Pro" Provenzano's history is a long one. On November 15, 1960 he was indicted in the District of New Jersey on one count of Hobbs Act Extortion (18 U.S.C. § 1951) relating to the demand and receipt of what commonly known as "labor peace" payoffs from the Dorn Transportation Company between 1952 and 1959. On July 12, 1963, having been convicted on this count, Anthony Provenzano was sentenced to a term of seven years. Between approximately May of 1966 and 1970 he was incarcerated on that sentence.

During 1962, Anthony Provenzano was indicted again in the District of New Jersey for Taft-Hartley violations (29 U.S.C. § 186) relating to the wrongful receipt of a house from Eastern Freightways Company. These charges were, however, dismissed during 1967.

In 1975, Anthony Provenzano was indicted in the Southern District of New York for conspiracy to violate the anti-kickback statute (18 U.S.C. §§ 371, 1954) relating to a proposed loan from the Utica Teamsters Benefit Fund for the renovation of the Woodstock Hotel. During July of 1978 he was convicted of these charges and sentenced to a four-year term of imprisonment.

On June 23, 1976, Provenzano was indicted in Ulster County, New York, along with Salvatore Briguglio and Harold "K.O." Konigsberg, on charges of conspiracy and murder (pursuant to New York Penal Law § 580-a and § 1044) relating to the 1961 death of Anthony Castellitto. On June 14, 1978, he was convicted on the murder count, while the conspiracy to commit murder count was dismissed. On June 21, 1978, Anthony Provenzano was sentenced to life imprisonment.

---

12. It should be noted that Gabriel Briguglio has as of yet not become a member of Local 560 by virtue of or following the merger of these two Locals.

Finally, on February 22, 1979, Anthony Provenzano was indicted in the District of New Jersey, along with Gabriel Briguglio, Stephen and Thomas Andretta and Ralph Pellecchia on RICO charges in the Seatrain Labor Peace Payoffs case. On May 25, 1977, he was convicted of these charges, and, on July 10, 1979, he was sentenced to a twenty-year term of imprisonment and remanded. He remains incarcerated on that conviction today. *See United States v. Provenzano*, 605 F.2d 85 (3d Cir. 1979).

Nunzio Provenzano, the brother of Anthony and Salvatore Provenzano, was employed by Local 560 as a Business Agent between approximately 1963 and August 6, 1966, as a clerk between approximately 1969 and 1970, again as a Business Agent between approximately 1970 and January 25, 1973, as Secretary-Treasurer between approximately January 25, 1973 and November 24, 1975, and as President between approximately November 24, 1975 and July of 1981.

On December 26, 1961, Nunzio Provenzano was indicted in New York County, New York, along with Salvatore Briguglio and a third defendant, on charges of conspiracy and Attempted Grand Larceny (New York Penal Law § 580-a and 1294) flowing from a scheme to demand what might be characterized as "labor peace" payments from the Braun Company and Hubert J. Braun, Jr. during December of 1961 (Braun Payoff Demand). On January 29, 1963, he was convicted of attempted grand larceny, and, on March 5, 1963, he was sentenced to a term of two to four years. He served this sentence in New York between approximately August of 1966 and February of 1969.

On September 4, 1980, Nunzio Provenzano was indicted in the District of New Jersey, along with Irving Cotler, Salvatore Provenzano, and Michael Sciarra, for RICO violations (specifically 18 U.S.C. § 1962(c) and (d)) stemming from the wrongful demand and receipt of "labor peace" payments from four trucking companies between 1971 and 1980, a series of incidents often referred to as the "City-Man Labor Peace Payoffs." On May 5, 1981, Nunzio Provenzano was convicted on these charges, and, on July 7, 1981, he was sentenced to a ten-year term of imprisonment. He is presently incarcerated on this conviction.

Finally, Thomas Andretta, the brother of Stephen Andretta, has been a member of Local 560 during several periods since 1955, including from approximately August 30, 1955 through November 30, 1956; from October 29, 1959 through January 15, 1960; from January 10, 1962 through November 29, 1965; and from February 27, 1978 through July of 1979.

On March 31, 1967, Thomas Andretta was indicted in Middlesex County, New Jersey, along with Armand Faugno, for having used threats to injure in the collection of a loan between March 13 and 23, 1967, in violation of N.J.S.A. 2A:105-4 (Middlesex County Loansharking Transaction). *See State v. Andretta*, 61 N.J. 544, 545, 296 A.2d 644 (1972). On May 17, 1973, Thomas Andretta pleaded guilty to that charge. On July 10, 1973, he was sentenced to serve from one to two and a half years in prison.

During early 1968, while free on bail in the Middlesex County Loansharking Transaction case, Thomas Andretta was indicted in the District of New Jersey, along with Frederick Salvatore Furino, on charges of Theft from Interstate Shipment, in violation of 18 U.S.C. § 659, relating to the theft of Skil Tools at the Canny Trucking terminal during January of 1968 (Skil Tools theft). Following his guilty plea in that case he was, on or about April 17, 1969, sentenced to a one-year term of imprisonment and remanded.

On July 22, 1971, Thomas Andretta was indicted in the District of New Jersey, along with Salvatore Briguglio, Armand Faugno and three others, on counterfeiting charges under 18 U.S.C. §§ 371, 472 and 474 (Counterfeiting case). He later pled guilty and, on July 10, 1973, was sentenced to fourteen months of imprisonment.

During the early 1970's except when he was incarcerated, Thomas Andretta, along with Ralph Picardo, was a regular and not infrequent visitor to the Local 560 offices, where he and Ralph Picardo were hosted by Salvatore Briguglio. During roughly this period—between approximately 1970 and late 1972, Thomas Andretta was apparently employed by Armand Faugno.

On February 22, 1979, Thomas Andretta was indicted in the District of New Jersey, along with Anthony Provenzano and others, in the Seatrain Labor Peace Payoffs case. Following his conviction in that matter, he was sentenced on July 10, 1979 to a twenty-year term of imprisonment. *United States v. Provenzano,* 620 F.2d 985, 989 (3d Cir. 1980). He is currently incarcerated on this sentence.

The other individuals who figure in this matter, but who are not named as defendants, include Robert A. Luizzi, who has been a Business Agent for Local 560 since September of 1978.

*   *   *

Credibility Findings

Salvatore (Sam) Provenzano

During the course of his direct testimony Salvatore Sinno was asked about Salvatore Provenzano:

Q. Did you ever engage in any illegal activity with Salvatore Provenzano?

A. No.

Q. Did you ever talk to Salvatore Provenzano about illegal activity?

A. No.

Q. Mr. Sinno, did you ever receive any instruction from Anthony Provenzano about what you could or should talk to Salvatore Provenzano about?

A. Yeah, they—he never wanted Salvatore Provenzano, to get involved in anything illegal. We discussed that many a times, yes.

Q. Can you tell us specifically what Mr. Anthony Provenzano's instructions to you were?

A. He wanted to keep him more or less clean. He didn't want to get him involved in any way or other in illegal activities.

Q. Did he give you the reason that, as you put it, he wanted to keep Salvatore Provenzano clean?

A. Well, I imagine—

MR. WEISSBARD: Objection.

THE COURT: Don't imagine. Objection sustained. Answer the question.

A. Yes. He mentioned that quite often, in regard, he didn't want Salvatore Provenzano with any kind of a record or anything, but, for the Union's sake.

Sam Provenzano presently is an International Vice President of the Teamsters Union, President of Joint Council #73, and President of Local 560. He thus wields great power on a national as well as local level.

He is intelligent, affable and likeable. Had Sam Provenzano decided to shed the company he has kept for at least 25 years, there is little doubt in my mind that he would occupy a prominent place on labor's scene today.

The evidence is highly persuasive that from the late 50's on into the 70's, Anthony (Tony Pro) Provenzano ran this union with an iron hand whether in or out of prison or office. Sam and Nunzio played musical chairs in minding the store for Tony to satisfy the technical requirements of the law.

At some point in the 70's Sam came into his own. With power at his fingertips, he ran the show and still does. Did he stay "more or less" clean as Sinno had testified? He did not. Most of the time he helped to steer the ship the way Tony wanted it and made sure the same crew remained on board.

I listened in amazement to him persistently proclaim his belief in the innocence of his brothers and other members of this criminal syndicate with respect to various crimes that they had been convicted of or pled guilty to.

Was he naive, blind or deaf? No. Salvatore Provenzano, in my judgment, knows the truth and is oblivious to it.

Why? A revealing answer was provided on April 27, 1983 when he was asked on cross examination:

Q. Today, given all that has happened with Local 560 and all the indictments and this civil complaint and everything like that, if another indictment came down like the Seatrain indictment, would you, today, think it a prudent thing as the president of the union to make an inquiry to try and find out what the circumstances were with respect to the union contract and the alleged violation of the contract?

A. To answer your question, yes. If I would have done it by reading the indictment is something else. I think it is prudent. I thought I answered that before, that I started to check out what was going on.

Q. Okay.

A. I never denied that. What I am saying is I didn't bother to read the indictments. But I was interested in what took place.

Q. All right, sir.

Now, I think I understand you. You were interested then—you were interested at the time of Seatrain in what was going on?

A. Yes. Because my brother was involved, and I couldn't see how he was involved in the situation. That was my main concern.

Q. Your brother?

A. Yes, sir.

Q. As opposed to the union?

A. *He comes first.* I will say that. (emphasis supplied)

He still does. For Sam Provenzano inherited a legacy of corruption which has been preserved by him to this very day. In speaking of Tony in partial response to my question he said: "He would never do anything to hurt this membership."

The record is otherwise.

Josephine Provenzano

Miss Provenzano, daughter of Anthony Provenzano, has been the Secretary-Treasurer of Local 560 since 1978 when she was elected to that office at the age of 23 to succeed her father who had been convicted of murder. She presently earns $64,000 per year plus perks.

She has an engaging personality and has no illusions as to why she was appointed. She said:

A. . . . what motivated them to do that, I have to say it is because—not only that I was a Provenzano, that counts for weight, but I was Tony's daughter. See, there is only one Tony to them. Now, there was a big issue in this case as to what members believe, what they read in papers or don't they believe, were they influenced by it? I have to tell you the truth. *I don't think they would have cared if it was true or not true.* Because they know what he did for them. To them, in their minds, what did the press ever do for me? What did the government ever do for me? They take my taxes and they go on about a whole platform of things they disagree with the government. Look what Tony did for me. He gave me pensions, eyeglasses, he gave me dental. I have welfare payments. He saw me on the street and took me in the bar. We had a drink. He remembered my wife's name. He asked me how my daughter was, that had the concussion in the hospital. There is something about my father, sir,—not that you can't get mad at him. You can get mad at him. There is something about the man. I mean you can't understand until you're like one of the guys from 560. They just—I would have never believed it, if I wasn't in those meetings and I didn't hear those people go wild about him. I mean they liked him, but it is just incredible to me. It is just absolutely incredible to me. And to them, I am Tony's daughter. . . .

There can be, to the members of Local 560, no higher recommendation in this entire world. And if I don't believe that, well, I wouldn't be here right now because I wouldn't be a member of the executive board of Local 560.

It is—I don't know how to put it into words. It is more like an emotion you feel. He has an uncanny ability of making people relax, and making them know he cares. He is not a big deal. He is not very well-educated, book-wise. He might have gone to the fourth or fifth grade. But you give him a contract, he can read it. I don't know how he can read it. He just can. You put him in a room with 500 truck drivers. Nobody in this world is going to talk to them that they will understand more than my father. You put him in a room with ladies, and you never see him. My girlfriends—when my father—there is articles in the papers or—they cry. They call me on the phone in tears. 'How could they say that about your father?'

I tell them, 'Hey, listen, everyone is entitled to their opinion. You know better. Don't cry. Don't get upset. Don't read it. That's all.'

He just commands such love and respect, and admiration and loyalty, not only from his family, but from the members of Local 560. Anyone that comes into contact with him. I don't know what else to say, your Honor. I mean. I don't even know if I expressed myself properly or adequately, but that is just how I feel. I am so proud to be my father's daughter. [Emphasis supplied].

Whatever experience Miss Provenzano lacks, she makes up in candor. Her understandable love for her father transcends everything else.

Stanley Jaronko

As pointed out previously, Mr. Jaronko has been a member of the Local since 1949 and a business agent since 1977. He was a shop steward for 17 years. He is a trustee of the union and a union representative to the Trucking Employees of North Jersey Fund (TENJ).

He was asked:

Q. Have you, to the best of your knowledge, ever done anything that a member might think was designed to intimidate him from coming to meetings or speaking out his mind?
A. Nope, never did it. Never will.

He was asked:

Q. Mr. Jaronko, if Nunzio Provenzano was able to come back to the union tomorrow, you as one member of the Executive Board would vote him on in a minute, I take it, right?
A. Yeah. I believe there is a law that he cannot come back. But after he does what is he supposed to do? Yes, I would.
Q. And if that law didn't exist and he could come back tomorrow, you would take him back tomorrow, right?

A. Yes. And I believe the members will, too.

Q. And you would do the same thing with Anthony Provenzano, assuming he could come back tomorrow, you would take him back tomorrow?

A. Yes.

With respect to the Maislin Terminal incident involving Local 560 member August Muller, described *infra*, I find Mr. Jaronko's testimony unconvincing and his version of the story unbelievable.

A careful review of Mr. Jaronko's testimony reveals that, with one exception, he steadfastly refused to accept a verdict of guilty involving the Provenzanos. His rationale—they were convicted on the testimony of an informer.

Overall, I found Mr. Jaronko to be fiercely loyal to the Provenzanos, completely indifferent to the history of criminal activity on the part of various individuals, including Anthony and Nunzio Provenzano. Mr. Jaronko's fealty to the present regime is steadfast beyond question. His testimony left much to be desired.

*   *   *

Joseph Sheridan

Shop Steward since 1965, Business Agent since 1972, Trustee since 1978, and Vice President of 560 since 1981, Mr. Sheridan presented a picture of an individual whose family had taken an active role in the union in the pre-Provenzano period and who had inherited the mantle. The other business agents, Mr. Sheridan appeared to me to feel very comfortable with his earnings of $995 per week. He is not a boat rocker. When asked about Nunzio Provenzano he said:

A. Sir, if you know Mr. Provenzano, Nunzio Provenzano like I know him, and I know him quite a few years, I don't believe those allegations.

I know him to be an excellent labor leader for his people, a good family man and a man I would be very proud to recognize in the morning. I don't believe them.

Q. And if he were eligible to serve tomorrow, you, as trustee and vice-president of the Local, would bring him back tomorrow?

A. I would be happy to.

When asked about Anthony Provenzano he said:

A. Sir, let me go back. I only served a couple of years with Mr. Anthony Provenzano. I believe he came back in '75 to '78. When I was on in '72, he wasn't there. So my experience with Anthony Provenzano is only as a member of Local 560 for that period of time.

I know the men idolized him and I can see why they idolized him. He was a man, he come off the trucks the hard way. I don't think that is something, I think I said in my testimony, I said the man has charisma that I wish I had. I don't have it. He is the type of man that can walk in a room with 5,000 hard hats could be in there, and he is well-respected no matter where he goes, because I don't think there is a man in our union, or in the labor movement, that can say anything against him, about this man.

He is a fighter. He fights hard. And I will give you an example like I respect him for. I think he just was incarcerated and he come out for a short time. I think it was a two-week period.

Q. Which incarceration?

A. I think, I don't know if it is on the murder one or on the Seatrain. He was out for about—a couple of weeks. And with all that was on that man's mind, the only conversation I had with Mr. Provenzano was hello, how are you, and nothing other than that.

I am telling this Court today, your Honor, just the way I feel about this man. I am choked up about it, that is the type of guy he was. He would come down to my desk. He says 'Joey, how are you? I am sorry to hear your wife has cancer.' He says, 'Anything I can do to help you, let me know.' I said, 'I appreciate it, Mr. Provenzano.' He says, 'Hang in there and do the best you can.'

That's the type of guy he is, with all that is on his mind, somebody else might not even think of it, but he thought, just a little something like that, that little charisma like that man has. Tomorrow morning, if you let him out of jail he would win the election overwhelmingly, with all the supervision you want to put up, he would walk away with the election.

THE COURT: If you felt he murdered Castellitto, would you still feel the same way?

THE WITNESS: No, I wouldn't.

THE COURT: Why?

THE WITNESS: If anyone takes anybody's life, I wouldn't even care if it was an animal, I certainly wouldn't respect him or want any part of him or have anything to do with him.

THE COURT: If you felt that he extorted Dorn's, how would you feel about it?

THE WITNESS: I certainly wouldn't respect him or admire him.

THE COURT: Would you vote for him?

THE WITNESS: Excuse me?

THE COURT: Would you vote for him?

THE WITNESS: I would have to weigh that one, sir, because if he was convicted in my conscience, he did something wrong like that, no, I don't think I would.

THE COURT: What about Nunzio's conviction in 1981, if you felt he was truly guilty?

THE WITNESS: If I thought Mr. Nunzio Provenzano was truly guilty of the crime, I know I wouldn't.

THE COURT: You know what?

THE WITNESS: I would not vote for him.

THE COURT: All right.

Let me ask you this. Mr. Dildine testified in this courtroom that he felt the government has pursued a vendetta. I think that was the word he used originally, and then I picked up on it, against Local 560.

THE WITNESS: Yes.

THE COURT: You were in the Courtroom for that?

THE WITNESS: Yes.

THE COURT: Okay. What does the government have to do, in your mind, I am talking about Joseph Sheridan's mind, if I may use the shopworn phrase, to put the ball across the line, to convince you that these individuals who Mr. Laufer has been talking about the last few minutes, were guilty of crimes. What—in other words—let me back up a moment.

Like all of us, I am sure you read the newspapers, right?

THE WITNESS: Yes, sir.

THE COURT: Every day we pick up the paper, we read Joe Smith convicted of murder or robbery in some hamlet in the United States; right?

THE WITNESS: Yes, your Honor.

THE COURT: Okay. You read that article, you don't know Joe Smith, I am assuming that. What reaction do you have, as a normal human being?

THE WITNESS: As reading that in the article, I certainly wouldn't think much of the individual who caused that crime.

THE COURT: Do you think the man has had a trial by a jury?

THE WITNESS: Yes.

THE COURT: The jury has deliberated and found him guilty beyond a reasonable doubt.

THE WITNESS: Yes, sir.

THE COURT: Would it be fair to conclude that, on the basis of what you read, the man is guilty? He has been found guilty; right?

THE WITNESS: Yes, sir.

THE COURT: All right. Now, all these cases that we have been talking about, with one exception, I think, I mentioned to Mr. Dildine the plea of guilty by Mr. Sal Briguglio, the counterfeiting case, there were verdicts handed down. Why, in your mind, Joseph Sheridan's mind, do you have a different reaction?

THE WITNESS: Sir, I guess, like you say, if you read something in the paper and you don't know somebody, you are fast to judge an opinion, which we all do. I do it, myself.

THE COURT: Right.

THE WITNESS: But I got to tell it to you the way I know it, is that I didn't really know the Provenzanos. I just knew of them being our leaders in the union and I personally, as Joe Sheridan, never really got to know them until I became part of an organization. I can speak for my family, my wife, and I am not just saying that in here, I consider myself a very devout man, a religious man, and I bring my family up this way. I have been in their company on not many occasions. They are respected people in their community. They have lovely children. They brought them up to respect their parents, and I don't see this aura of, you know, what we are talking about, because I am there almost—I am there 11 years, and I can say that, as God is my judge, all I know these people to be is, no one ever, in the 11 years I am up there, said to me, Joe Sheridan, this is the contract.

Your Honor, I believe you asked me the question yesterday, when you said, can you, as Joe Sheridan, make a decision without picking the phone up? I can tell you companies where—and this is not done in all unions, where if I go out to negotiate a contract and if I know I got the best that I can, I don't have to go to that phone, sir, and I never have.

I will just say, that's the contract. If the people ratify it, I will come in the next day and I will tell whoever the president is at the time, sir, this is our contract. I got this and I got that. That is how I know these people, sir.

THE COURT: I understand that. But as a devout individual, and that is the way you have described yourself.

THE WITNESS: Yes, sir.

THE COURT: Haven't you ever questioned, that is my—haven't you ever questioned in your own mind, I mean aside from the fact that you are on the payroll, and I am being real up front with you—

*   *   *

THE WITNESS: I am sitting in the courtroom when Mr. Sinno was here, and we are going through testimony, and they are talking about the Mafia, and the 'hit men,' and all these here people, your Honor, like I said, unless I am the most naive person in the world, I am up there 11 years, I never met that type of individual, I never come in contact with them, and I don't know these people to be anything but good labor leaders, and responsible family men. I will go to my grave saying that.

They are good fighting people for the people they represent. Sure, the things that went on in the past, you can say quarterbacking on a Monday morning, maybe this or that should have been done, but they try, even to the membership, Sam said to me, he says, we have the contract for the Meadowlands, he said Joey, do you think you can get the Brendan Bryne Arena, he says, I got to try something and see if we can't get this membership out.

*   *   *

THE WITNESS: Your Honor, you know the hardest thing I think you have to fight, being a member of our Local, you can be invited out for a party, has nothing to do with unions or any union officials there, and it has happened to me quite a lot. The conversation, what do you do for a living. Business agent for 560. Oh, boy. You know, it is that type of stuff where, I think the papers have done a job, and it is a household word, as far as, you know, I think everyone thinks that this is a racketeer local, and it is a dominated local.

Joseph Sheridan: decent, devout, blind and bought.

II.

[1, 2] Continuously between approximately the late 1940's and the present, Anthony Provenzano has been the leader of a group of individuals who have been associated together in fact as an enterprise within the meaning of 18 U.S.C. § 1961(4), the activities of which have affected interstate commerce. This group of individuals, the "Provenzano Group," has included (in addition to Anthony Provenzano), Nunzio Provenzano, Stephen Andretta, Thomas Andretta, Gabriel Briguglio, Andrew Reynolds, Salvatore Briguglio (until his murder in 1968), Salvatore Sinno (until his defection in 1961), Harold "K.O." Konigsberg (until his incarceration in the mid-1960's), Armand Faugno (until his "disappearance" in 1972), Ralph Michael Picardo (until his defection in 1975), Ralph Pellecchia (until his imprisonment), and Frederick Salvatore Furino (until his murder in 1982). The evidence adduced at trial clearly demonstrates that these individuals conspired to and actually did conduct the affairs of the Provenzano Group Enterprise through a pattern of racketeering activity, in violation of 18 U.S.C. § 1962(c) and (d), involving murder and labor racketeering offenses on a protracted and continuing basis so as to enrich themselves and perpetuate the existence of their criminal association. The evidence further demonstrates that the Provenzano Group has maintained an ongoing organizational structure in the form of a hierarchy and protocol, which has controlled the affairs and conduct of the Provenzano Group's associates during approximately the past thirty-five years. Finally, it has also been conclusively demonstrated that the Provenzano Group has had an existence separate and apart from simply the pattern of activity in which it has engaged.

A.

Sometime during the late 1940's, Anthony Provenzano invited Salvatore Sinno to become associated with him and others in a criminal organization, the Provenzano Group herein. Sinno accepted this invitation. From this association, Sinno learned that the Provenzano Group operated as an organized racketeering enterprise, and, through its leader, was a faction of a larger New York–based criminal organization. This larger organization was at that time headed by Mike Miranda, who was serving as "acting boss" while its former head Vito Genovese was imprisoned. Prior thereto the organization was led by an individual whom Sinno identified as "Lucky" Luciano.

The larger criminal organization of which the Provenzano Group was a faction had a settled hierarchy. The positions which constituted this hierarchy were "boss," "underboss," "captains," and "soldiers," which were also known as "made members" or "button men." Anthony Provenzano was a part of this hierarchy and held the position of "made member" within the larger organization. Others who held such positions during Sinno's period of association with the Provenzano Group included Toby D'Amico, Mike Sabella, Earl Collucio, Tony Salerno, Peter LaPlaca, Bobby Manna, Gyp DeCarlo, Nick Perry, Pete DiFeo and Jerry Catena (the latter four of whom were "captains").

The associates or members of this larger criminal organization were then permitted by its protocol to engage in a variety of criminal activities, such as gambling, extortion, trafficking in stolen property and the corruption of law enforcement authorities to ignore criminal violations, but were prohibited from involvement in narcotics, prostitution and counterfeiting. Pursuant to the directions of Anthony Provenzano, and apparently in accordance with the larger organization's protocol, Sinno and others participated in the commission of a number of criminal offenses indicative of the relationship between the larger criminal organization and the Provenzano Group. One such criminal offense was the operation by Sinno and others of an illegal monte card game in New York City over a period of several years, from which the larger organization received a "tribute" payment of three percent for having allowed the game to operate. An illegal monte card game was also operated in Hoboken over a period of time which involved the payment of money to law enforcement authorities for "protection." Jersey City was the situs for the operation of an illegal dice game over a several year period prior to 1961, another criminal offense. Anthony Provenzano provided Sinno with $5,000 in operating capital for the Jersey City game in exchange for a ten percent share in the profits.[15]

In September of 1961, Salvatore Sinno disassociated himself from the Provenzano Group. At that time, Nunzio Provenzano was an associate of the Provenzano Group and, like Sinno, had been proposed for full membership in the larger criminal organization. Nunzio Provenzano's involvement in both organizations is highlighted by his presence at the "drop" where, by prearrangement, Sinno "gave up" his truck to be "hijacked."

Following the period described by Salvatore Sinno, the Provenzano Group continued to exist as a racketeering enterprise, notwithstanding the incarceration of Anthony Provenzano between approximately the mid-1960's and 1970 and the incarceration of Nunzio Provenzano (as well as Salvatore Briguglio) between approximately 1966 and 1969. First, I find that between approximately 1969 and 1977, Anthony Provenzano, Gabriel Briguglio, Stephen Andretta and Thomas Andretta unlawfully conspired to and did conduct the affairs of an enterprise (the Provenzano Group) through a pattern of racketeering activity, consisting of multiple violations of the Taft-Hartley Act, 29 U.S.C. § 186, and involving both Local 560 and several carriers for Seatrain Lines. Further, between approximately 1971 and 1980, Nunzio Provenzano and others conspired to and did conduct the affairs of an enterprise through a pattern of racketeering activity, again consisting of multiple violations of the Taft-Hartley Act, and involving four interstate carriers.

*　　*　　*

15. Anthony Provenzano also caused an employer to place Salvatore Sinno's name on its payroll so that Sinno's tax records would reflect a legitimate source for his income from the various gambling activities seemingly undertaken at Anthony Provenzano's behest. This provides another example of an act consistent with and reinforcing of the organizational structure of the enterprise and which promoted both organizational and individual well-being.

B.

During the past thirty years, Anthony Provenzano and other members of the Provenzano Group have engaged in a pattern of criminal and other improper acts, the object of which was to gain control over and to exploit the Local 560 Enterprise.

First, between approximately January 1, 1952 and June 1, 1959, within the District of New Jersey and elsewhere, Anthony Provenzano, while an official of Local 560, extorted "labor peace" payoffs from Walter Dorn and his company, Dorn Transport, Inc. of Rensselaer, New York. During this period, Anthony Provenzano held the positions of Business Agent, and later, of President, and obtained a total of $17,100 from Dorn.[18]

Next, at the time of his nomination and appointment as a Business Agent for Local 560, Anthony Provenzano directed Salvatore Sinno and Earl Coluccio to attend the membership meeting in question in order to intimidate and if necessary discipline any "rambunctious people"—meaning those members who might presume to voice opposition to his appointment. Similar tactics were employed by the Group in preparation for Local 560's January 10, 1960 election, which was hotly contested. As one such step, Anthony Provenzano directed Nunzio Provenzano, Thomas Reynolds and Robert Luizzi to "sign up" ineligible members in order to increase the Group's voting strength. Salvatore Sinno, at Anthony Provenzano's behest, persuaded some six of his friends to vote for the Provenzano slate in that election, although each of them was, in fact, ineligible to so vote. Salvatore Sinno himself was able to (and did) vote in the 1960 election because Anthony Provenzano had brought Sinno's membership "book" up to date by falsifying entries to show that Sinno was a member of Local 560 in good standing.

Third, in order to enhance his own power and that of the Provenzano Group within Local 560, and apparently to punish what he regarded as a breach of the Group's protocol, Anthony Provenzano recruited Harold "K.O." Konigsberg and Salvatore Briguglio to kill Anthony Castellitto—which they, together with Salvatore Sinno and others, did on June 6, 1961. Prior to his "disappearance," Anthony Castellitto was one of the most popular members of Local 560. He had been, for example, the only candidate to run unopposed in Local 560's 1960 election. Anthony Provenzano considered Anthony Castellitto to be a serious threat to his control over Local 560 and felt that Anthony Castellitto might be assisting the opposition party within Local 560.

To carry out Anthony Provenzano's directive, Harold "K.O." Konigsberg enlisted Salvatore Sinno and others sometime shortly before June 6, 1961 to assist him with the planned murder. On June 6, 1961, in Ulster County, New York, Konigsberg, Sinno, Salvatore Briguglio and others killed Anthony Castellitto by striking him on the head with a blunt object and strangling him about the neck with a cord.

18. This pattern was to some extent repeated when, between November 30 and December 12, 1961, Salvatore Briguglio and Nunzio Provenzano attempted to extort labor peace payments (attempted grand larceny) in the Braun Payoff Demand case, discussed *infra*.

Thereafter, Anthony Provenzano rewarded Konigsberg for his part in the Castellitto murder by paying him the sum of $15,000. Anthony Provenzano rewarded Salvatore Briguglio for his part in the Castellitto murder by making him a Business Agent in Local 560.

On or about December 20, 1962, approximately one month after Anthony Provenzano had been indicted in the Eastern Freightways case, the membership of Local 560 voted, upon the motion of Michael Sciarra, to increase the salary of its President, Anthony Provenzano, from approximately $20,800 to approximately $45,800 annually. Sciarra testified that his motivation in making the motion was the common knowledge within the Local that Anthony Provenzano faced substantial legal expenses in connection with his defense on the Dorn charges. His salary was again increased on February 14, 1963, and upon the motion of Stephen Andretta, from approximately $45,800 to approximately $95,800 annually. Andretta testified, in turn, that he was prompted to make the motion because of the feeling that Anthony Provenzano should make as much money as Jimmy Hoffa, who was at the time President of the International Union. Hoffa disappeared on July 30, 1975.

On or about March 13, 1963, Anthony Provenzano announced to the attendees of a membership meeting of Local 560 that he was not taking these two salary increases and would not do anything to impoverish the Local. This was again confirmed at the October 13, 1963 membership meeting, when Anthony Provenzano told those attending that, "as of today, I have not taken either of the salary increases granted me." On or about July 21, 1966, the membership of Local 560 voted, upon the motion of Michael Sciarra, as seconded by Stephen Andretta, to reduce the salary for the office of the President from $95,000 to $20,800, to be effective with the appointment of Salvatore Provenzano as President on May 6, 1966.

On or about January 30, 1969, Anthony Provenzano (then in prison) caused his attorney, Joseph F. Walsh, to mail a letter to Local 560 requesting that it issue a check to Anthony Provenzano in the amount of $25,000 (less appropriate deductions) "on account of back salary due and owing to him." This letter was subsequently received by the Local 560 Executive Board. As a result of this request, the Local 560 Executive Board paid to Anthony Provenzano the sum of $25,000 annually each year between 1969 and 1976. These payments together represented all but approximately $48,785 of the amount accumulated through his salary increases. During the period encompassed by these payments, Anthony Provenzano did not hold office in Local 560, being in fact disqualified until November of 1975 from holding any union office.

Local 560 received no benefit in exchange for the payment of these funds to Anthony Provenzano. Contrary to his representation to the membership on March 13, 1963, the payments (totalling $223,785) did in fact "impoverish" the Local. His ability to exact these payments from Local 560 provides further evidence of the strength and dominance of the Provenzano Group and its exploitation of Local 560 for its own purposes.

Next, on May 24, 1963, in Hudson County, New Jersey, Walter Glockner was murdered. Prior to his death, Glockner had been a vocal critic and opponent of the

Provenzano brothers. In particular, on the evening before his death, during the course of a Local 560 meeting chaired by Salvatore Provenzano, Glockner had voiced opposition to the appointment of J. W. Dildine as a Business Agent. After the meeting, Glockner attempted to approach Salvatore Provenzano in order to further vent his feelings on the matter. As he did so, he became embroiled in a heated exchange and shoving match with Thomas Reynolds. Ralph Pellechia, Local 560's Sergeant-at-Arms at the time, restrained Glockner and forceably evicted him from the premises. The following morning, Glockner was shot to death in front of his residence in Hoboken.

*　　*　　*

During the mid-1960's, Anthony Provenzano consolidated his power and control over Local 560. Shortly after his election victory in 1965, he, Nunzio Provenzano and Salvatore Briguglio commenced serving prison terms resulting from their respective convictions in the Dorn Extortion and Braun Payoff Demand cases. Nevertheless, the Provenzano Group remained strong, and new associates came to prominence. The new associates—Stephen Andretta, Thomas Andretta, Armand Faugno, Ralph Michael Picardo and Frederick Salvatore Furino—were "tied in" to the Group principally through Salvatore Briguglio. Andrew Reynolds was also later brought in through Nunzio Provenzano. Certain of these new associates joined forces with the other members of the Provenzano Group in continuing to further acquire, maintain and exploit control over Local 560.

Between approximately December of 1969 and June of 1977, Anthony Provenzano, Stephen Andretta, Thomas Andretta and Gabriel Briguglio, together with others unlawfully accepted "labor peace" payments from certain employers— namely, Interocean Services, Inc. (between approximately mid-1969 and mid-1974) and Di-Jub Leasing, Inc. (between late 1974 and early 1977).

Between approximately early 1974 and late 1977, Anthony Provenzano, aided and abetted by the other associates of the Provenzano Group (and in particular by Salvatore Briguglio and Stephen Andretta), did receive and agree to receive certain fees, kickbacks, gifts and things of value because of and with intent to be influenced with respect to his actions and decisions relating to certain questions and matters concerning the Local 560 Benefit Plan (the Trucking Employees of Passaic and Bergen Counties Welfare and Pension Fund), in violation of Sections 1954 and 2 of Title 18 of the United States Code.

*　　*　　*

Further, I find that the circumstantial evidence is strong and convincing that Anthony Provenzano, aided and abetted by Salvatore Briguglio and Stephen Andretta (whose involvement is clear despite the government's specific failure to include him as to this incident in the complaint) engineered the entire Romano loan/kickback deal for their gain and at the membership's expense. Salvatore Provenzano testified that he remonstrated with his brother when he (Salvatore) learned of the first property sale. While his instincts were correct, his fervor to protect the union membership was subordinated to his brother's will. His brother came first.

Next, continuously between approximately January of 1971 and July of 1980, Nunzio Provenzano, Irving Cotler and others, unlawfully received and accepted and agreed to receive and accept certain payments, loans and deliveries of money and other things of value from certain employers—namely, Pacific Intermountain Express Company (between approximately January of 1971 and July of 1980), Mason and Dixon Lines, Inc. (between approximately November of 1976 and June of 1979), T.I.M.E.–DC, Inc. (between approximately November of 1975 and April of 1979) and Helms Express (between approximately January of 1977 and April of 1979), the employees of which companies were employed in an industry affecting commerce. Specifically, it was found that (a) Nunzio Provenzano and others were officers and employees of Local 560; (b) Local 560 did represent and would admit to membership certain employees of the said employer companies, and (c) the said payments, loans and deliveries were made with the intent on the part of the said employer companies to secure "labor peace" from Local 560 by influencing the officers and employees of Local 560 with respect to their official actions and duties—all of which violated 29 U.S.C. § 186(b) and 18 U.S.C. § 2.

The power of the Provenzano Group and its ability to exploit Local 560 for its own purposes was again apparent in 1979. On or about November 9th of that year, the membership of Local 560 voted to award Anthony Provenzano an annual "pension" which would equal one-half of his salary at the time of his retirement. This step had been necessitated, in the view of the Group, by the fact that a break in service (resulting from his imprisonment between 1966 and 1970 in the *Dorn* case) had disqualified him from receiving a pension from the Teamsters.

Thereafter, on June 21, 1978, Anthony Provenzano was sentenced to life imprisonment for the murder of Anthony Castellitto. As a result, he was forced to "retire" from Local 560. On November 21, 1978, Nunzio Provenzano told the attendees at a Local 560 membership meeting that the Executive Board had acted on the membership's vote to grant Anthony Provenzano a pension, and he thanked the membership for having supported the motion. Pursuant to this action, Anthony Provenzano received the following amounts as his "pension" from Local 560: 1979—$27,612; 1980—$27,612; 1981—$28,143.

In his testimony, Salvatore Provenzano stated that he had "no idea" how Local 560 would benefit from the payment of this one-half pension. Trustee Michael Sciarra also knows of no benefit to Local 560 which flows from these payments other than to keep "the members happy—they voted for it." The ability of the Provenzano Group to exact these payments is clearly demonstrative of its strength, influence and continuing ability to control and exploit Local 560 for its own purposes—at the expense of the membership. The audacity of these payments in the face of Anthony Provenzano's conviction (and sentence of life imprisonment) for murder is remarkable.

As part of the effort to gain control over and exploit Local 560, continuously throughout the period between June of 1961 and the present, Anthony Provenzano and other associates of the Provenzano Group—aided and abetted by various past and present members of the Local 560 Executive Board—systematically used extortion in order to induce a significant portion or segment of Local 560's membership to surrender certain property. Specifically, this extortion took the form of the wrongful use of actual and threatened force, violence and fear of physical and economic harm, particularly the loss of the ability to earn a livelihood, and it was used to induce or coerce the membership into surrendering their federally protected rights to participate in the affairs of Local 560 in a democratic manner. This extortion affected interstate commerce and the movement of articles and commodities in such commerce.

The extortion of these intangible property rights occurred through a series of actions committed by the Provenzano Group. The first of these was the "disappearance" of Anthony Castellitto in 1961.

The extortionate effect of the Castellitto "disappearance" was further amplified or highlighted by the ambush slaying of Walter Glockner in 1963. Again the pattern was repeated: As previously noted, Glockner had, on the night before his murder, spoken out at a Local 560 membership meeting in opposition to a Provenzano Group proposal—even more critically, a proposal to move a Provenzano Group associate into the position of Business Agent. Almost immediately after the murder took place, Thomas Reynolds, Sr. was arrested and held for a number of weeks as a "material witness." This prompted widespread speculation among the membership that Glockner's murder had been the direct result of, and was in retaliation for, his outspoken criticism at the meeting.

One can have a grave suspicion that Glockner's death was caused by the Provenzano Group. As I have previously found, however, the record will not support a finding to that effect, even by a preponderance of the evidence. But it is clear from a review of the entire record that Glockner's violent demise has been used by the Provenzano Group either directly or subtly as a mechanism of intimidation. For example, it is apparent from the testimony of August Muller that two decades later the members of the Local still have a perception that the Group annihilated Glockner. Even if they did not, this perception has been exploited by the defendants as a means of instilling fear and stifling opposition.

The degree to which perceptions linger that the Glockner murder was an act of retaliation by the Provenzano Group and the dramatic effect that such a perception can have at the present time is illustrated by the August Muller incident, which developed during the course of the trial in this matter.

* * *

The perception which initially flowed from the Castellitto "disappearance" and the Glockner murder gradually developed into a pervasive climate of intimidation within Local 560. An important factor in the process of generating and maintaining this climate of intimidation has been the systematic appointment and reappointment of associates of the Provenzano Group, particularly of those associates who had serious and extended criminal records or whose propensity for violence or criminal activity was otherwise known to those who were principally responsible for the particular appointment as well as the membership.

* * *

This pattern of appointments and reappointments following convictions and incarceration, as well as the related pattern of criminal offenses committed while in office, is, according to testimony I deem credible, unique to Local 560 and unparalleled in the history of United States labor organizations. I find it to be a shameful horror story, the effect of which has been the extortion of the membership's LMRDA–created property rights to union democracy, and the creation, as a result, of a Provenzano Group "fiefdom" within Local 560.

Another factor in the process of generating and maintaining the climate of intimidation within the membership of Local 560 has been the conspicuous and studied indifference of the Provenzano Group, and particularly of its associates who held officer positions in Local 560, to the frequent presence of known or reputed criminals and "undesirables" around the Local's offices. The fact of this presence tended to foster a perception among the membership that the incumbent officers and the Provenzano Group had available to them the support and resources of persons who were not adverse to the use of criminal methods in attaining their desired results. These visitors included:

(a) Thomas Andretta, the brother of Business Agent Stephen Andretta, who had been convicted of the use of extortionate means in the collection of debt in Middlesex County in 1967 (indicted together with Armand Faugno), the theft of Skil Tools from the Canny terminal during 1968 (convicted together with Frederick Salvatore Furino), and counterfeiting during 1971 (convicted along with Salvatore Briguglio, Armand Faugno and three others). In addition, Thomas Andretta had been convicted in or around 1960 for theft from Interstate Shipment. Notwithstanding these convictions, Thomas Andretta was a frequent visitor at the office of Local 560 during the late 1960's and early 1970's.

(b) Armand Faugno had been convicted in 1967 with Thomas Andretta in the Middlesex County Loansharking Transaction and with various other in the 1971 Counterfeiting case. In spite of this record, Faugno sometimes visited the offices of Local 560 before his disappearance in December of 1972. While there is no evidence introduced at trial that Faugno was known to any rank and file member of Local 560 who might have been visiting the office at the same time, word of his relationships with Provenzano Group associates most certainly spread among certain segments of the membership following his disappearance while under indictment together with Thomas Andretta and Salvatore Briguglio.

* * *

The pervasiveness of the climate of intimidation within Local 560 and the intensity of its impact upon the membership's ability or willingness to exercise their "union democracy" rights under the LMRDA are evinced by the complete absence of publicly voiced opposition to, disagreement with or critical discussion of the (non-contract related) policies, proposals, decisions and actions of the Provenzano Group incumbents. According to the testimony of Professor Clyde Summers, which testimony I credit, the true test of union democracy is whether the members feel free to openly criticize the policies and practices of the incumbents, and not merely whether there are any opposition candidates. There have been a large number of occasions in the recent history of Local 560 during which an objective observer might have expected to hear such criticism or discussion at membership meetings. For example, the murder of Walter Glockner on the morning after his public display of opposition at a union meeting, and the subsequent arrest and detention (for several weeks) of Thomas Reynolds as a material witness in the murder, should have been "fodder" for the opposition in 1963 and should still be "fodder" today, particularly in light of the Local's history. The evidence suggests that the question of Glockner's murder has never been raised at a membership meeting, at least not since 1965.

Further, Professor Summers also testified that the conviction of an official on a union-related offense will normally trigger criticism or even encourage the opposition to come forth and make a challenge. The failure of an Executive Board to take any remedial action when a responsible official is indicted or convicted can only add fuel to such a situation. Professor Summers noted that it would matter little that such an offense related to a union other than the one in which the defendant was an official (such as was true in the Braun Payoff Demand case). To have appointed persons who are prepared to raid a union is "to bring foxes into the henhouse." Consequently, anyone who is appointed by a person who was himself sent to jail for selling labor peace should normally be a target of criticism. There has, of course, been no such criticism within Local 560 since the emergence of the Provenzano Group.

*   *   *

III.

In order to prevent future racketeering violations by the Provenzano Group and its aiders and abettors, it is necessary to enjoin Stephen Andretta and Gabriel Briguglio from any future dealings with Local 560 and to remove the current Executive Board members from their positions, appointing in their place one or more trustees to administer the Local during a curative period of appropriate length. Following this period, the trustees would conduct a carefully supervised election to restore union democracy within Local 560.

Stephen Andretta and Gabriel Briguglio, while holding positions of trust within their respective labor organizations, committed serious and protracted labor racketeering violations as associates of the Provenzano Group. If given the opportunity, they are likely to do so again. Stephen Andretta was given an opportunity at trial to make expiation for his conduct, particularly including that involved in the Seatrain Case. Instead, his testimony, which, at best, lacked candor and strained credibility, demonstrated no hint of atonement. Gabriel Briguglio presented no evidence in his defense, and his silence under the circumstances supports an inference that his own evidence would be unfavorable to his cause.

The current Executive Board members must be removed as a predicate to the restoration of union democracy within Local 560 and to ameliorate and remedy the conditions which have enabled the associates of the Provenzano Group to dominate and exploit the Local for the past thirty years. The evidence clearly points to the fact that the members view the leadership of the Local as a single, monolithic control organization. So long as it, or any portion of it, remains in actual control of Local 560, Professor Summers' testimony indicates that it will be very difficult to remove the sense of fear which the members now experience. This sense of fear within the Local—causing members to believe that it is not safe to protest or organize—is so overwhelming that it is not likely to correct itself in the foreseeable future.

Removal of each Executive Board member is also necessary because each one is either unwilling or unable to evaluate objectively the criminal conduct of fellow officers or business agents, or to institute prophylactic measures to ensure as much as possible that past criminal conduct will not be repeated. Moreover, the pervasive attitude of arrogance and insolence in the face of these circumstances continues to impress upon the membership that the Local's leadership at the very least condones criminal conduct. This, too, serves to perpetuate the atmosphere of intimidation and to suppress any dissent.

*　　*　　*

Continuously throughout approximately the last quarter of a century, the associates of the Provenzano Group have dominated Local 560 through fear and intimidation, extorting the membership's union democracy rights, and have exploited it through fraud and corruption. Because the conditions within Local 560 which have been the *sine qua non* for the reported commission of acts of these defendants remain, I must conclude that future [RICO] violations are likely to occur, thereby resulting in irreparable harm to the membership of Local 560, its contract employers, and the public. In order to prevent and restrain such future violations of § 1962, it is necessary to enjoin defendants Stephen Andretta and Gabriel Briguglio from any future contacts with Local 560, and to remove the current members of the Local 560 Executive Board in favor of the imposition of a trusteeship for an appropriate period of time, which will terminate following the completion of supervised elections.

I have additionally determined to exculpate the institutional defendants herein, specifically Local 560 itself and its Funds and Plan. In order to attribute the misconduct of the individual defendants to these institutional defendants, I must find (1) that the individual defendants committed the acts of racketeering in the scope of their employment, and (2) that they thereby intended to advance the affairs of the institutional defendants.

While it is clear that the individual defendants acted within the scope of their employment in committing the various criminal acts previously recited, it is equally obvious that their intent was not to advance the affairs of their employers. To the contrary, the institutional defendants in this action were the victims. The associates of the Provenzano Group, aided and abetted by the other defendants herein, intended by their actions to control and exploit Local 560 to its detriment. I therefore conclude that there is no basis for retaining either Local 560, the Funds or the Plan as a defendant in this action, except insofar as it is necessary to retain Local 560 as a nominal defendant to effectuate the equitable relief heretofore specified and as may be ordered in the future.

VI.

In sum, I have determined that the individual defendants herein have violated 18 U.S.C. § 1962(b), (c) and (d). Because of the likelihood of continued violations, I have determined to enjoin defendants Stephen Andretta and Gabriel Briguglio from any future contacts of any kind with Local 560, and to remove the current members of the Local 560 Executive Board in favor of a trusteeship. This trusteeship shall continue for such time as is necessary to foster the conditions under which reasonably free supervised elections can be held, presumptively for eighteen months. I have, however, decided to stay the effect of this injunctive relief pending appeal, and have also decided to defer the naming of the trustee(s) until the completion of any such appellate proceedings. Finally, I have decided to dismiss Local 560, the Funds and the Plan from this action, except insofar as I must maintain jurisdiction over Local 560 as a nominal defendant in order to effectuate the equitable relief heretofore specified or as may be ordered in the future.

Plaintiff shall submit an order in conformance with this opinion within seven (7) days.

United States v. Local 560 and Michael Sciarra, Opinion of Judge Dickinson Debevoise
(January 7, 1991)

In this proceeding the government seeks a permanent injunction against Michael Sciarra prohibiting him from further participation in the affairs of Local 560. The trial was conducted on July 16, 1990, but only two witnesses were presented, and the bulk of the evidence upon which a decision must be based was introduced upon applications for preliminary injunctive relief. Fed.R.Civ.P. 65(a)(2). This opinion constitutes my findings of fact and conclusions of law.

Judge Ackerman stayed his March 16, 1984 Judgment Order pending appeal. In consequence Sciarra and the other members of the Executive Board of Local 560 remained in office.

On December 26, 1985 the Court of Appeals for the Third Circuit affirmed the judgment of the district court, and the Supreme Court denied a petition for certiorari. On June 23, 1986 Judge Ackerman lifted the stay and implemented the Trusteeship provided for in the Judgment Order. Thus, there was a period of approximately two years, four and one-half months between Judge Ackerman's February 1984 opinion detailing the racketeering activity and the 1986 appointment of the trustee and ouster of the Executive Board. During that period, on October 19, 1984 to be precise, Sciarra succeeded Salvatore Provenzano (who had been convicted of defrauding the welfare benefit fund and of receiving kickbacks) as President of Local 560. What transpired during that period is one of the principal subjects of the present proceeding.

Judge Ackerman appointed Joel Jacobson Trustee of Local 560 on June 23, 1986. On May 12, 1987 Judge Ackerman appointed Edwin H. Stier, Esq., in place of Jacobson, and he appointed as Associate Trustee Frank Jackiewicz. Stier undertook numerous measures to achieve his three principal objectives: (a) conducting the day-to-day operations of the union so as to provide effective representation to the membership, (b) using his own background in conducting investigations to organize and oversee inquiries into the affairs of the union and of the pension and welfare funds, and (c) encouraging the members of Local 560 to throw off years of passivity in the face of Provenzano domination and to participate in the affairs of the union.

In early 1988 Stier concluded that although the forces conducive to an uncoerced atmosphere within Local 560 were still fragile and still threatened with organized crime efforts to regain control, an election with suitable controls was feasible.

On February 11, 1988 Judge Ackerman extended the Trusteeship until December 6, 1988 and ordered that general elections be held prior to that date. Nominations were to be made at a membership meeting called for October 9, 1988 and the election by secret ballot was scheduled for November, ballots to be mailed to each member's home to reduce the opportunities for undue pressure.

Certain developments came to the attention of the government which led it to believe that unless injunctive relief were obtained, the result of the election would be to return Local 560 to the control of organized crime, specifically the Genovese Family. The strongest faction competing for control of Local 560 was Teamsters for Liberty, a group which had never evidenced a critical view of the former leadership and which was dedicated to termination of the Trusteeship. That stance of itself was no reason to interfere with the efforts of Teamsters for Liberty. However, the government had come into possession of evidence which led it to believe that the Genovese Family had determined to regain control of Local 560 and that it had designated Michael Sciarra as the person through whom it would exercise control. Sciarra was a dominant force in Teamsters for Liberty, and he and Joseph Sheridan, also a former Executive Board member when the Provenzano Group was in control, were Teamsters for Liberty's candidates for President and Vice-President, respectively.

Faced with that situation and with the fragile nature of Local 560's democratic forces the Government instituted the present proceedings, seeking an order prohibiting Sciarra and Sheridan from further participation in the affairs of Local 560.

On September 14, 1988, after a six-day hearing, I granted preliminary injunctive relief, barring Sciarra and Sheridan from seeking elective office. Teamsters for Liberty substituted as its candidates for President and Vice-President Sciarra's brother Daniel Sciarra and Sheridan's nephew Mark Sheridan.

The election was carefully monitored and fairly conducted, and on December 6, 1988 it was announced that the Teamsters for Liberty slate had won. As a result Daniel Sciarra and Mark Sheridan assumed the offices for which they ran. Other Teamsters for Liberty candidates had been elected to complete the Executive Board. Stier, the Trustee, turned over the day-to-day administration of Local 560 to the newly elected officers and Executive Board but continued to serve in a monitoring role.

On January 9, 1989 the newly elected Board appointed both Michael Sciarra and Joseph Sheridan to fill business agent positions. Thereupon the government obtained an order to show cause why they should not be immediately barred from holding any appointed position within Local 560 pending the outcome of the trial in the matter. The government urged that Sciarra and Sheridan gave the appearance of acting as *de facto* officers of the Local and of exercising actual power consistent with that of incumbent Executive Board members, thus creating the risk of reemergence of Genovese Family control of the Union.

At a hearing on January 30, 1989 I concluded that the development was troubling but that I should not assume without more that the new officers and Executive Board would not exercise full control of the Union or that they would be subject to Sciarra's domination and influence. Consequently I denied the government's application at that time.

The Trustee, pursuant to orders of Judge Ackerman, continued to monitor closely the management of the Union. The new officers and Executive Board members entered upon their duties. Subsequently, Sheridan entered into a settlement with the government, resigning as business agent and agreeing not to involve himself in the future in the management of Local 560. Michael Sciarra, however, remained highly involved in the Union's affairs.

On February 6, 1990 the government moved once again to bar Sciarra from holding any position of trust in the Union, asserting that evidence relating to events during the previous 13 months showed that Sciarra had used his hold on a large and vocal segment of the Local 560 membership and his position as business agent to acquire control of the Union. A second preliminary injunction hearing was held on March 20 and 21, and I concluded that Sciarra had indeed become virtually *de facto* President of Local 560. On May 8, 1990 I signed an order preliminarily enjoining Sciarra from holding any position of trust within Local 560 and from attempting to influence its affairs.

I scheduled a trial on an expedited basis. The trial began on July 16, 1990.

＊　　＊　　＊

On three occasions in the last two years I have held evidentiary hearings concerning Sciarra's continuing role in Local 560. My findings upon the conclusion of the first application for a preliminary injunction are set forth in 694 F.Supp. 1158 (*Local 560* No. 2); my findings upon conclusion of the second application for a preliminary injunction are set forth in 736 F.Supp. 601 (*Local 560* No. 3). The evidence which was submitted at the trial of the matter consisted of the testimony of Special Agent Mark Dowd of the Federal Bureau of Investigation, the testimony of Michael Sciarra and certain documents. Nothing that developed at the trial leads me to alter the findings set forth in *Local 560* No. 2 or *Local 560* No. 3. In fact the evidence at the trial fortifies those findings.

The totality of the evidence establishes that: (i) Since March 16, 1984 when Judge Ackerman signed the order granting relief the Genovese Family has sought to maintain or reestablish its control over Local 560; (ii) Michael Sciarra was the person through whom the Genovese Family sought to effectuate its control; (iii) Sciarra accepted this role; (iv) Sciarra has a dominating and forceful personality, and there are no leaders or factions within Local 560 who are able to resist him and the forces within the Union which he controls; and (v) unless Sciarra is removed from any position within Local 560 he will assume control of the Union, directly or indirectly, and thereby subjugate Local 560 once again to the control of the Genovese organized crime family.

[2] The continuing determination of the Genovese Family to maintain control of Local 560 is evidenced by the tape recordings of three conversations held in a

construction shed in Edgewater, New Jersey and by one tape recording of a conversation held at the Palma Boy Social Club in East Harlem. When viewed in conjunction with the findings in *Local 560* No. 1; they demonstrate that the efforts of this organized crime group to control Local 560 did not cease with the entry of Judge Ackerman's order. The personnel changed somewhat, but many old faces continued to appear.

I quoted extensively from those tape recordings in my opinion in *Local 560* No. 2, at pp. 1170–1178. I incorporate my earlier findings with respect to the tapes herein and at this point will only summarize them.

The first conversation took place on November 1, 1984 and involved Milton Parness, Matthew Ianniello (a captain in the Genovese Family), Stanley Jaronko (who served on Local 560's Executive Board with Sciarra) and an unidentified male. Ianniello and Jaronko discussed continued control of Local 560. Jaronko stated that he would "just lay low for eighteen months" (the period during which it was expected a court-appointed trustee would be in office). It was in that conversation that Ianniello directed Jaronko to "let Mike run the show." The reference was to "Mikey Sciarra."

The second tape records a November 6, 1984 conversation between Ianniello and Stephen Andretta (one of the defendants who was a member of the Provenzano Group). It was a lengthy conversation concerning numerous persons in the Genovese Family, past and pending criminal endeavors, and the Local 560 RICO case. As to the situation at Local 560, Ianniello stated, "I think Mike Sciarra should take over there. Who can you trust there, anybody else?" Andretta responded, "Mike and I were born and raised together." Later Ianniello stated, "I'll send word to [Mike]. I'll make sure that he knows that you can talk to him as one." There followed this interchange:

IANNIELLO: No, no, I'll send word to Mike (unintelligible).

ANDRETTA: I can see Mike any time you want me to.

IANNIELLO: You?

ANDRETTA: Yeah.

The third tape records a December 7, 1984 conversation between Ianniello, Stephen Andretta and an unidentified male. That too was a lengthy conversation which dealt with a number of subjects of significance in this case, one of the more important subjects being the New England Motor Freight ("NEMF") contract. As to the role which Sciarra was to play, the following is illustrative:

ANDRETTA: I understand at this point. But with Mikey and then you, you have direct control of Mikey.

IANNIELLO: Yeah.

ANDRETTA: No question.

IANNIELLO: Yeah, he does what I tell him.

A fourth tape recorded conversation had taken place on November 28, 1984 in the Palma Boy Social Club in New York City. The participants were then Genovese

Family boss Anthony Salerno, Louis Gatto, one of his caporegimes, Giuseppe Sabato and Cirino Salerno. The conversation turned to Local 560, and the following exchange took place:

A. SALERNO: But they threw everybody out of office there.
SABATO: Yeah, they're all out.
A. SALERNO: Everybody's out.
SABATO: They're all out.
A. SALERNO: So how can you control it?
SABATO: What do you mean? They got the control in there.
A. SALERNO: Who is that now?
SABATO: Matty (Ianniello).
A. SALERNO: Oh, we got a guy in there?
SABATO: Sure.

These taped conversations must be viewed in the light of the facts disclosed in the 1984 *Local 560* No. 1 opinion. When so viewed there can be no doubt that the Genovese Organized Crime Family intended to maintain its control over Local 560 during the pendency of the appeal from Judge Ackerman's March 16, 1984 Judgment Order, during any period of trusteeship and thereafter. I concluded after the first preliminary injunction hearing and I conclude now that the tapes constitute strong evidence that this control was to be exercised through Anthony Salerno's caporegime Matthew Ianniello and that Ianniello, upon the advice of Stephen Andretta, selected Michael Sciarra to be the man on the scene at Local 560 to whom orders and instructions could be given.

Thus, notwithstanding the issuance of the March 16, 1984 Judgment Order and the appointment of a trustee on June 23, 1986 the Provenzano Group as it existed in 1984 and as its personnel changed somewhat during the years that followed, never ceased the unlawful conduct described in Judge Ackerman's opinion in *Local 560* No. 1.

* * *

After March 16, 1984 Sciarra continued to profess his loyalty to Anthony Provenzano and could not bring himself to disavow the criminal and other unlawful tactics of the Provenzano Group nor to admit the existence of the Provenzano Group conspiracy and Genovese Family involvement in the affairs of Local 560. As recently as September 24, 1989, Sciarra, then a Local 560 business agent, proclaimed to an enthusiastic Local 560 membership his love for Provenzano. I do not take seriously Sciarra's belated mea culpa delivered on July 17, 1990 at the conclusion of the trial in this matter. That declaration, like so many of Sciarra's statements over the years, was designed to meet his needs of the moment.

Most of the evidence in this case was introduced at the 1988 preliminary injunction hearing. That evidence disclosed actions on Sciarra's past which tied him personally to the taped conversations and the continuing conspiracy. Neither Sciarra's testimony at the trial nor the arguments advanced in his post-trial briefs lead me to change the findings and conclusions with respect to these actions set forth in my 1988 opinion, *Local 560* No. 2. I incorporate those findings and conclusions herein.

The evidence and findings with respect to the New England Motor Freight ("NEMF") sweetheart arrangements are set forth at 694 F.Supp. at 1173–1177, 1179–1181.

* * *

I cited two other circumstances in my 1988 opinion which tended to confirm Sciarra's continued participation in the Genovese Family efforts to maintain control over Local 560.

The first was the failure to take steps to remove Marvin Zalk as administrator of the Local 560 Welfare Plans after he had been convicted of obstruction of justice in a case involving fraud upon the [Pension and Welfare] Plans. The second was the failure to terminate a contract with a provider of legal services to Local 560 members under circumstances so eggregious to defy belief.

* * *

I probably should have granted the government's application to enjoin Michael Sciarra from assuming the position of business agent, but perhaps it is fortunate that I did not do so. Permitting Sciarra to serve as business agent during the January 12, 1989 to May 8, 1990 period when he was supposedly under the control of the Executive Board, provided a demonstration of what would happen if he were given any position within Local 560. He immediately became de facto President of the Union, pushing his brother aside, figuratively and literally, whenever it suited his purpose to do so. Were it not for the continuing intervention of the court appointed Trustee he would have had himself appointed a trustee of two pension and welfare funds maintained for the benefit of Local 560 members. These funds had been grossly misused during the Provenzano years, and one of the principal tasks of the court appointed trustee was to ensure their honest and effective administration.

I issued the 1988 order enjoining Sciarra from becoming President of Local 560 because were he to assume that office there was a strong likelihood that he would lead Local 560 back into the control of the Genovese Organized Crime Family. The evidence submitted at the 1990 second preliminary injunction hearing showed that Sciarra, through his position as business agent, had assumed the power which the first preliminary injunction was intended to keep from him. Therefore on May 8, 1990 I issued a new order preliminarily enjoining Sciarra from holding any office in Local 560.

At the trial of this matter two additional items of evidence further demonstrated Sciarra's continuing ties to the Genovese Family. It will be recalled that Matthew

Ianniello and Stephen Andretta were the principal participants in the tape recorded conversations which established the Genovese Family's continuing plan to control Local 560 and the decision to use Sciarra as the person through whom control would be exercised.

At the trial Special Agent Mark Dowd of the F.B.I. testified that on the morning of June 4, 1990 (less than a month after I had enjoined Sciarra from participating in Local 560 affairs) he and Special Agent Thomas Browne conducted a physical surveillance of Sciarra. This led them to a diner on Route 46 near Little Falls. When the two agents entered, Sciarra was using the pay telephone in the vestibule. They proceeded by him to a booth just inside the dining area. About ten minutes later Sciarra entered this area from the vestibule and walked across the room to two men who occupied a table. The Agent identified one of these men, who was seated in the courtroom, as Local 560 business agent David Keitt. Sciarra conversed with the two men for some minutes. At that point, a fourth individual entered the dining area. Sciarra immediately left Keitt and his companion and walked back towards the entrance where the other man had paused. They exchanged greetings and sat down together at the first booth inside the dining area. Agent Dowd identified this man as Stephen Andretta. After approximately twenty-five minutes, the agents left the diner and waited outside. Keitt and his companion left the diner moments after the two agents. Approximately forty-five minutes thereafter, Michael Sciarra and Stephen Andretta left the diner together. They conversed in the parking lot for a few more minutes, and then departed from the area in their respective vehicles.

The other item of evidence showing Sciarra's continuing association with the Genovese Family was elicited on cross-examination of Sciarra. The Government asked about Jimmy Ida, who had been identified during the August, 1988 proceedings as "Matty" Ianniello's chauffeur and as one of his designated messengers to Michael Sciarra on Local 560 matters. In the monitored conversation of December 7, 1984 Ianniello had told Andretta that Ida could serve as a contact with Sciarra if Andretta were having difficulty with the assignment. On cross-examination Sciarra admitted that he had met with Ida on some seven occasions since 1987 in a cafe in Manhattan's "Little Italy" Section.

Sciarra's explanation of the meetings with Andretta and with Ida was that there was a need to discuss Sciarra's being a defense witness in an upcoming criminal trial at which Andretta and Ida would be defendants. I have little confidence in Sciarra's explanations of events and circumstances generally. At the very least this evidence shows Sciarra's continuing association with the Genovese Family members who devised the plan to exercise control of Local 560 through him.

* * *

As long as Sciarra holds any position within Local 560 he will be able through his forceful personality and through his hold on a large and vocal segment of the membership to dominate and control the Local and its pension and welfare funds. If he assumes power within the Union it is highly likely that upon termination of the court appointed trustee's oversight the Genovese Family would reassert control over Local 560, undoing all the efforts of the past eight years. Great strides towards the establishment of union democracy have been made during the period of the trusteeship. The return of Sciarra and, through him, Genovese Family influence, would crush the movement towards membership control and bring back the dark night of the strong arm and repression.

Control by Sciarra and through him by the Genovese Family would place the welfare and pension funds at great risk. They were looted before the court appointed trustee assumed office and if Genovese Family influence were reestablished it is almost a foregone conclusion that they would be looted again upon the departure of the Trustee.

In sum, Sciarra's presence within Local 560 would subject the union, its members and its pension and welfare funds to irreparable injury. This injury can be avoided only by injunctive relief which would prevent Sciarra's return to any leadership capacity in Local 560.

*　　*　　*

For all the foregoing reasons I conclude that additional relief is required. An order will be entered permanently enjoining Michael Sciarra from holding any office or position of trust within or otherwise endeavoring to influence the affairs of Local 560 or any of its benefit plans. The government is requested to submit a form of order.

Interim Settlement Agreement and Consent Decree

(February 6, 1992)*

* * *

3. OBJECTIVES AND INTENT: The parties recognize that Local 560 has historically suffered from a serious labor racketeering problem which has been associated with the destruction of union democracy and intimidation of the individual members. Accordingly, the objective and purpose of this Interim Settlement is to create within Local 560 remedial conditions which will—to the extent possible but in the least intrusive manner—eliminate the vestiges of the documented racketeering problem, forestall the reemergence of any such racketeering problem in the future, and otherwise ensure that any incipient racketeering problem is quickly detected and effectively eradicated. To that end, the remedial effort structured herein seeks (a) to promote and protect union democracy; (b) to protect all union members from invidious economic discrimination; and (c) to foster the existence of an Executive Board which is responsive to the legitimate interests of the entire membership, which is vigilant in the protection of their economic and political rights, which is dedicated to the principles of honest trade unionism, and which will serve as an effective bulwark against the reemergence of an externally induced racketeering problem.

4. THE EXECUTIVE BOARD: Effective upon the first working day after the entry of this Interim Settlement Decree, the Executive Board of Local 560 shall be reconstituted as follows:

a. DANIEL SCIARRA shall resign from the position of President. Thereafter, he shall be eligible to serve in the capacity of shop steward. The office of President shall remain vacant until such time as the District Court shall direct that an election be held to fill the position.

b. Secretary-Treasurer ROBERT MARRA, Recording Secretary ALFRED VALLEE and Trustee PETER GRANELLO shall continue to serve in their present positions and discharge all obligations and responsibilities thereof.

c. From among the remaining three Executive Board positions (Vice President and two Trustees), the current Executive Board shall before the entry of

---

* [The interim settlement was amended on February 6, 1992. The changes primarily affect the size and composition of the executive board (paragraph 4 of this interim settlement) and permit the board to appoint Alfred Vallee as president of Local 560.]

this Decree select one incumbent to continue in the position of Union Trustee. The two incumbents who are not selected by the process specified herein shall nevertheless remain eligible to serve in any and all positions of trust within the union—including, but not limited to, the position of business agent.

d. Upon entry of this Consent Decree, the Court's Trustee, Edwin H. Stier, shall promptly appoint from among the members of Local 560 in good standing two suitable members each of whom shall serve in the capacity of Union Trustee upon the Executive Board and shall exercise all powers, duties and responsibilities thereof as specified in the Constitution and By-laws. Those appointees shall serve for the same term and under the same economic and working conditions as pertain to the four remaining incumbents.

e. Thereafter, the Executive Board will function with six members as aforesaid until further order of the Court.

f. The incumbents of the Executive Board acknowledge and the new members of the Executive Board shall acknowledge that they have a heightened awareness of their fiduciary duty to the membership because of the serious racketeering problem within Local 560 as discussed in the five published court opinions which are central to the litigation. In light of the special circumstances discussed therein, each such Executive Board member shall be diligent with respect to discharging the said fiduciary duty and in implementing both in letter and spirit the terms and conditions of this Agreement in order to achieve the remedial objectives of the Court Opinions. Each such member has an affirmative and continuing obligation to be vigilant with respect to preventing or otherwise detecting and remedying the types of derelictions, abuses and corrupt practices which the various court opinions have identified as having contributed to the racketeering problem of the past. Any incumbent who shall hereafter violate the fiduciary duty in a manner which materially endangers the remedial objectives of the Court Trusteeship or whose conduct shall otherwise bring discredit upon Local 560 or the International Brotherhood of Teamsters under the standards established by the Independent Administrator of the I.B.T. or who otherwise engages in a course of conduct which is inimical to or obstructive of the remedial process of the Court Trusteeship shall, in addition to internal remedies, be subject to removal from office upon a finding of such misconduct after notice and a hearing before the District Court.

g. ROBERT MARRA, PETER GRANELLO and the third incumbent named by the Executive Board pursuant to subparagraph "c" above shall promptly select and designate a Co-Chair of the Executive Board. ALFRED VALLEE and the two Union Trustees appointed pursuant to subparagraph "d" above shall also promptly select and designate a Co-Chair of the Executive Board. The designation of the two Co-Chairs shall be subject to approval by the Court Trustees. The Co-Chairs of the Executive Board shall jointly perform the responsibilities and functions of the President as long as that position remains vacant pursuant to the provision of subparagraph "a" above.

5. THE CONSTRUCTION FIELD: The following special provisions shall apply to the area of construction within the jurisdiction of Local 560:

a. The Executive Board and its successors shall not in the future appoint former Business Agent Onofrio Mezzina to any position of trust (including particularly "shop steward" or "business agent"). In the event that Onofrio Mezzina, is, in accordance with the then-existing union practices, employed as the sole union member upon a construction site or at some other place of employment, he shall not thereby gain the position of "steward" nor shall the Executive Board permit him to exercise the responsibilities of nor otherwise hold himself out to be a "steward" nor to derive any status or benefit of the steward's position thereby. Moreover, Mezzina shall not be employed as nor otherwise permitted to act in the capacity of a service provider for Local 560 unless specifically authorized by this Court after notice to the Government and an evidentiary hearing upon his suitability. Notwithstanding the foregoing, the Executive Board may compensate Mezzina at the hourly rate of a business agent for services rendered during any brief period which is necessary to accomplish an orderly transition, and it may otherwise compensate him from time to time for lost wages and benefits necessitated by his services as a witness.

* * *

b. The Court's Trustee shall promptly appoint to the Business Agent position which Mezzina has just vacated a suitable candidate from among the eligible members of Local 560.

c. The Business Agent thereby appointed shall also hold the title of Local 560 Construction Referral Administrator and shall administer the Local 560 construction referral system referred to in subparagraph "d" below.

d. Within thirty days of the entry of this Decree, the Executive Board shall present to the Trustee and the Government for their approval a comprehensive plan for a fair system for job referrals in the construction field. The new system will have as its primary objective the allocation of the available work based upon rational principles and fundamental fairness. The system shall ensure to the extent possible that the membership is able to ascertain without undue difficulty the actual operation of the system with respect to particular job referrals. The system shall incorporate safeguards reasonably available to protect its integrity.

6. THE COURT TRUSTEE: Nothing contained herein shall be construed as limiting the powers, duties and responsibilities presently assigned to the Court's Trustee.

a. Incidental to the discharge of the Court Trustee's general oversight responsibility, the Executive Board shall on a weekly basis provide the Court

Trustee with a certified report or minutes of all Executive Board meetings and of all other decisions of the Executive Board, whether or not made within the confines of a formal meeting. These certified minutes or reports shall be detailed and complete.

b. The Executive Board shall inform the Court Trustee in particular detail about its proposed actions with respect to the appointment or removal of all subordinate officials, the retention, performance and/or termination of service providers and vendors (when the aggregate cost exceeds $5,000 per annum), and the hiring or dismissal of employees.

c. The Trustee shall have plenary powers to investigate and to report to the Court upon the operations of the union and the progress of the remedial effort of the Court Trusteeship—particularly with respect to the potential reemergence of the racketeering problem and the various conditions affecting union democracy. In conducting any such investigation, the Court Trustee shall have complete and unfettered access to all records, officials and employees of Local 560.

d. Local 560 shall provide reasonable compensation for such auditors or investigative accountants and support personnel as the Trustee deems necessary to discharge his investigative duties and responsibility.

7. REMEDIES: Any party herein and the Trustee may, upon notice to others concerned, make application to the Court for enforcement of or relief from any of the terms and provisions contained herein; and the Court may grant such relief as shall be equitable and just, having due regard for the purpose of the underlying litigation, the remedial objectives of the Court Trusteeship and the Opinions related thereto, and circumstances existing at the time of the application. Any willful violation of any restriction or prohibition contained herein, or other disobedience of any mandate of this Decree shall be punishable as a contempt of court.

3

The Commission:
United States v. Salerno

(Trial: September–November 1986)

Introduction

United States v. Salerno aimed to fell all of New York City's Cosa Nostra leaders with a single stroke. The indictment charged the bosses of New York City's Cosa Nostra crime families and several of their subordinates with constituting and operating a "commission" that served as a board of directors and supreme court for the mob. In proving its case, the government sought to place the defendants within the history of Cosa Nostra. In a real sense, the case was about whether it is a crime, meriting life imprisonment, to be a Cosa Nostra boss. Ultimately, the jury, the judge, and the appellate court answered that question in the affirmative.

Background

The background of the Commission case is the history of Cosa Nostra itself. For many years, law enforcement personnel asserted the existence of a commission that coordinated the activities of the mob. This theory seemed to be confirmed when Joseph Bonanno, the former boss of the Bonanno crime family, published *A Man of Honor*.[1]

According to Bonanno's romanticized account, the commission was founded in 1931 as a mechanism for resolving interfamily conflicts ranging from economic disputes to bloody struggles such as the Castellammarese War of the late 1920s.[2] The commission was comprised of prominent bosses who were elected to five-year terms at national meetings of Cosa Nostra leaders from around the country. The last such meeting, according to Bonanno, occurred in Apalachin, New York, in 1956; since then, the commission has been composed of the five New York bosses. Rudolph Giuliani, then U.S. attorney for the Southern District of New York, has been quoted as saying, "If Bonanno can write about a Commission, I can indict it."

Investigation

United States v. Salerno began in 1980, when the FBI's New York City office initiated operation GENUS, assigning teams to build RICO cases against each of the five New York crime families. Ultimately, over two hundred agents were involved in this operation, aided by a number of assistant U.S. attorneys.

Operation GENUS coordinated federal, state, and local agencies: FBI agents, New York City detectives and officers, assistant U.S. attorneys, as well as New York State Organized Crime Task Force attorneys and investigators. It utilized electronic surveillance on a scale previously unknown. Investigators gathered over four thousand hours of conversations pursuant to 171 court-authorized bugs and wiretaps.[3] Agents planted bugs in locations ranging from Genovese crime family boss Anthony Salerno's headquarters, the Palma Boy Social Club in East Harlem, to automobiles driven by defendants Ralph Scopo and Anthony Corallo, to the home of Paul Castellano, Gambino family boss and reputed head of the commission. These bugs were extraordinarily productive. Over the Castellano bug, two agents listened around the clock for four months to discussions of criminal activity, Gambino family internal politics, Cosa Nostra interventions in the construction industry, and turf disputes among the families involved in garment industry racketeering. Over the Corallo bug, agents of the New York State Organized Crime Task Force listened for four months to sensitive discussions of Lucchese crime family and commission activities.

Infiltration and intensive surveillance of the Bonanno family proved particularly fruitful. FBI Agent Joseph Pistone passed along extensive information about the disorder within that family, which had caused its earlier takeover by the commission.

Over five years, the investigators obtained sufficient information to fill in the structure, hierarchy, and activities of each of the crime families. While law enforcement officials had previously obtained glimpses of Cosa Nostra's organization, the information had never before been as thoroughly and systematically collected, assembled, and analyzed.

The intelligence information generated by operation GENUS resulted in separate RICO prosecutions of each of the five New York crime families[4] and in the Commission case. Each family RICO case indicted the leaders of a crime family, charging that they had participated in the affairs of an enterprise (their mob family) through a pattern of racketeering activity. *United States v. Salerno* indicted in one case the bosses and underbosses of the four New York families represented on the commission, along with their key underlings, for running the commission. (The Bonanno family was not represented on the commission at this time because it was in the throes of civil war.) According to Giuliani, "The [Commission] case should be seen as the apex of the family cases. . . . It is an attempt, if we can prove our charges, to dismantle the structure that has been used since the beginning of organized crime in the United States."

The Indictment

The indictment, unsealed on February 26, 1985, named as defendants more Cosa Nostra leaders than had ever before been indicted at one time.[5] The defendants were Paul Castellano, boss of the Gambino family (dropped after he was murdered on December 16, 1985); Aniello Dellacroce, Gambino underboss; Anthony Salerno, boss of the Genovese family; Anthony Corallo, boss of the Lucchese family; Carmine Persico, boss of the Colombo family; Gennaro Langella, Colombo underboss; Ralph Scopo, Colombo soldier; Salvatore Santoro, Lucchese underboss; Christopher Furnari, Lucchese *consigliere*; and Anthony Indelicato, Bonanno capo.[6] Although they had never represented their respective families on the commission, Scopo and Indelicato were named as defendants because they executed the commission's orders.

The theory of the government's case was that the Cosa Nostra commission constituted a criminal enterprise; that each defendant was a member or functionary of the commission; and that each defendant had committed two or more racketeering acts in furtherance of the commission's goals. According to the prosecution, the defendants' predicate racketeering acts fell into three categories: first, management of a multifamily bid-rigging and extortion scheme in the New York concrete industry; second, conspiracy to organize loansharking territories in Staten Island; and, third, the murders of Bonanno family boss Carmine Galante and two of his associates in furtherance of the commission's effort to resolve a Bonanno family leadership dispute.

The indictment charged these defendants both with operating the commission through a pattern of racketeering activity and with conspiring to operate it as a racketeering enterprise. The government alleged that the commission's raison d'etre was to "regulate and facilitate the relationships between and among La Cosa Nostra families." Through the enterprise, the defendants were alleged to have engaged in or aided and abetted authorization of murders, narcotics trafficking, loansharking, and infiltration of labor unions. The indictment also charged that the commission "maintained its authority by identifying itself with threats and violence."

In support of the commission's existence, the indictment included a history of the commission's membership and activities. It named the leaders of the five families that had been represented on the commission since its formation in 1931, including, among others, Vito Genovese, Thomas Lucchese, Joseph Colombo, Carlo Gambino, and Albert Anastasia.

The indictment charged all of the defendants except Indelicato with utilizing their dominance over the District Council of the Concrete and Cement Workers Union to organize and oversee a "concrete club," a cartel of concrete contractors. The operation of the concrete club was the basis for thirteen counts of extorting money from contractors and six labor bribery counts. In addition, Corallo and Santoro were charged with participating in a Staten Island loansharking conspiracy, and Indelicato was charged with furthering the purposes of the commission by murdering Carmine Galante, Leonard Coppola, and Giuseppe Turano, three mob figures who opposed the commission's chosen candidate during its reorganization of the Bonanno crime family.

Thus, the government painted organized crime as a sprawling criminal conglomerate whose activities ranged from garden-variety vice rackets to murder, labor racketeering, bid rigging, and unfair competition in the construction industry. It also presented a vague picture of the commission as a Cosa Nostra court and as a board of managers pursuing its own criminal enterprises.

The Prosecution

The trial began on September 8, 1986.[7] Assistant U.S. Attorneys Michael Chertoff, John Savarese, and John Childers conducted the prosecution. Federal district judge Richard Owen presided at the trial. Carmine Persico represented himself, a strategy that enabled him to address the jury directly without exposing himself to cross-examination; some of the nine-week-long trial's most dramatic moments involved Persico's cross-examinations of former mob associates and members who were testifying for the government.

The prosecution took advantage of the requirement under RICO that it prove the existence of an organization in fact. The prosecutors put into evidence a history of organized crime and of the commission. They began their case with evidence of the Apalachin meeting that had occurred thirty years previously and they adduced testimony about infamous mobsters who had died long before the events charged in the case. Not surprisingly, the defendants strenuously, but unsuccessfully, objected to the recitation of the history of Cosa Nostra and its commission, arguing that such evidence was irrelevant and prejudicial.

The government's first witnesses were several state troopers who had conducted the famous 1959 Apalachin raid. The prosecution's best witness on Cosa Nostra history and customs was Angelo Lonardo, the underboss defector from the Cleveland crime family. His testimony touched on the lives and careers of legendary gangsters—Vito Genovese, Thomas Lucchese, Joseph Colombo, Carlo Gambino, Albert Anastasia. His vivid testimony provided exquisite detail on the Mafia's traditions, codes, structure, and activities. Further, Lonardo identified each of the defendants and named his organizational status within the Cosa Nostra hierarchy.

In addition to Angelo Lonardo, the government called Fred DeChristopher, a cousin with whom Carmine Persico had lived while he was a fugitive from November 1984 to February 1985; Joseph Cantalupo, a former Colombo family member; and Joseph Pistone, the FBI agent who had infiltrated the Bonanno family. They also testified as to the traditions and methods of Cosa Nostra and its commission, the Mafia's initiation rituals, and the intrafamily politics of the New York families. These rules and customs of Cosa Nostra, which traditionally insulated the bosses from prosecution, now were offered as evidence proving the existence of an enterprise that passed on its structure, rules, and criminal franchises from generation to generation. Assistant U.S. Attorney John Savarese described the defendants as "[t]he board of directors of a vast criminal enterprise";[8] the jury cannot have helped being impressed by such references and testimony.

Moving from a historical exposé of Cosa Nostra, the prosecution proceeded to establish the defendants' violations of RICO by proving their membership on the commission and their predicate acts: the authorization of the 1978 murders of Carmine Galante, Giuseppe Turano, and Leonard Coppola; the aiding and abetting of Staten Island loansharking; and the management of a cartel that controlled the New York concrete industry. The case against Scopo was proved by showing his collection of "extortionate" payments on behalf of the commission from concrete contractors. The government's case against Indelicato hinged upon evidence that the commission had authorized his murder of Carmine Galante.

The prosecutors sought to prove that the concrete cartel permitted only its seven members to bid on concrete contracts in New York City that were worth more than $2 million. The District Council of the Concrete and Cement Workers Union enforced the cartel by refusing to carry out (or by subverting) unauthorized contracts. This enabled the club to allocate contracts among its members, contracts that were especially profitable because the cartel could name its own price. In exchange for this lucrative opportunity, the contractors had to kick back to the commission 2 percent of the contract prices. For purposes of federal criminal law, the government cast this scheme as an extortion of contractors. As the New York State Organized Crime Task Force reported, in reality the contractors were willing participants who passed the 2-percent surcharge on to their customers.[9]

The club's operations were extensively detailed through direct testimony and dozens of taped conversations. Stanley Sternchos of Technical Concrete Construction Company and James Costigan of X.L.O. Concrete Company, contractors who had both been charged with Taft-Hartley Act violations (making payoffs to a labor official, Ralph Scopo, bagman for the cartel) and had been granted immunity in exchange for their testimony, described the operation of the club.[10]

In making its case against Corallo and Santoro, the government argued that they had facilitated loansharking by resolving a territorial dispute between the Lucchese and Gambino families. This was a RICO predicate act because it (1) constituted aiding and abetting of loansharking, and (2) furthered the goals of the commission as an enterprise.

The government argued that the Carmine Galante murder was ordered by the commission in order to resolve a power struggle within the Bonanno family. Fred DeChristopher, Carmine Persico's cousin by marriage, testified that Persico had told him that he had voted against the murder in a commission meeting. From this, the jury was asked to infer that the commission had voted to kill Galante.

Joseph Pistone also testified on the commission's involvement in the Galante murder. He had been informed, while undercover in the Bonanno family, that the family had been taken under commission control because of instability resulting from a leadership dispute between Carmine Galante and Philip Rastelli. After the murder, he was told that the commission had reorganized the family under Rastelli, returning it to autonomous control for the first time in a decade.

Indelicato's palm print was found on the Galante murderers' getaway car, firmly linking him to the crime. Further, the prosecution showed a surveillance video of Indelicato being congratulated at the Gambino family headquarters, the Ravenite Social Club, by Bonanno family *consigliere* Stefano Canone and Gambino family underboss Aniello Dellacroce less than half an hour after the murders. The government offered this after-the-fact approval to show that the commission had authorized Indelicato to kill Galante.

The Defense Case

The scope and depth of the prosecution case confronted the defendants with a difficult task. The defendants' primary trial strategy was to attempt, through cross-examination, to discredit the witnesses who testified against them, and to argue that the government's electronic surveillance demonstrated only the existence of an organization, not its involvement in any criminal activities. The defense conceded the existence of a concrete club, but argued that its members were contractors.

Corallo's attorney admitted the existence of Cosa Nostra and its commission, the first such admission in the history of Mafia defendants. The defense argued, however, that the commission was not involved in any criminal activity and that membership in either Cosa Nostra or the commission alone was not proof of criminality. The defendants argued that the commission's only roles were the mediation of internal Cosa Nostra family conflicts and the approval of new members; they denied any involvement in loansharking, murder, or extortion. Further, they denied any connection between the commission and the concrete club, arguing that the latter was an industry cartel operating on its own.

Ralph Scopo's attorney, John Jacobs, admitted in his closing arguments that his client had accepted payoffs from employers, but he denied that they were extortionate or collected on the commission's behalf. The defendants argued that the contractors were willing participants in an extremely profitable cartel and should themselves have been prosecuted for bid rigging. According to Anthony Cardinale, the lawyer for Anthony Salerno,

It is a club of contractors, not of commission members . . . the commission had nothing to do with the concrete payments. . . . Listen to the words that are actually being spoken, they do not contain any threats or any pressure. . . . The concrete companies gladly paid to gain an advantage in the industry.[11]

Further, the defendants argued that there was a long tradition of bid rigging in New York's construction industry, predating the alleged influence of a

Cosa Nostra commission. Later, in their appeals, the defendants would argue that life sentences for bid rigging were cruel and unusual.

The defendants attempted to discredit Lonardo and the government's other Cosa Nostra witnesses as traitors looking to even old scores and save themselves from long prison terms. Lonardo was branded a turncoat who had promised to serve the government in any way possible to get himself out of prison. Persico, representing himself, argued that Joseph Cantalupo, a former Colombo associate, had a grudge against him because of a beating by Persico's brother over an unpaid loansharking debt. "You was angry because you was beat up, and you was beat up because you didn't pay back the money," argued Persico. This argumentative "question" may have backfired by revealing Persico's own involvement in loansharking, rather than discrediting Cantalupo. Persico ran into similar difficulties in his cross-examination of Sternchos, who, according to Persico, had demonstrated his untrustworthiness by failing to make necessary payoffs to Ralph Scopo, an argument that the jury may have found more inculpatory than exculpatory.

Unfortunately for the defense, the multitude of government photographs of gatherings of the Cosa Nostra defendants, combined with intercepted references to commission meetings, provided convincing evidence of the commission's activities. Recordings of Scopo explaining the commission's rules for the concrete club and of Corallo discussing his plans to murder Cosa Nostra drug dealers, were equally hard for the defendants to rebut. Ultimately, the prosecution's overwhelming evidence was too much for the defense to overcome.

The Verdict and Sentence

On November 19, 1986, after six days of deliberation, the jury found the *Salerno* defendants guilty of all seventeen racketeering acts and twenty related charges of extortion, labor payoffs, and loansharking. The verdict was hailed by law enforcement officials and commentators: Rudolph Giuliani announced, "The verdict reached today has resulted in dismantling the ruling council of La Cosa Nostra."

In pronouncing sentence on the *Salerno* defendants, Judge Owen stated that "the sentence has to be fashioned to speak to [future crime bosses]." Despite the fact that Salerno's predicate crimes were "extortion" (in reality, bid rigging), Judge Owen excoriated him at sentencing: "You have spent your lifetime terrorizing your community." He then sentenced all of the defendants, except Anthony Indelicato, to one hundred years in prison; Indelicato received forty years. In addition, he imposed fines on Corallo and Santoro of $250,000, on Indelicato of $50,000, and on the other defendants of $240,000 each.

Although some organized-crime bosses in the past have retained their leadership positions while imprisoned, running family business through trusted subordinates, the life sentences in *Salerno* have almost certainly ended these defendants' careers.[12]

The Appeal

The defendants appealed their convictions on numerous grounds. Among their many arguments,[13] they claimed that the evidence was insufficient to prove (1) the extortion of five concrete companies whose principles did not testify; (2) Corallo's involvement in the concrete club; (3) the existence of a loansharking conspiracy; and (4) the commission's involvement in the murders of Carmine Galante, Giuseppe Turano, and Leonard Coppola. Anthony Indelicato appealed his RICO conviction for participation in the 1978 Galante murder on the ground that the five-year RICO statute of limitations had expired.[14] All of the defendants challenged the admissibility of the extensive evidence on the history of Cosa Nostra, and all of them challenged the severity of their sentences.

The Second Circuit Court of Appeals rejected all of the insufficiency-of-evidence arguments.[15] It held that there was sufficient evidence to prove the existence of the concrete club, as well as systematic bribery and extortion in the concrete industry. While there was no direct evidence of Corallo's participation in the cartel, the court found him to be a cartel member because he was a member of the commission that managed the cartel and because his subordinate, Lucchese family *consigliere* Christopher Furnari, had participated in the cartel's allocations of concrete contracts.

The Second Circuit also rejected the argument that there was insufficient evidence to prove that the defendants' loansharking and murder conspiracies were carried out in furtherance of the commission's objectives. With respect to the loansharking charge, the court held that

[t]he jury could reasonably conclude that the efforts of Corallo and Santoro were not only related to the Commission's activities, but actually furthered the Commission's goal of arbitrating interfamily disputes and coordinating criminal activities among the families.[16]

Similarly, with respect to the relationship between the commission and the Galante murders, the Second Circuit held that

[t]here was evidence at trial that the Commission had established a "death penalty" for anyone who might murder a boss without prior Commission approval. After the Galante murders, however, Indelicato was not eliminated, but was promoted by the Commission. . . . The murders were a product of multifamily coordination, which is one of the functions of the Commission. . . . The jury could reasonably conclude that the Commission approved the murder of Galante in order to resolve the Rastelli-Galante dispute and to restore order and autonomy to the Bonanno family.[17]

The Second Circuit's opinion could be interpreted to mean that all the commission members are responsible for crimes that fall within the commission's jurisdiction, broadly defined, without proof of direct participation or even aiding and abetting. If so, Cosa Nostra leaders would face expansive RICO liability simply for their status in organized crime. As the *Salerno* dissent argued,

That the Commission's role as peace-keeper among the families should subject its officers to criminal liability for all crimes engaged in by any individual or family member of the Mafia would eviscerate the requirement of improper intent in our conspiracy laws.[18]

It is not clear, indeed it is unlikely, that the commission enforces its rules so automatically that criminal liability should follow without specific proof of commission action in particular instances. As the dissent observed, "testimony that the 'common law' of La Cosa Nostra requires Commission authorization before a family boss can be killed does not prove that the law was observed in Galante's case."[19] In several other cases where bosses have been killed, including Paul Castellano, a prior commission vote has not been shown.

The defendants further argued that the admission of evidence of Cosa Nostra's history was reversible error because it had no relevance to the charges and was highly prejudicial. The appellate court disagreed, holding that Cosa Nostra's history and traditions were relevant because they tended to show the purposes the commission served for Cosa Nostra:

[D]iscussions of Commission rules and structures . . . served the Commission conspiracy by educating family members concerning Commission policy and control, thus insuring obedience and knowledgeable participation within the highly structured and secretive criminal network.[20]

Cosa Nostra's traditions and methods, which had served as means of insulating the bosses from prosecution, were here used as proof of both Cosa Nostra's existence and the commission's managerial role.

Finally, the Second Circuit acknowledged the severity of the 100-year sentences but concluded that the judge acted well within his discretion in handing them down. Judge Owen's "message to future bosses" was affirmed.

Conclusion

As late as 1983, defendants in a major Chicago organized-crime trial had dismissed "Cosa Nostra" as a fictional construction of media and government.[21] Many sociologists and other academics continued to deny the existence of a coordinated organized-crime group in the United States.[22] In *Salerno*, the government conclusively rebutted these denials. As Giuliani stated, "If we can prove the existence of the Mafia in court beyond a reasonable doubt, we can end this debate about whether the Mafia exists. We can prove that the Mafia is as touchable and convictable as anyone."[23] After nearly five decades, U.S. law enforcement had addressed a phenomenon long taken for granted by Hollywood and popular folklore. *Salerno* exhaustively proved Cosa Nostra's existence, organization, rules, and involvement in criminal activities as diverse as loansharking, murder, and labor and corporate racketeering.

In proving the concrete club cartel, the government revealed how entrenched and sophisticated Cosa Nostra has become in exploiting opportunities in the legitimate economy. After the commission case, Cosa Nostra's control of more than a dozen trade unions in the New York construction industry was exposed in the New York State Organized Crime Task Force report *Corruption and Racketeering in the New York City Construction Industry*[24] and in many criminal and civil RICO cases. The upper tier of the concrete cartel, controlling concrete contracts in excess of $5 million, was later targeted in a prosecution of S & A Concrete and its chief operating officer,[25] and several subsequent government racketeering suits and criminal prosecutions have attempted to break Cosa Nostra's control over New York's construction unions.

However, while *Salerno* undoubtedly proved the existence of Cosa Nostra and some sort of commission made up of the bosses of the New York families, it raised as many questions as it answered. At times, the prosecution referred to the commission as a *national* board of directors for the mob, but its membership was said to be limited to the New York City crime families, and all of the predicate acts charged in the case involved New York mobsters. The prosecution offered testimony concerning commission influence in Cleveland and Buffalo and historical evidence of commission representation for families outside of New York, but it did little to develop a thorough picture of Cosa Nostra as a national organization or of the commission as a nationwide court and/or board of directors. In our view, there is not sufficient evidence to conclude that there exists a national decisionmaking body with authority to adjudicate disputes among all of the Cosa Nostra families in the United States, much less direct their criminal activities.

The mechanisms of commission and Cosa Nostra decisionmaking are similarly obscure. The case leaves us in doubt about how the commission makes decisions—for example, by unanimity or majority rule—and how the commission enforces its judgments. We are also left wondering how the commission goes about voting (if it does) to assassinate one of its own members. Did John Gotti obtain approval from the commission to assassinate Paul Castellano? If so, how was it that three members of the commission would have voted, if they did, to kill a fourth? If Gotti did go to the commission, how could he have been confident that his intentions would not have been communicated to Paul Castellano?[26] And what about the plot by members of the Genovese family to kill John Gotti, which the FBI overheard?

Neither the authority nor the power of the commission was made clear in *Salerno.* Can the commission take jurisdiction over disputes on its own or is its jurisdiction conferred by parties (families) to a dispute? Does the commission act on its own initiative to "punish" rule violations or conduct not in the best interest of Cosa Nostra as a whole, or does it wait for a complaint? When does the commission intervene in intrafamily disputes? In cases where rival factions vie for control of a family, on what basis does the commission decide which party to support?

Taken at its broadest, *Salerno* stands for the proposition that Cosa Nostra leaders can be convicted of committing RICO offenses at any time. The government need only show (1) that the defendant participated in an enterprise, namely a crime family, the commission, or Cosa Nostra generally, and (2) that he did so through a pattern of racketeering activity—in effect, any two crimes committed (a) by himself or (b) by his underlings if he "conspired" in, "authorized," or "aided and abetted" those crimes. Proof of this "authorization" can be satisfied by proof of the defendant's status in the hierarchy. The use of RICO in this case and in the family RICO cases came close to convicting mobsters simply for being mobsters, if it did not actually cross that line.

Despite the questions it left unanswered, *Salerno's* expansion of RICO liability—and the prominence of its defendants—supports the claim that it was the most ambitious, and among the most successful, of the hundreds of federal Cosa Nostra prosecutions during the 1980s. Professor G. Robert Blakey, the principle draftsman of RICO, summed it up well:

The Commission case is to RICO what the Standard Oil case was to the Sherman Act. The Sherman Act was written in 1890 to get at the Standard Oil trust, and that case wasn't brought until twenty years later. So we're five years ahead.[27]

Notes

1. Joseph Bonanno, *A Man of Honor: The Autobiography of Joe Bonanno* (Simon and Schuster, 1983).

2. See Virgil W. Peterson, *The Mob: 200 Years of Organized Crime in New York* (Green Hill Publishers, 1983).

3. *U.S.–Italian Teamwork Bringing Organized-Crime Chiefs to Trial*, New York Times, 18 October 1985, A1.

4. See, e.g., Bonanno family: *U.S. v The Bonanno organized Crime Family*, 87 Civ 2974 (EDNY 1987); Gambino family: *United States v Gotti*, 641 F Supp 283 (SDNY 1986); Genovese family: *United States v Salerno*, 868 F2d 524 (2d Cir 1989); Lucchese family: *United States v Luchese Organized Crime Family* (EDNY 1989); Colombo family: *United States v Persico*, 832 F2d 705 (2d Cir 1987), *United States v Colombo*, 616 F Supp 780 (EDNY 1985).

5. *United States v Salerno*, 85 CR 139 (SDNY 1985).

6. In an interlocutory ruling, the Second Circuit, sitting en banc, issued a holding that significantly expanded the scope of the RICO statute. Indelicato had appealed from the RICO charges against him, arguing that three simultaneous murders could not support RICO's requirement of pattern of predicate acts. The Second Circuit disagreed, holding that "acts may constitute a pattern even though they are nearly simultaneous." The court reasoned that, although the three murders were nearly simultaneous, they constituted more than one act, were related by design, and were part of the activities of the commission and Bonanno family enterprises and thus were part of continuing racketeering activity. *United States v Indelicato*, 865 F2d 1370 (2d Cir 1989).

7. During the eighteen months between indictment and trial, several of the defendants were held without bail, pursuant to the Bail Reform Act. In ruling on the challenge to this detention (*United States v Salerno*, 481 US 739 [1987]), the Supreme Court upheld the constitutionality of the Bail Reform Act provision that permits judges to detain defendants without bail upon a finding that they present "a danger to the community."

8. Arnold H. Lubasch, *Persico Jury Is Told of "Vast Criminal Enterprise,"* New York Times, 7 November 1986, B4.

9. The Commission prosecution did not address the highest tier of the concrete club, which assigned contracts worth more than $5 million exclusively to S & A Concrete, which was jointly owned by the Genovese and Gambino families. See testimony of Vincent Cafaro before the Permanent Subcommittee on Investigations of the Committee on Government Affairs, 100th Cong., 2d session, 11, 15, 21, 22, 29 April 1988. In another case called *United States v Salerno*, the RICO convictions

of Salerno and several other defendants for managing the upper tier of the cartel were ultimately reversed by the Second Circuit; *United States v Salerno*, 937 F2d 797 (2d Cir 1991) (reversing convictions), 1125 S Ct 2503 (1992) (reversed and remanded), 952 F2d 623 (2d Cir 1992) (reversing convictions on remand).

10. The government's efforts to purge the mob from New York's concrete industry continued after the *Salerno* trial (see *Quadrozzi v City of New York*, 1989 US Dist LEXIS 8119 [SDNY. 1989]; *United States v Salerno*, supra note 9), and the larger effort to remove the mob from New York's construction industry continued into the 1990s.

11. *Mafia Commission Trial Hears Persico Sum Up*, New York Times, 12 November 1986, B3.

12. There have been reports that convicted Gambino boss John Gotti retains influence within the Gambino family; *From Prison, Gotti Reportedly Keeps Control of Mafia Group*, New York Times, 13 November 1993, 27.

13. The Second Circuit listed the arguments it considered for reversal:

The ones which merit consideration are: (a) claims of insufficiency of the evidence as to (1) extortion, (2) Corallo's involvement in the Club operations, (3) loansharking conspiracy, and (4) the nexus of the predicate acts of murder to the Commission; (b) Indelicato's claim that his prosecution for substantive RICO and RICO conspiracy violations is barred by the applicable statute of limitations; (c) challenges to the admissability of certain evidence; (d) claims by Corallo, Salerno and Santero that certain exculpatory tape recordings were erroneously excluded; (e) double jeopardy and jurisdictional claims asserted by Persico and Langella; (f) a claim by Persico that the jury should have been sequestered for the entire trial, rather than only during the deliberations; (g) a claim by Furnari that his counsel was burdened by a conflict of interest; (h) a claim by all appellants that certain *Brady* material was improperly withheld by the government, necessitating a new trial; and (i) challenges by all defendants to the severity of their sentences. Indelicato also raised a substantial question whether the simultaneous murders of Carmine Gallante, Leonard Coppola and Giuseppe Turano constituted a "pattern of racketeering activity" within the meaning of 18 U.S.C. sect. 1962(c)(1982). . . . this question was determined by the Second Circuit in banc, rather than by this panel. (*United States v Salerno*, 868 F2d 524, 529 [2d Cir 1989])

14. Following its own decision in *United States v Persico*, 832 F2d 705 (2d Cir 1987), *cert. denied*, 486 US 1022 (1988), the Second Circuit reversed Indelicato's predicate RICO convictions but affirmed his RICO conspiracy conviction, holding:

A RICO conspiracy offense is complete, thus commencing the running of the five-year statute of limitations, only when the purposes of the conspiracy have either been accomplished or abandoned. . . . but a substantive RICO charge is barred by limitations as to any defendant unless that defendant committed a predicate act within the five-year limitations period. (*United States v Salerno*, 868 F2d 524, 534 [2d Cir 1989])

15. In his partial dissent, Judge Bright argued that the government had presented insufficient proof to convict Corallo and Santoro for the loansharking conspiracy, and that it had failed to prove the connection between the commission and the Gallante murders.

16. *United States v Salerno*, 868 F2d 524, 532 (2d Cir 1989).

17. Id. at 533.

18. Id. at 545.

19. Id.

20. Id. at 537.

21. *U.S.—Italian Teamwork Bringing Organized-Crime Chiefs to Trial*, New York Times, 18 October 1985, A1.

22. See Joseph Albini, *The American Mafia: Genesis of a Legend* (Irvington, 1979); Norval Morris and Gordon Hawkins, *The Honest Politician's Guide to Crime Control* (University of Chicago Press, 1979); Dwight C. Smith, *The Mafia Mystique* (Basic Books, 1975).

23. Michael Winerip, *High-Profile Prosecutor*, New York Times, 9 June 1985, sec. 6, p. 37.

24. Ronald Goldstock, Martin Marcus, Thomas Thacher, and James Jacobs, *Corruption and Racketeering in the New York City Construction Industry: The Final Report of the New York State Organized Crime Task Force* (New York University Press, 1990).

25. See *United States v Salerno*, supra note 9.

26. See Howard Blum, *Gangland: How the FBI Broke the Mob* (Simon and Schuster, 1993).

27. *U.S.—Italian Teamwork Bringing Organized-Crime Chiefs to Trial*, New York Times, 18 October 1985, A1. (This quote appears in several sources.)

United States v. Salerno, Indictment

Count One

The Grand Jury charges:
   That at all times material to this Indictment:

The Enterprise

1. ANTHONY SALERNO, a/k/a "Fat Tony," PAUL CASTELLANO, a/k/a "Paulie," a/k/a "Mr. Paul," a/k/a "Big Paul," ANIELLO DELLACROCE, a/k/a "Neil," a/k/a "O'Neil," GENNARO LANGELLA, a/k/a "Gerry Lang," ANTHONY CORALLO, a/k/a "Tony Ducks," SALVATORE SANTORO, a/k/a "Tom Mix," CHRISTOPHER FURNARI, a/k/a "Christie Tick," PHILIP RASTELLI, a/k/a "Rusty," and RALPH SCOPO, the defendants, and others known and unknown to the Grand Jury who are not named as defendants in this Indictment, constituted an enterprise as defined in Title 18, United States Code, Section 1961(4), that is, a group of individuals associated in fact, which enterprise is often described as the "Commission" of La Cosa Nostra ("The Commission"), and which operated in New York and other locations in the United States and other countries.

2. From in or about 1900 up to and including the date of the filing of this Indictment, there existed in the United States a criminal society known by various names, including "La Cosa Nostra" and "the Mafia," which society operated through entities known as "Families." Each such Family had as its leader a person known as "Boss," or "Father," or "Acting Boss," a deputy leader known as "Underboss" or "Second," and a high ranking official known as "Consigliere." Each Family further operated through the participation of officers known as "Capos" or "Group Leaders," and members known as "Soldiers" and "Associates."

3. The Boss of each Family, with the assistance of the Underboss and Consigliere, supervised, promoted, and protected the criminal activities of the Capos, Soldiers and Associates of the Family, and, in return, received a part of the illegal earnings of those Capos, Soldiers and Associates.

4. Five of the La Cosa Nostra Families had their principal headquarters in New York City, although they operated throughout the United States and abroad. The Families were often identified by the name of their Boss or of a former Boss. From 1931 up to and including the date of the filing of this Indictment the succession of Bosses or Acting Bosses of the five New York City La Cosa Nostra Families included the following individuals:

I	II	III
Charles Luciano a/k/a "Charlie Lucky"	Frank Scalise	Joseph Profaci
Frank Costello	Vincent Mangano	Salvatore Magliocco
Vito Genovese	Albert Anastasia a/k/a "The Earthquake"	Joseph Colombo
Frank Tieri, a/k/a "Funzi"	Carlo Gambino a/k/a "Carl"	Carmine Persico a/k/a "Junior"
Anthony Salerno a/k/a "Fat Tony"	Paul Castellano a/k/a "Paulie" a/k/a "Mr. Paul" a/k/a "Big Paul"	Thomas DiBella
		Gennaro Langella a/k/a "Gerry Lang"

IV	V
Gaetano Gagliano	Angelo Caruso
Thomas Lucchese a/k/a "Tommy Brown"	Joseph Bonanno
Anthony Corallo a/k/a "Tony Ducks"	Carmine Galante
	Philip Rastelli a/k/a "Rusty"

Throughout this Indictment, the five Families headquartered in New York will be described respectively as the Genovese Organized Crime Family ("The Genovese Family"), the Gambino Organized Crime Family ("The Gambino Family"), the Colombo Organized Crime Family ("The Colombo Family"), the Lucchese Organized Crime Family ("The Lucchese Family"), and the Bonanno Organized Crime Family ("The Bonanno Family").

5. Each La Cosa Nostra Family was a separate organization. Normally, the Boss and ruling officers of each Family possessed the full authority to supervise, regulate, and direct all illegal activities which involved or affected the interests of officers and members of that particular Family exclusively. However, illegal activities involving or affecting the interests of officers or members of two or more La Cosa Nostra Families exceeded the jurisdiction of any single Family. To avoid "wars" between Families, disputes between and among Families over the control of illegal activities had to be resolved by a supreme leader or body. In or about 1931, the Bosses of the New York and other La Cosa Nostra Families associated to form the "Commission" to serve as the council for La Cosa Nostra Families. From 1931 up to and including the date of the filing of this Indictment, the Commission had the power to resolve disputes and to regulate relations between and among La Cosa Nostra Families. Furthermore, from in or about the mid-1950's up to and including the filing of the Indictment, the Commission occasionally assumed the power to intervene in Family leadership disputes that could not be resolved within a particular Family.

6. The Commission was an enterprise distinct from the individual Families, but it was comprised of Bosses and Acting Bosses—acting in concert with other high ranking officers—from the five La Cosa Nostra Families which had their headquarters in New York City. At different times the Commission also included influential Bosses from a number of La Cosa Nostra Families with their headquarters elsewhere in the United States, including, but not limited to, Families in Chicago, Illinois, Buffalo, New York, Detroit, Michigan, Philadelphia, Pennsylvania and New Jersey.

7. The Commission reached decisions and issued orders through votes of all or some of the Commission members, or through the action or decisions of an individual Commission member or members. From time to time, an individual Commission member or Commission members (or delegates) adjudicated disputes or acted as spokesman in authorizing action on behalf of the Commission.

Purposes of the Enterprise

8. The general purpose of the Commission enterprise was to regulate and facilitate the relationships between and among La Cosa Nostra Families. Specific purposes of the Commission included the following:

a. Promoting and carrying out joint ventures between and among La Cosa Nostra Families to obtain money through illegal activities. These Commission joint ventures included a joint venture among several La Cosa Nostra Families which controlled and dominated certain concrete contractors and allocated payoffs on certain concrete contracts in New York City.

b. Resolving actual and potential disputes and regulating among the several La Cosa Nostra Families regarding the operation, conduct, and control of illegal activities. These illegal activities included interference with interstate commerce through extortion; extortionate extentions of credit, commonly called "loansharking" or "shylocking"; gambling or "bookmaking"; infiltration and control of labor unions and labor organizations; and narcotics trafficking.

c. Extending formal recognition to newly elected Bosses of La Cosa Nostra Families, and, from time to time, resolving leadership disputes within a Family.

d. Taking such steps as were necessary to preserve order in, between and among the La Cosa Nostra Families, including authorizing acts of murder of certain La Cosa Nostra Family members.

e. Approving the initiation or "making" of new members or soldiers in the several La Cosa Nostra Families.

f. Controlling relations between La Cosa Nostra and members of the Sicilian La Cosa Nostra, also variously described as the "Sicilian Mafia," an enterprise distinct from La Cosa Nostra of the United States.

g. Establishing certain rules governing the Families, officers and members of La Cosa Nostra.

h. Keeping persons inside and outside La Cosa Nostra in fear of the Commission by identifying the Commission with threats, violence, and murder.

Means and Methods of the Enterprise

9. Among the means and methods whereby the said defendants and others conducted and participated in the conduct of the enterprise's affairs at all times relevant to the Indictment were the following:

a. The Commission established a "Club" of certain construction contractors who poured concrete. The Commission controlled the allocation of contracts to pour concrete on construction jobs where concrete costs exceeded two million dollars. The Commission and its co-conspirators and agents would designate which contractor would be permitted to make the successful bid on a particular contract. Often other concrete contractors would be directed to submit bids higher than that of the designated winner. The Commission enforced the rules of the "Club" with the threat of punishing disobedient contractors, by causing the contractors' supplies of cement to be stopped, or by causing certain labor union leaders to create "labor problems" for the contractors. The Commission exploited its control over these concrete pouring contracts in order to demand and receive payoffs from concrete contractors. Among the illegal ways in which the Commission implemented and exploited its control over these concrete pouring contracts were the following:

(1) The defendants and their co-racketeers and agents would and did extort, and conspire and attempt to extort money and property from certain concrete contractors who sought to bid for, who bid for, and who obtained concrete pouring contracts in connection with certain construction projects.

(2) The defendants and their co-racketeers and agents would and did exercise control over and influence the decisions of the Concrete Workers District Council and would and did agree to the payment of bribes to an official thereof to wit, defendant RALPH SCOPO.

b. The Commission resolved a leadership dispute within the Bonanno Family, and between the Bonanno Family and other La Cosa Nostra Families, by authorizing the murders of Carmine Galante, a/k/a "Lilo," who was Boss of the Bonanno Family, and Leonard Coppola, and by later authorizing the murders of Bonanno Family Capos Alphonse Indelicato, a/k/a "Sonny Red," Dominic Trinchera, a/k/a "Trin," Philip Giaccone, a/k/a "Philly Lucky," and the attempted murder of Bonanno Family Soldier Anthony Indelicato, a/k/a "Bruno."

c. The Commission authorized certain other murders.

d. The Commission participated in the selection of a new Boss for the La Cosa Nostra Family in Buffalo, New York.

e. The Commission approved the admission of new members to the La Cosa Nostra society of criminals.

f. The Commission promoted and encouraged a climate of fear to enhance the ability of the Commission and its members to control La Cosa Nostra and to obstruct justice.

Roles of the Defendants

10. The defendants played the following roles, among others, in furthering the affairs of the enterprise:

a. At times relevant to this Indictment, the defendant ANTHONY SALERNO, a/k/a "Fat Tony," was Consigliere, Acting Boss and Boss of the Genovese Family, and was associated in fact with and a member of the Commission. [Similar statements about each of the other defendants have been omitted.]

The Racketeering Conspiracy

11. From in or about 1970 up to and including the date of the filing of this Indictment, in the Southern District of New York and elsewhere, ANTHONY SALERNO [and the other defendants] did combine, confederate, conspire, and agree together and with each other to conduct and participate, directly and indirectly, in the conduct of the affairs of that enterprise through a pattern of racketeering activity.

a. The defendants each participated in the conduct of the affairs of the enterprise through the commission of multiple racketeering acts, as set forth in Paragraphs 12 through 21 below.

The Pattern of Racketeering

12. The pattern of racketeering activity consisted of the following acts:

Conspiracy to Extort Payoffs From Certain Concrete Companies

Racketeering Act # 1

13. It was a part of the pattern of racketeering activity that from in or about 1981 up to the date of the filing of this Indictment, in the Southern District of New York and elsewhere, the defendants and others known and unknown to the Grand Jury, unlawfully, wilfully, and knowingly would and did combine, conspire, confederate, and agree together and with each other to obstruct, delay, and affect commerce by

extortion, in that they would and did combine, conspire, confederate, and agree together and with each other to obtain property, to wit, sums of money, from and with the consent of certain New York City area construction companies engaged in interstate commerce in the concrete-pouring business, to wit, members of a group called the "Club," and others, and their officers, employees and representatives, which consent had been induced by the defendants' wrongful use of actual and threatened force, violence, and fear of economic loss, in violation of Title 18, United States Code, Section 1951.

Concrete Extortions and Payoffs

Racketeering Act # 2

A.

14. It was a part of the pattern of racketeering activity that in or about May, 1983, in the Southern District of New York and elsewhere, the defendants and others known and unknown to the Grand Jury, unlawfully, wilfully, and knowingly would and did obstruct, delay, and affect commerce by extortion and would and did attempt to do so, in that they would and did obtain and attempt to obtain property, to wit, money in the approximate amount of $326,000 from and with the consent of the X.L.O. Concrete Corporation, which company was engaged in interstate commerce, and its officers, employees and representatives, which consent had been induced by the defendants' wrongful use of actual and threatened force, violence, and fear of economic loss, in violation of Title 18, United States Code, Section 1951.

B.

15. It was a part of the pattern of racketeering activity that in or about May, 1983, in the Southern District of New York and elsewhere, the defendant RALPH SCOPO, president and business manager of the Concrete Workers District Council, being a representative of, and being an officer of a labor organization which represents and would admit to membership the employees of the X.L.O. Concrete Corporation, who are employed in an industry affecting commerce, aided and abetted by the [other] defendants and others known and unknown to the Grand Jury, unlawfully, wilfully, and knowingly would and did request, demand, receive, and accept, and agree to receive and accept the payment of money in the approximate amount of $326,000 from the X.L.O. Concrete Corporation in violation of Title 29, United States Code, Section 186(b)(1) and Title 18, United States Code, Section 2.

[Racketeering Acts 3–10 parallel Racketeering Act 2 except that different companies are named as the victims of the alleged extortion.]

Murder of Carmine Galante

Racketeering Act # 11

26. It was a part of the pattern of racketeering that from in or about January 1979 up to and including July 31, 1979, in the Southern District of New York and elsewhere, the defendants ANIELLO DELLACROCE, a/k/a "Neil," a/k/a "O'Neil," PHILIP RASTELLI, a/k/a "Rusty," and others known and unknown to the Grand Jury did unlawfully, wilfully, and knowingly conspire to murder and solicited, facilitated, and aided and abetted the murder of Carmine Galante, a/k/a "Lilo."

Murder of Leonard Coppola

Racketeering Act # 12

27. It was a part of the pattern of racketeering that from in or about January 1979 up to and including July 31, 1979, in the Southern District of New York and elsewhere, the defendants ANIELLO DELLACROCE, a/k/a "Neil," a/k/a "O'Neil," PHILIP RASTELLI, a/k/a "Rusty," and others known and unknown to the Grand Jury did unlawfully, wilfully, and knowingly conspire to murder and solicited, facilitated, and aided and abetted the murder of Leonard Coppola.

Murder of Alphonse Indelicato

Racketeering Act # 13

28. It was a part of the pattern of racketeering that in or about April and May, 1981, in the Southern District of New York and elsewhere, the defendants PAUL CASTELLANO, a/k/a "Paulie," a/k/a "Mr. Paul," a/k/a "Big Paul," ANTHONY CORALLO, a/k/a "Tony Ducks," PHILIP RASTELLI, a/k/a "Rusty," and others known and unknown to the Grand Jury did unlawfully, wilfully, and knowingly conspire to murder and solicited, facilitated, and aided and abetted the murder of Alphonse Indelicato, a/k/a "Sonny Red."

[In Racketeering Acts 14–16, the government alleged that the defendants conspired to murder Dominic Trinchera, Philip Giaccone, and Anthony Indelicato.

[Counts 2–15 realleged the extortions having to do with the concrete club.]

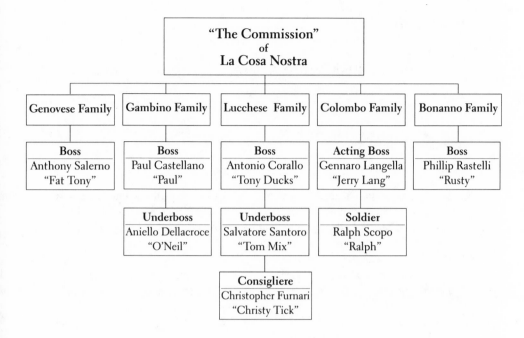

Testimony of FBI Agent Joseph Pistone

[By Mr. Savarese]

Q. Did he [Benjamin Ruggiero, Bonanno family] tell you anything about a process that would go on concerning what he would tell you about the Bonanno family?

A. Yes, he said that from this point on that he would, as I said, start schooling me in things that I would have to do and things that I would have to know now that I was associated with the family.

Q. And that phrase that you just used, "schooling," was that one that Mr. Ruggiero used on any other occasions?

A. He used that phrase right up until the end of the operation.

Q. In the course of Mr. Ruggiero's explaining to you his having gone on record, did he tell you anything with respect to his being responsible for you?

A. Yes, he said that since he had gone on record with me, or with the family, that I was going to be under him, that he was now responsible for any actions that I took and that I had a responsibility to him to show that I conducted myself in the proper manner.

Q. Did he explain anything to you further about your responsibilities and about your conduct?

A. Well, he said that there were certain things that I would have to know regarding individuals in the family and who to treat with respect and that how to act around a made guy and how to act around individuals that had status in the family.

Q. And what did Ruggiero tell you in conversation when he was schooling you about the Bonanno family?

A. Well, he told me that the first thing I had to learn is that, again, the respect for made guys. He said, if you ever get in an argument with a made guy, don't ever raise your hand to him. He said don't ever get in a argument with a made guy.
Also said that anything—any monies that I made from any activities I would have to share with him and then also again with whoever the captain was at that time.

Q. Did he discuss with you anything concerning the operations of the family business and how you should conduct yourself with respect to that?

A. Yes.

Q. What did he tell you?

A. Well, he said one thing that I should learn not to get involved in any businesses or don't worry about business that another family member's involved in and if you don't have any stake in it. He said just mind your own business if it doesn't concern you.

Q. What, if anything, did Lefty Ruggiero tell you about the manner in which people would be introduced to other individuals within the family?

A. Well, he said that when there's two made guys and one of the made guys is making an introduction of an individual, that if the individual being introduced is a made guy, he says he's a friend of ours. And what that does is clues in the person that he is being introduced to another made guy.

Q. Was there any other way of introducing that he told you about with respect to someone who is not a made guy?

A. If he's not a made guy, the way you introduce him is he's a friend of mine. That means he's just a friend of mine, not a friend of ours, not a made guy.

Q. Did he explain anything else to you about the significance of saying somebody was a friend of mine?

A. That clues the other individual in that not to be talking about any kind of business if you don't want, you know, family business because this individual isn't made.

Q. And did you have any conversations with Mr. Ruggiero about the general responsibility to share the proceeds that you would get from your various activities?

A. Yes, he said that I would have to share with him and he would have to share with Mike and in reality Mike as a captain, or any captain, would—is supposed to share with the boss of the family.

Q. Did Lefty Ruggiero ever discuss with you the consequences of not following the rules?

A. Yes, he did.

Q. What did he tell you about that?

A. Well, he said if I ever messed up—he put it in other words—but what would happen was that we'd both be killed.

Q. Did he have any particular phrase that he used?

A. Yes; the phrase that he liked was that we'd be going bye-bye.

Q. Did you understand from the context of your conversations what he meant by going bye-bye?

A. He meant that we'd be killed.

Q. Did Mr. Ruggiero ever personally discuss with you your chances of actually becoming a made member within the Bonanno Family?

A. Yes.

Q. What did he tell you?

A. Again, if I kept my nose clean, did what I was supposed to do, continued to demonstrate that I was an earner, and loyal-type guy, that I had a good shot at it.

Q. As part of your undercover activities for the FBI, did you take any steps to show that you were a good earner in this period?

A. Yes, I did.

Q. And could you just briefly describe to us in general how you went about doing that.

A. Well, one of the methods was by showing Ruggiero that I was involved in obtaining stolen property; by becoming involved in Ruggiero's bookmaking operation, and also during the course of the whole undercover operation, introduced Ruggiero and other members of the Bonanno Family into a couple of other FBI undercover operations that they were able to earn some money from, and they thought that I had moved in on these operations and took them over for them.

*   *   *

Q. Now, sir, let me direct your attention to the month of July, 1979. Do you recall having a telephone conversation with Lefty Ruggiero during that month?

A. Yes, sir.

Q. And what was said in the first conversation?

A. Well, in the first conversation Ruggiero had asked me if I had read the New York papers, and I told him no, I didn't. I had not at that point. And he instructed me to go buy a New York paper, he said "You'll be in for a surprise."

Q. What did you do after that first conversation?

A. I went and I bought the New York paper.

Q. And did you come to have a second telephone conversation with Mr. Ruggiero soon after that?

A. Yes.

Q. Would you tell us what you said and what he said?

A. I told him I had bought the paper and I was surprised.

Q. What if anything did he tell you?

A. He said he wanted to see me in New York. .

Q. Following that conversation did you go to New York?

A. Yes, I did.

Q. When was that?

A. It was the latter part of July of '79, cause those conversations were the middle part of July.

Q. And did you meet with Ruggiero when you got to New York?

A. Yes, I did.

Q. And where did that meeting take place?

A. I went down to his club on Madison Street.

Q. Who was present for this conversation?

A. Myself and Ruggiero.

Q. Would you please tell the ladies and gentlemen of the jury what you had and what Mr. Ruggiero told you in that conversation?

A. I told Lefty that I was really surprised that Carmine Galante had gotten murdered. That was why he had instructed me to buy the newspaper because it was in the newspaper about Galante getting murdered, and he said that due to Galante getting murdered there were some changes in the Family, that he was going to make me aware of that I should know of.

Q. What were the changes that he specifically told you about in the Bonanno Family?

A. Well, he said now that Galante had gotten whacked out that Rusty Rastelli was going to be the boss of the Family and he said that Nicholas Marangello and Sabella were due to get hit with Galante, but individuals intervened on their behalf and instead of getting killed that Mike was knocked down as captain, reduced to the rank of soldier and Marangello was knocked down, he was no longer the underboss.

Q. You just used two phrases that Mr. Ruggiero told you, "whacked out" and "hit." What did those phrases mean?

A. Got killed.

Q. Now, what if anything else did Ruggiero tell you in this conversation as he was explaining what would happen in the Bonanno Family after Galante had been killed?

A. Well, he told me that Sonny Black Napolitano was now a captain and that's who Ruggiero was—and myself were going to be under. That Joey Messino had been elevated to the rank of a captain and that Cesare had been made a captain and that he said at the time that Cesare was the youngest captain in the Family.

Q. When you say Cesare, who are you referring to?

A. Cesare Bonventre.

Q. That same individual that you identified in the photograph?

A. That's correct.

Q. Did he tell you anything else?

A. He told me that Sal Catalano—he said Sal had been elevated to the position of street boss of the Zips.

Q. When he said street boss of the Zips, what did you understand that to mean?

A. Well, that he was the boss of the Sicilian faction within the Bonanno Family.

*   *   *

Q. When Ruggiero came down to [Tampa, Florida, to] discuss the situation with Rossi, what happened?

A. Well, we went out to dinner and over dinner I told Rossi to explain to Ruggiero what his problems were with these wise guys from Chicago and New York, and he did, and then we went to the club, showed Ruggiero around the club, introduced him to some of the individuals that were from New York and were from Chicago, and—

Q. Would you describe, please, what you mean by the phrase "wise guy"?

A. Wise guy is another term for made guy.

Q. And these were other made guys from New York or Chicago who were in Florida and you were meeting with Ruggiero, correct?

A. Individuals who claimed they were wise guys, that's correct.

Q. Now, what happened as a result of these discussions?

A. Well, as a result of on-going discussions between Ruggiero and Rossi, what it came down is that Ruggiero made himself a 50 percent partner in Kings Court, being that this was going to be Rossi's protection from the other wise guys moving in and taking over the Kings Court.

Q. Now, you testified before that you met Sonny Black Napolitano in Florida in April of 1980, correct?

A. Correct.

Q. And how was it that he came to Florida on that occasion?

A. Well, since he was our captain at the time, and that the Kings Court was a club that was supposedly making money, a lot of money, Sonny came down to look it over and help us engage in other activities in the area.

Q. When Mr. Napolitano came down to speak with you at the club, did you have a specific conversation with him?

A. Yes, I did.

Q. And where did that occur?

A. Well, that occurred inside the nightclub. Myself, Ruggiero, Napolitano and Rossi and a couple of other individuals were at the club that evening, and at one point during the conversation we were having, Sonny Black said that he wanted to speak to me in private.

So we moved to another table and held a discussion in private.

Q. In that private discussion with Napolitano what did he tell you?

A. Well, Sonny said that he had been talking to Ruggiero about me and Ruggiero had given him a good rundown about me. He had been talking to other people in New York that knew me and he liked what he had heard from these people and the fact that I was a good earner, I was always out hustling, I minded my own business, I stayed out of people's way if I didn't have to get—wasn't involved with them, and that I was basically an all right guy.

He went on to inquire what we wanted to get started down there, so I told him that I think we should get possibly some gambling, shylock going, and he said that that was a good idea because gambling was a good source of income.

He said that he would have—we would have all the backing from his people in New York that we needed and that I should start in right away and get a gambling operation, bookmaking and shylock operation going.

Q. And those operations would be working out of the club that you had established with the FBI down there, correct?

* * *

Q. During that dinner conversation on December 18, 1980, did you have a conversation with Mr. Napolitano?

A. Yes.

Q. Would you please tell us what he told you during the course of that dinner conversation?

A. Well, during one portion of the conversation Sonny mentioned that he was pleased with the way I was handling things in Florida, that I was earning money and wasn't always running to him for money like other members of his crew. And he said that shortly that the Commission was going to open up the books for membership in the family and that he was—he could nominate five individuals and the number one guy was going to be John Sarisante and the other four slots he was obligated to either sons or relatives of members, other members in the family.

Q. Did he tell you anything else with respect to you and your chances for membership?

A. He said that the books would open up again, were going to open up again next year and that he was going to propose me for membership in the family.

Q. When he used the phrase "the Commission is going to open up the books," what did he mean?

A. That the Commission had given permission for families to induct members.

Q. Was he referring to families in the New York area?

A. That's what I understood him to mean, yes.

Q. What if anything else did Sonny Black Napolitano say to you about your possible membership in the Family?

A. He said that when the books opened up next year he was going to propose me for membership.

Q. Did he ask you any information about yourself in connection with that?

A. Yes, he asked me if I had had any drug arrest, and I told him no, I didn't.

Q. What if anything did he say in response when you told him that you had no drug arrests?

A. Well, he said that was good and the reason being that the cops, you know— would be less heat I would take, less heat from the cops, they wouldn't be looking at me as strong if I didn't have any drug arrests.

Q. You remained in the New York City area through December, is that correct?

A. Through the new year, that's correct.

Q. And did you continue to meet with Mr. Ruggiero and Mr. Napolitano during the time that you were there?

A. Yes, we would meet every day at the Motion Lounge.

Q. In particular, let me direct your attention to December 24 of that year, 1980, did you have occasion to have any conversations on that day?

A. Yes.

Q. With whom did you speak?

A. Well, on the 24th we were at the Motion Lounge and it was myself, Napolitano, Ruggiero, Santura, Sarisante and other individuals who were—who hung out and were members of Sonny's crew.

Q. In the course of that conversation did the subject of Neil Dellacroce come up?

A. Yes, it did.

Q. What was said?

A. There was a lot of conversation going on about different activities and at one point Napolitano said that Neil Dellacroce was a power and that—on the Commission—and that he was the one that was designated to settle disputes among the families.

Q. Directing your attention to three days later, December 27, 1980, did you have occasion to have any conversation on that day?

A. Yes, I did.

Q. Again, would you tell us where that conversation took place?

A. Well, again, we were at the Motion Lounge doing what we normally did, hanging out, playing cards, discussing the various activities that we are currently involved in or activities that we had participated in in the past. And at one point Ruggiero was relating a story about Milwaukee, back in '78.

* * *

A. We were involved in a vending machine business in Milwaukee, Wisconsin, and we were partners with Frank Balistrieri who was the boss of the Milwaukee family.

Q. Let me ask you this. The discussion that he was referring to in Milwaukee, had that also been a part of your ongoing undercover operation?

A. That's correct.

Q. And what was the operation that was going on out in Milwaukee, just briefly?

A. It was a vending machine business that we had.

Q. What was the arrangement that was attempting to be made with Mr. Balistrieri, the boss of Milwaukee?

A. To become partners with Balistrieri in this vending machine business in which Ruggiero succeeded in doing.

Q. Going back to this conversation in December of 1980, what did Mr. Ruggiero tell you?

A. As he was relaying this conversation at one point he said that the initial sit-down that we had with Balistrieri regarding the vendings machine business was arranged by Tony Ducks, the New York end of it.

Q. When he said Tony Ducks, did you know who he was referring to?

A. Tony Ducks Corallo.

Q. Had you at any point ever met Mr. Corallo in the course of your undercover operation?

A. Sure did.

Q. Who did you understand Mr. Corallo to be at that time?

A. At that time I understood him to be a boss.

Q. Did you know then which specific family?

A. Lucchese family.

* * *

Q. In the course of your visits and meetings did you ever have him pointed out to you by any of the people that you were meeting with, such as Ruggiero or Napolitano?

A. Not that I can recall.

Q. Let me back up for one moment, sir, and direct your attention back to the conversation that you had in July of 1979 after Carmine Galante had been killed. Do you recall you testified that you had been told that Salvatore Catalano had been promoted to be the street boss of what you described as the Zips, do you recall that?

A. Yes.

Q. Do you recall whether there was any further conversation concerning the role of the Zips within the Bonanno family?

A. Yes, I had had conversation regarding their role within the Family.

Q. What was their role, what was the—

A. That prior to that, that they were close with Galante and that they were involved with drug traffic with Galante.

Q. Directing your attention back again to March of 1981 did you have any conversation or further discussion with Mr. Ruggiero concerning both the Zips and any factions that were developing within the Bonanno family at the time?

A. During March of when?

Q. March of 1981. Or just simply with respect to any factions that were developing in that period of time.

A. Yes, he had discussion with me regarding a split that had developed in the Family regarding Sonny Black Napolitano and Rusty Rastelli and other individuals in the Family.

Q. During these discussions concerning the factions within the Bonanno family did Mr. Ruggiero ever describe to you who the principal persons were on each side of that factional dispute?

A. Yes.

Q. Was there a particular side that Lefty Ruggiero identified himself with?

A. Well, he had identified himself of course with Napolitano and Napolitano was on the side of Rusty Rastelli.

Q. Did he describe to you who was on the other side of the factional dispute?

A. Yes.

Q. Who was that?

A. Well, Sonny Red Indelicato, Dominic Trinchera and Philip Giaccone.

Q. What position did those three persons, Indelicato, Trinchera and Giaccone, have at that time?

A. I was told they were captains.

* * *

Q. Now, Mr. Pistone, again I had asked you about a conversation that you had with Lefty Ruggiero on April 2, 1981. Could you tell us what that conversation was about, in substance?

A. Well, basically Ruggiero was discussing a confrontation or sit-downs that had occurred regarding whether I belonged to him or Tony Mirra. Mirra had brought up this problem with the Family and other individuals, and Ruggiero was relating the outcome of the sit-down and also relating Sonny Black's position, how he had risen in the Family.

Q. Did you have any conversation concerning Rusty Rastelli at that point?

A. Well, he said that everything—as long as Rusty was in jail we'd have to wait until Rusty got out of jail and that there had been orders that nobody starts any trouble or any problems until—while Rusty's away.

Q. Did he explain to you who it was that had made that order?

A. The Commission.

* * *

Q. Did you meet with Mr. Napolitano?

A. Yes, I did.

Q. Did you have occasion at that time to speak with Mr. Napolitano, again concerning the same issues of resolving the factional disputes within the Bonanno Family.

A. Yes, I did.

Q. What if anything did Mr. Napolitano tell you at that time?

A. Well, after our discussion regarding the situation that he wanted me to handle, Napolitano made the statement that it's the first time in ten years that the Bonanno Family is running itself and not the Commission running it.

Testimony of Angelo Lonardo

Q. What does "button" mean?

A. He is a member of the Mafia.

Q. What about the term "made guy?"

A. That he is a member.

Q. What about the term "wiseguy"?

A. That he is a member.

Q. Can you tell us how decisions are made within a La Cosa Nostra family?

A. In the city you belong to?

Q. Yes.

A. Well, the boss, the underboss, they get together—

Q. You say the boss and the underboss within a family?

A. Right, capos and consiglieri, counselor.

Q. Who has the final authority within a family to make a decision?

A. The boss has.

Q. What is the job of the consiglieri or counselor?

A. Well, when a soldier does something wrong he usually brings it up to the underboss or the boss and he kind of defends him, straightens everything out for him.

Q. When you say he brings it up, you mean the consiglieri brings it up?

A. Yes, he does.

Q. How does the soldier get orders?

A. Through the capo.

Q. Now, you testified there are families in a number of cities. Is it possible to transfer from one family to another?

A. Yes.

Q. Can you explain how that is done?

A. Well, you go to your boss and you tell him that I am moving away from here. I am going to, say, San Francisco and can I have permission to leave. So the boss says it's okay but as long as you know somebody there. Go meet the boss and tell them what you are doing there and that you are going to live there and become a soldier in his family.

Q. Now, you indicated there are 5 families in New York. Can you tell us the names of those families?

A. Yes.

Q. What are they?

A. Well, there is the Lucchese family, Colombo family, the Gambino family, the Genovese family and the Bonanno family.

Q. Of which of these families do you know Anthony Salerno to be the boss?

A. Genovese family.

Q. Who is the Genovese family named after?

A. Vito Genovese.

Q. Is there any body which controls the Cosa Nostra families in many cities?

A. Yes, there is.

Q. What is that called?

A. The Commission.

Q. Who sits on The Commission?

A. The 5 bosses of New York.

Q. Do you know of any other people who have sat on The Commission who have not been bosses of New York?

A. Well, years ago I know Frank Milano was, Al Polizzi, Angelo Bruno.

Q. Who were Frank Milano and Angelo Polizzi?

A. They were the ex-bosses of Cleveland.

Q. Who is Angelo Bruno?

A. He was a boss of Philadelphia.

Q. What are The Commission's functions within La Cosa Nostra?

A. Well, if there is a dispute about anything they get together and iron it out.

Q. Are there any other functions The Commission performs?

A. Well—

Q. Are there any other functions The Commission performs?

A. They make all the rules and regulations, what you can do, what you can't do.

Q. Can you tell us any rules or regulations, as you sit here now; that you are aware of The Commission having made concerning La Cosa Nostra?

A. That they have made?

Q. Yes.

A. For instance, nobody can sell narcotics.

Q. What was the reason for that rule?

A. That would bring too much heat on everybody.

Q. Is there another rule you are familiar with?

A. Well, you always have to do the right thing. You can't have no prostitutes.

＊　　＊　　＊

A. Well, the rules are that they can't kill a boss in other cities or in New York City without them knowing anything about it.

Q. When you say "without them knowing anything about it," who is the "them" you are referring to?

A. The Commission.

Q. Incidentally, you mentioned earlier that members must do the right thing. What do you mean by "the right thing"?

A. Well, before they do anything they got to get permission.

Q. From whom do they have to get permission?

A. From their capo and the capo takes it up with the underboss and the boss.

Q. Now, sir, when you were the underboss or acting boss in Cleveland did you ever personally sit with The Commission?

A. I never did.

Q. Did you ever meet the entire Commission?

A. No, I never did.

Q. How did the Cleveland family communicate with The Commission?

A. We used to communicate with the Genovese family.

Q. And was there anybody in this courtroom that you communicated with in order to be in touch with The Commission?

A. Yes.

Q. Who is that?

A. Tony Salerno.

Q. I am sorry, you said Anthony Salerno?

A. Anthony Salerno.

Q. And what was his position on The Commission, if you know?

A. He was a member.

Q. Now, sir, I would like to direct your attention back to the 1920's when you first became associated with La Cosa Nostra.

Who was the boss at that time?

A. My father.

Q. What was his name?

A. Joseph Lonardo.

Q. Did there come a time something happened to him?

A. Yes.

Q. What was that?

A. My father got killed.

Q. As a result of that did you do something?

A. Yes, I did.

Q. What did you do?

A. I killed the man that was responsible for killing my father.

Q. And what was that man's name?

A. Sam Todaro.

Q. What position, if any, did he have in the Cosa Nostra?

A. I found out he was the counselor.

Q. Can you describe how you killed him?

A. Well, one day my cousin said to me "the best way to get Sam Todaro is to talk to your mother and tell her that we need—that your family needs money and if Sam

Todaro would help her with some money, but don't tell her why you are going down there to talk to him." So I said, "okay, I will talk to my mother and tell her that." So I told my mother. I said, "Ma, we have to go see—"

Q. What did you tell your mother?

A. I told my mother "let's go see Sam Todaro, maybe he can help us with some money," and I said, "would you come along," and so she said "yes." And we got in the car and we drove down to 110th Street and I told somebody there on the corner if he would call Sam Todaro, that my mother would like to talk to him. So he said, "yes, I will." So he went, got Sam Todaro, and Sam Todaro came over and as he got close to the car I pulled out a gun and shot him.

Q. Were you arrested?

A. No, I was not at the time.

Q. Did there come a time you wound up getting tried for that murder?

A. I gave myself up, yes.

Q. Were you involved in planning this murder with any other people?

A. Yes.

Q. Who were you involved with?

A. With my cousins.

Q. What were your cousins' names?

A. John DeMarco, Dominic DeMarco, Dominic Esprado.

Q. What position if any did John DeMarco have in the Cosa Nostra?

A. He was a member.

Q. Now, sir, were you tried for killing Sam Todaro?

A. Yes, I was.

Q. Did you testify?

A. Yes, I did.

Q. Did you deny killing him on the witness stand?

A. Yes, I did.

Q. Were you convicted?

A. Yes, I was.

Q. Was your conviction reversed?

A. Yes, it was.

Q. How long during this period were you in jail?

A. 23 months.

Q. During this period did the other people who you had agreed with to kill Sam Todaro, did they kill any other people?

A. While I was in the county jail 2 others died, yes.

Q. Had you agreed to have those people killed?

A. Yes.

Q. And had you agreed with these people to have other people killed?

A. Yes.

Q. How many other people?

A. Well, there was the 5 Pirello brothers and Sam Tolocca.

Q. Of those 6 two of them were killed while you were in the county jail?

A. That's right.

Q. Did you personally participate in any of these other killings?

A. No, I did not.

Q. But you did agree to them?

A. Yes, I did.

Q. How, if at all, were these killings related to the matter of your father's death?

A. They were responsible for my father's death, all of them.

Q. Now, sir, did there come a time in the early to mid-1930's that you were familiar with a man by the name of Dr. Romano?

A. Yes, he was also involved in my father's death.

Q. Had he at one point occupied a position in La Cosa Nostra?

A. Yes.

Q. What had that position been?

A. He had been the boss.

Q. Of which city?

A. Cleveland.

Q. Did he retire at one point?

A. Yes, he did retire.

Q. Did there come a time you were involved in his death?

A. I didn't get the question.

Q. Did there come a time you were involved in his death?

A. Yes, I was.

Q. Can you explain what happened?

A. Well, my cousin Dominic DeMarco got sick. He had an appendicitis attack and his brother wanted to rush him to the hospital and my cousin Dominic said to his brother, he said, "let Dr. Romano operate on me. I want to show him that we want to be friends with him," and so there would be peace.

*   *   *

A. And my cousin Johnny insisted that he didn't want Dr. Romano to operate on his brother but his brother Dominic insisted and he said, "okay, I will let Dr. Romano operate on you." So he called up Dr. Romano and Dr. Romano says, "we will rush him to St. John's hospital." And he operated on him and he died.

Q. As a result of that did you and John DeMarco agree to do something?

A. Yes, we did.

Q. Would you tell us what you did?

A. We decided that Dr. Romano had killed my cousin and he was also responsible in the death of my father and we decided to kill him.

Q. Did you in fact do that?

A. Yes, I did.

Q. Now, did there come a time after you killed Dr. Romano that you heard something from a man by the name of Al Polizzi?

A. Yes, I did.

Q. Who was Al Polizzi?

A. He was the boss of Cleveland.

Q. Do you recall approximately when this conversation with Al Polizzi was?

A. It was the next day or 2.

Q. After the killing of Dr. Romano?

A. Yes.

Q. Do you remember where the conversation took place?

A. That I don't remember now.

Q. Do you know the year that Dr. Romano was killed?

A. I know it was in the early 30's, '34, '33, something like that. I don't remember.

Q. Now, will you tell us what Al Polizzi told you a couple of days after Dr. Romano was killed?

A. "Jeez, you should have said something to me about this before you did anything." He said, "you got us in a spot now, you know," but Al Polizzi didn't know at the time—

Q. Let me stop you there. What else did Al Polizzi tell you?

A. That we shouldn't have done it the way we did it.

Q. What reason, if any, did he give you for that?

A. He says, "the way you did it, the way you guys did it, the same thing could happen to us."

Q. And did he have any other conversation with you concerning John DeMarco and your situation?

A. Well, yes, there was.

Q. Tell us about that.

A. There was a fellow by the name of Jim Mangano. He raised hell about it.

Q. Who was Jim Mangano?

A. He was a boss of a family here in New York.

Q. Tell us what Al Polizzi told you about Jim Mangano.

A. That he didn't like it and Al Polizzi had to go to New York and tell them what happened and why it happened and they met with other people there.

Q. When you say other people, whom do you mean?

A. The Commission.

Q. Is this from Al Polizzi?

A. Yes.

Q. Al Polizzi was then the boss or acting boss of Cleveland?

A. That's right.

Q. Would you tell us what Al Polizzi told you about this meeting in New York with Mangano and The Commission?

A. Jim Mangano raised hell about it and he wanted John DeMarco to be condemned to death. And as far as for me he says, "Angelo didn't know any better because he is not a member so he listened to his cousins, so we will exonerate him."

Q. Did there come a time after this conversation with Al Polizzi that John DeMarco left the area?

A. Yes, he did.

Q. Then did there come a time he returned?

A. Yes, he did.

Q. Did you have any conversation with Al Polizzi concerning that return?

A. Yes.

Q. Tell us what he said to you.

A. That he had straightened Johnny DeMarco out to come back to Cleveland.

Q. And what if anything did he tell you about who he had straightened it out with?

A. Well, there was a meeting between New York and Chicago and between them they decided to exonerate him.

Q. When you say a meeting between New York and Chicago, can you be more specific as to what you mean?

A. Well, there were different fellows from Chicago and also from New York and they met in Miami Beach.

Q. In fact, were you present in Miami Beach at such a meeting?

A. I was but I was not in the meeting.

Q. Can you tell us where you were and what you saw?

A. I was in the living room and they were out in the backyard.

Q. Who was out in the backyard?

A. Fellows from New York and fellows from Chicago plus Al Polizzi.

Q. When you say fellows from New York, what positions, if any, did they hold in La Cosa Nostra?

A. They were some of the higher-ups from both cities.

Q. When you say higher-up, what do you mean?

A. Like the bosses or maybe underboss.

Q. Now, sir, did there come a time when you were proposed to become an actual member?

A. Yes.

Q. When were you proposed?

A. I remember I was proposed somebody told me in the 30's, late 30's but there was a freeze on after that. You couldn't make any members.

Q. When you say a freeze, were you told who had imposed the freeze?

A. The Commission.

Q. Do you remember who it is that proposed you?

A. Proposed me?

Q. Yes.

A. Yes.

Q. Who was that?

A. Thomas Agenti.

Q. What position if any did he hold in the La Cosa Nostra?

A. At that time I believe he was the counselor.

Q. Did you have conversations with any member of La Cosa Nostra concerning the freeze at that time?

A. Well, they told me that "right now we can't make you. There is a freeze on."

Q. When you say "they" who are you referring to?

A. Like my cousin, cousins, and even Al Polizzi told me. He says "but in due time you will be made."

Q. Did your cousins or Al Polizzi describe to you or tell you the reason why there was a freeze on?

A. I know one of the reasons was that they were making too many fellows in New York City and some of them weren't the right fellows to be made and there were fellows buying their way into the Mafia, paying money out to an underboss or a counselor and they wanted to put a stop to it.

Q. Did there come a time that you actually were made as a member?

A. Yes.

Q. When was that?

A. The late 40's.

Q. Was there a ceremony?

A. Yes.

Q. Where did it take place?

A. At the Statler Hotel in Cleveland.

Q. What location in the Statler Hotel?

A. The location?

Q. Where in the Statler Hotel?

A. In a suite.

Q. Was it a private suite?

A. Yes, it was.

Q. Can you tell us who was present that you remember?

A. At that time John Scalish, who was acting boss; Tony Milano, he was the underboss; my cousin Johnny DeMarco. I don't remember if he was a capo or the counselor at the time.

Q. And were there other people being made along with you?

A. Yes, there were.

Q. Can you physically describe the setting of the ceremony?

A. Well, you walk into a room and they tell you to sit down and they ask you, "do you know what you are doing here," and naturally you say no. So then they tell you. They say, "we want to make you a member of this family but before we make you a family we want to tell you different things about it." He said, "do you understand that," and I said "yes."

So they went on and spoke and says, "you know, if you become a member you can't sell no narcotics. You can't have no girls working for you on the street. You can't be a pimp. Before you do anything you always got to get permission, talk to your capo and get permission for what you want to do, and if we ever need you to do something, no matter what time of the day, night, that we call you, even if there is somebody dying in your family you got to leave and do it."

Q. Did he tell you the kind of thing you might be asked to do?

A. Well, to give you a contract to kill somebody.

Q. Was anything said concerning secrecy?

A. He said, "you can't tell nobody anything about this to anyone."

Q. As you were sitting there listening to this was there anything placed before you?

A. There was a table with a cloth over it.

Q. After you were told these rules and regulations what happened with respect to the cloth?

A. Well, they say to you "do you understand what we are talking about? Do you want to become a member? You still have a chance to refuse or to become a member." So naturally I said, "yes, I will become a member." Then they flipped the cloth over and there is a gun there with a dagger and they say, "that is the way you live from now on, with the gun and the dagger, and you die with the gun and the dagger, do you understand that," and I said "yes."

Q. Then what happened?

A. Then they give you a card with a picture of a saint and they light it up and you let it burn to ashes.

Q. Then what happens?

A. Then they pinch your finger and you kind of suck the blood and they all shake your hands and kiss you on your cheek and they say, "you are a member from now on."

Q. Were you told by any member of La Cosa Nostra what the reason was for not being able to be involved with drugs?

A. They said it would bring too much heat.

Q. At the ceremony were you told what the penalty was for breaking those rules?

A. Yes, you could die.

Testimony of James Costigan

Q. During the course of these meetings did Mr. Scopo inform you and give you more of the details about the Club?

A. A little bit more, yes.

Q. And did he explain the operation of the Club to you?

A. Yes.

Q. Tell us what he told you during the course of these meetings about the operations of the Club and who ran it and anything else he told you about the Club.

A. He said that, like I said, the Club was run by these heads—not the heads, representatives of the four families; that the work was going to be whacked up, that the contractors were in it.

Q. Did you have conversations with him during this series of meetings concerning what he meant by "families"?

A. I knew what he was talking about.

Q. Did you—did he use the word and you would respond and you would use the word and he would respond?

A. Yes.

Q. And based on that you had an understanding of what he meant, correct?

A. Yes.

Q. What did you understand him to mean by "families"?

A. The Mafia families in New York.

Q. Now, sir, you mentioned a two percent fee had to be paid. What if anything did he tell you about who it would go to?

A. He said it was going into a pot and it would be divided up amongst the families.

Q. And what if anything did he tell you about the category of jobs that was covered by this arrangement?

A. They were jobs over two million in price.

Q. What if anything did he tell you about jobs under two million dollars in price?

A. They were not allowed to sought by Club members.

Q. What if anything did he tell you about—

A. As to what?

Q. Why people in the Club would not be or shouldn't be bidding below two million.

A. Well, there was a lot of small contractors, and he said they had to eat too.

Q. What if anything did he tell you about the geographical area within which the Club arrangement functioned?

A. Manhattan.

Q. What if anything did he tell you about who would actually decide the allocations on a job by job basis?

A. I don't know if he ever articulated that. My understanding was that these—

Q. Was your understanding based on what Mr. Scopo told you during these meetings?

A. Pretty much.

Q. Tell us what your understanding was?

A. It was that these four guys would meet and decide who was going to get what jobs.

Q. Incidentally, you mentioned two percent. Are you familiar with the term points?

A. Yes.

Q. And in your understanding what—in the industry, what does the term point mean?

A. A point? A percentage point.

Q. So two points would be two percent?

A. Yes.

Q. Now, sir, again directing your attention to this entire series of meetings, what, if anything, did Mr. Scopo tell you concerning how a company that was allocated a job would go about setting the price on the job?

A. The guy would figure out what his cost was. He would add 15 percent, a markup, and two percent for the Club.

Q. And what, if anything, did he tell you about the bidding process that would be followed by those companies that had not been allocated a particular job?

A. Well, they would put in inflated numbers.

Q. And what, if anything, did he tell you about the reason for that?

A. I don't know if he ever specifically outlined the reason. He just said that they would put in a higher number and I understood, you know, to help the guy get the job that was supposed to get it.

Q. What, if anything, did he tell you about how the contractors would get those inflated numbers?

A. They'd get their information through Al Chattin. He was like the line of communication with the thing.

Q. Now, sir, what if anything during these conversations did Mr. Scopo tell you about what would happen if a company took a job that it wasn't allocated?

A. They'd have to pay a penalty.

Q. Would that penalty be in addition to the two percent?

A. Yes.

Q. During these conversations what, if anything, did Ralph Scopo say to you concerning his own role or his own activities concerning the Club?

A. As to what?

Q. In other words, what did Ralph Scopo tell you was his own role in the club arrangement, what was his function, if any?

A. Well, he'd go to the meetings, he'd speak for the people he represented.

Q. Did he tell you who he represented at these meetings?

A. He represented us, I believe he represented Century.

Q. And when you mentioned meetings, what, if anything, did he tell you about who attended these meetings he would go to?

A. The other three guys that were making, you know, the allocations and Chattin.

Q. When you say the other three guys making allocations, are you referring to the three guys from the families?

A. Yes.

Q. What, if anything, did Mr. Scopo ever tell you concerning his power to affect a contractor's ability to work on a job?

A. That's a tough question to answer, you know.

Q. Let me rephrase the question this way. Directing your attention to sometime later, like 1983 or 1984, did you ever have a conversation with Ralph Scopo concerning a strike at that point?

A. Yes.

Q. What did he tell you on that occasion?

A. I think one of his union was involved in the strike and there was talk of someone getting concrete on their job from a non-union supplier and he said, my guys won't handle the concrete if it comes. That's all, that is what I mean.

Q. Incidentally, can you tell us, sir, based on your experience, what the daily cost would be—would have been to XLO during the period from 1981 to 1984 had you had one day of stoppage on a job due to a labor dispute?

A. You mean what the overhead would be?

Q. Yes, what would be the cost to XLO of a one day stoppage?

A. Well, you mean on one job?

Q. On one job, one dispute, one day stoppage.

A. Could be any job.

Q. Tell us what would be the cost to the company, the loss.

A. I'd say in that time, from that five-year pull?

Q. Yes, during that time period.

A. Anywhere from five to ten thousand.

Q. And can you explain how it is that a company would sustain that kind of a cost?

A. Where that cost came from?

Q. Yes, how do you figure that cost?

A. There's about 20 odd people that get carried on a job.

Q. When you say "get carried" what do you mean?

A. They get paid no matter what.

Q. They are paid no matter what?

A. Yes. There's rentals that go on, like the crane rentals. Then there's some trades where the job stops they get paid the day anyhow. You know, it adds up.

Q. You indicated that until approximately May or June of 1981 you said no to Ralph Scopo's invitation to you to join the Club. What was your state of mind before May or June of 1981 concerning that invitation to join the Club?

A. You mean—

Q. What was your thinking?

A. What was my inclination?

Q. Yes.

A. I didn't want to join it.

Q. Why not?

A. I didn't want to do it, that's all. I didn't want to be controlled.

Q. And did there come a time in May or June of 1981 when you said yes to Ralph Scopo about the Club?

A. Yes.

Q. And do you remember, where did you meet with Mr. Ralph Scopo on that occasion?

A. In his office.

Q. Did he call you or did you call him?

A. Probably he called me.

Q. Would you tell us what he said to you and what you said to him on that occasion?

A. As to my decision to join the Club?

Q. Yes. What did he say to you?

A. He said, you know, like,—I'm trying to think. He said, look, I can't hold these guys back any more, you're going to have to make up your mind, either you are in or you are out. And I had discussed that with my partners, you know, all along, you know, if we were put up against the wall, we didn't want to go out of business.

Q. When he said he couldn't hold these guys back any more, what, if anything, did you understand him to mean about "these guys," who these guys were?

A. What I understood?

Q. Yes, what did you understand?

A. I understood him to mean that even if he didn't want to, he'd have to give me labor problems, if I didn't go along.

Q. What did you understand the effect that those labor problems would have on your business?

A. Say it again.

Q. What did you understand would be the effect of labor problems like that on your business?

A. Cost a lot of money, you know, to the point where you may as well not be in business.

Q. How long did you remain a member of the Club after you joined in May or June of 1981?

A. Till September of '84.

Q. What happened then to change the situation?

A. Two FBI guys came into my office with a carton full of tapes and played them for six or eight hours.

Q. Now, sir, during your time in the Club, did you have further meetings with Ralph Scopo?

A. Yes.

Q. And did you meet Al Chattin?

A. Yes.

Q. And did you have numerous meetings with him?

A. Uh-huh.

Q. And did you have discussions with Mr. Scopo and Mr. Chattin concerning the Club?

A. Yeah.

Q. Did you learn from these conversations who the members of the Club were?

A. Yes.

Q. Who were they besides XLO?

Q. S & A, Cedar Park, Northberry, Century Maxim and G & G, that is as I recall.

Prosecution Rebuttal Summation, Assistant U.S. Attorney Michael Chertoff

Mr. Gaudelli said yesterday that the government threw in this Mafia stuff in order to prejudice you and inflame you and get you to thinking about things that you are not supposed to think about. Well, you know, the word "prejudice" means prejudge, and when you came into this courtroom eight weeks ago, almost to the day, and I gave you my opening statement, I said to you put out of your mind all the baggage, all the media stuff, everything you think you have heard about the Mafia, because that doesn't belong here. And that was before you came into the courtroom, because you had to listen to the evidence in the case and make up your mind based on what you heard here.

But you have listened to evidence for eight weeks, so it is not a question of prejudging anymore or preconceptions. It is a question of what you learned from the tapes, from the surveillances, from what these defendants said and did as you heard about it in this courtroom.

This isn't something that was designed by the government, as you heard in the opening. The government didn't make up the word "La Cosa Nostra" or the word "boss" or "captain" or all of the things you heard about that the Mafia does. The defendants did that. The defendants designed that. What the government did was present you with the evidence about that.

What did the evidence show you? The evidence showed you that because of this organization called La Cosa Nostra, these men were able to direct and to commit crimes on a vast scale, nationwide in scope.

You know, you have sat here for eight weeks and you have heard people talk about the Mafia and you have heard about killing and you have heard about extortion and you have heard about loan-sharking, and it is hard not to get a little numb. You sit in a courtroom and everything is nice and calm here. We all sit around tables. Generally speaking, we talk in low voices. But, remember, what the proof in this case is about is what happens on the street, out there, outside of the walls of this courtroom. You have to keep that sense of reality with you when you think about the evidence that you have seen and you have heard in this case, because that is what the case is about.

These crimes you have heard about here, whatever defense counsel would like you to think, were not isolated crimes that had nothing to do with each other. It is not just about an extortion here or an extortion there, or a killing here or a loan-sharking there. These crimes were connected. And they were connected to something called the Commission of La Cosa Nostra, which is the enterprise in this case. These crimes were interdependent. The pattern of this criminal activity which you heard about was made possible only because of the organization of the Mafia, what that represents.

Mr. LaRossa told you, and this was true, he reminded you that when you came in to be sworn as jurors, you were asked whether you could accept the proposition that just because a person is a member of the Mafia, that alone does not make him guilty of the crimes here, and that is correct. Merely the fact that a person is a member of the Mafia does not make him guilty of the crimes. But, part of the crime charged here is being part of the Mafia and part of the Commission of La Cosa Nostra. That is one of the elements, that is one half of the crime, because the crime that is charged here is racketeering and what racketeering is about is setting up, joining, associating with a criminal enterprise, organized criminal activity, and using that organization to commit crimes like extortion and murder and loan-sharking.

So it is not true to say that this case has nothing to do with the Mafia or the Mafia is irrelevant. The Mafia is very relevant in this case. The Mafia is relevant because it is the Mafia that makes possible this kind of concerted criminal activity. The Mafia is relevant because what racketeering is, the evil that racketeering laws are designed to prevent, is people banding together in an organized and disciplined fashion for one purpose; to commit crimes.

You know that the organization we are talking about here was not the Kiwanis, it wasn't the Elks Club, and that is important too, because these men weren't just thrown together in this organization. No one just scooped them up off the street and labeled them Mafia and then sent them off on their way. They took oaths to join this organization. They joined an organization which was disciplined, which had rules that were enforceable by punishment, including the punishment of death.

You know something about the secret society and the rules and the principles that these men voluntarily adopted, that they embraced, because you heard them talk about it. You have heard a conversation, for example, in a Jaguar on June 14 of 1983, with three of the defendants here—Mr. Furnari sitting over there, Mr. Santoro and Mr. Corallo—and they were talking about the membership requirements for the Mafia, for La Cosa Nostra. What was one of the cardinal principles, the main rules, that they were interested in? You can't testify. If you testify, you can't be a member; in fact, you are lucky to be alive. That was the word that Mr. Furnari used and Mr. Corallo used. He is lucky to be alive because he testified.

What is the reason for having that rule? The reason for having that rule is so that the people who run this criminal organization can count on their subordinates. They know if they tell someone to go out and do something, he is going to do it, and he is going to keep his mouth shut. And that increases their power, because you could not take over an industry, you could not take over labor unions, if you didn't have the power to direct others to help you.

One man, even a conspiracy of short duration, a few men, they couldn't have taken over the concrete industry in New York, and you know that, ladies and gentlemen. They couldn't have approved the selection of the president of the International Teamsters Union. They could not be making decisions about delegates for the Masons Union. They couldn't be getting $200,000 from the Carpenters Union. They couldn't be running the Concrete Workers Union. One man, a few men, couldn't do that. A disciplined criminal organization is what is necessary to do that.

4

The Pizza Connection:
United States v. Badalamenti

(Trial: October 1985–February 1987)

Introduction

United States v. Badalamenti exposed a heroin-trafficking conspiracy that emerged in the aftermath of the breakup of the French Connection in the early 1970s.[1] The case came to be known as the "Pizza Connection case" because several of the defendants used pizzerias as fronts for engaging in heroin distribution. It was the longest organized-crime trial and culminated the largest and most complex of the decade's organized-crime investigations. *Badalamenti* exposed organized crime's involvement in drug trafficking and the extensive cooperation between the American Cosa Nostra and the Sicilian Mafia. The case also demonstrated the extraordinary efforts American and foreign law enforcement agencies are capable of in their pursuit of organized crime.

The Indictment

The final superseding indictment, filed on February 19, 1985, charged thirty-five defendants with conspiracy to import drugs and to evade banking and money-laundering statutes. The entire trafficking network allegedly involved over two hundred additional participants. In addition to the

Badalamenti defendants, some conspirators were prosecuted in Italy and Switzerland; others were later prosecuted in *United States v. Adamita*.[2]

The indictment charged numerous specific violations of currency importation and transaction reporting statutes;[3] thirty-one defendants were charged with participating in a RICO conspiracy, and ten were charged with managing a "continuing criminal enterprise."[4]

The indictment named as defendants senior Mafia figures, including Gaetano Badalamenti and Salvatore Catalano, along with lower-level participants in the drug traffic, such as investors, drug couriers, and messengers responsible for coordinating the conspiracy's far-flung factions. In effect, *United States v. Badalamenti* brought to trial an international Cosa Nostra drug-trafficking operation.

Twenty of the defendants were connected to two groups: eight relatives of Gaetano Badalamenti, once head of the Sicilian Mafia commission, and twelve members and associates of the Sicilian Mafia, some of whom had become important figures in New York's Bonanno crime family. Two defendants, couriers of money and messages, belonged to neither of these factions.

Gaetano Badalamenti was the most prominent defendant. As a result of the Sicilian Mafia wars of the early 1970s, the Corleonese crime family had driven him out of Italy and murdered numerous members of his family.[5] The indictment charged that he had conspired to export narcotics from Brazil, where he was living, to the United States. Seven of his relatives were also named as defendants: Salvatore Evola, a contractor in Temperance, Michigan, accused of being an investor and distributor in the operation; Emanuele Palazzolo and Pietro Alfano, pizzeria owners in Wisconsin and Michigan, accused of being investors and organizers of the trafficking; Giuseppe Trupiano, Giuseppe Vitale, and Vincenzo Randazzo, accused of participating as couriers; and Vito Badalamenti, Gaetano's son, accused of assisting his father in the conspiracy.

Salvatore Catalano, a capo in the Bonanno family, was the highest-ranking Cosa Nostra member of the trial's New York defendants. He was also allegedly a member of the Sicilian Mafia and was accused of running the Bonanno drug importation business, which purchased drugs from the Corleonese organization in Sicily and from Badalamenti's organization in Brazil. The indictment charged Giuseppe Ganci with being a key organizer of the drug importation and distribution joint venture in America. Salvatore Lamberti, a member of the Sicilian Mafia's Borgetto family, his cousin Giuseppe Lamberti, a partner of Catalano and Ganci, and Giuseppe's brother-in-law Salvatore Mazzurco, another Catalano/Ganci partner, were named as investors in the drug business and charged with negotiating purchases of drugs in Sicily for the Catalano/Ganci group. The indictment charged Gaetano Mazzara and Frank Castronovo with storing drug money for the consortium in their New Jersey restaurant. Salvatore Greco, a New Jersey pizzeria owner and the brother of Sicilian Mafia boss Leonardo Greco of Bagheria (Sicily), was charged with money laundering. The indictment charged Francesco Polizzi with being an "investor" in and customer of the Catalano/Ganci joint venture. Defendants Baldassare Amato and Cesare Bonventre were charged with being investors in and wholesale distributors for the operation, while Filippo Casamento was accused of being Ganci's wholesale drug customer.

The indictment charged Giovanni Cangiolosi, a representative of the Corleonese family, with participation in the conspiracy. It alleged that he had been sent to the United States to resolve disputes among the traffickers.

The Investigation

The investigation which led to the Pizza Connection trial was different from the investigations that led to the other prosecutions considered in this book. Those began with the targeting of known Cosa Nostra leaders and involved gathering enough evidence to make a case. In the Pizza Connection, the FBI built a massive case from the ground up. Several Bureau offices began by responding to bits and pieces of information about different criminal groups and crimes. Only after years of following different trails did a coherent picture of the Pizza Connection emerge. More than any other prosecution of the 1980s, this case demonstrated the FBI's ability to conduct a massive and complex investigation into organized crime.

The case[6] began with the FBI's New York City office's investigation into the 1979 murder of Carmine Galante, the Bonanno family boss. Law enforcement officials believed that he was assassinated by a rival Bonanno family faction competing for control of the New York Cosa Nostra heroin trade. Eventually, they identified the rival faction as the "Zips," a cadre of Sicilian immigrants who resented Galante's control over the New York–Sicilian heroin trade. The investigation initially focused on Salvatore Catalano, a Bonanno capo and leader of the Zips, and on Cesare Bonventre, Galante's bodyguard.

Over the next five years, the Galante investigation intersected with Buffalo and Detroit FBI drug investigations; a New Rochelle (New York) FBI international money-laundering investigation; a DEA undercover drug operation in Philadelphia; and Italian investigations directed by the Palermo magistrate,

Giovanni Falcone.[7] The Swiss police became involved when Swiss financial institutions were implicated in the conspiracy's money-laundering schemes. The Spanish and Brazilian police assisted the United States in tracking conspirators whom the FBI traced to their countries.

As the scope of the activities of the Zips suspected of assassinating Galante became apparent, the FBI expanded its operation into a massive investigation of international drug trafficking. This evolution began in October 1980, when a white-collar criminal investigation conducted by the FBI's New Rochelle office, tracing a rumored overseas transfer of more than $60 million through a variety of money-laundering channels, identified several members of the Zips as the source of the funds. Over eighteen months later, the FBI uncovered a different money-laundering method using international brokerage houses in New York and Zurich to transfer some $20 million. Discovery of the Swiss connection proved particularly fruitful. With the cooperation of the Swiss government, the FBI eventually interrogated several Swiss money launderers who had extensive contacts in Italian banking and Turkish morphine smuggling.

The money-laundering investigations led the FBI to a vast network of New York and New Jersey organized-crime figures as the sources of the money, and the money-laundering routes all led to Sicily, which, in the late 1970s, had become the leading European center for heroin processing.

Shared intelligence enabled parallel investigations to progress in both Italy and the United States. In October 1982, United States and Italian officials gathered at Quantico, Virginia, for a joint conference on organized crime. These meetings were valuable for both governments. They contributed to the Italian arrests, three months later, of 153 mafiosi throughout Italy, while the Italians provided the FBI with surveillance photographs that confirmed the identities of several New York conspirators and were extremely useful at trial.

In spring 1983, the FBI launched a massive electronic surveillance operation in support of the expanding investigation. Over the next thirteen months, the case developed into the largest wire tapping operation ever mounted by the FBI. The FBI tapped the home phones of dozens of East Coast and Midwest conspirators, as well as numerous pay phones. The seventy-five authorized wiretaps led to the interception of over one hundred thousand conversations. One year after the wiretaps began, over one hundred of the 165 agents assigned to the organized-crime division of the FBI's New York office were working full time on the case; in addition, several dozen FBI and DEA agents in other states were involved.

The electronic surveillance provided the agents with new insight into the dynamics and structure of the drug network. Investigators were able to identify the roles played by the conspirators on both sides of the Atlantic. Initially, Sicily appeared to be the sole source of the drugs acquired by the New York-New Jersey-based joint venture headed by Catalano. However, as the exhaustive surveillance continued, agents realized that the Catalano organization was dealing with a Brazilian contact who had both cocaine sources in Latin America and heroin sources in Italy.

By early 1984, the FBI had tentatively identified the Brazilian drug source for Catalano's group as Gaetano Badalamenti, a surprise because the Sicilian Mafia had declared him an outcast. The hypothesis was all but confirmed when Tommaso Buscetta, a senior Mafia figure, long wanted in both Italy and the United States for his role in the French Connection, was captured in Brazil and, after agreeing to cooperate with the authorities, confirmed that Badalamenti was living in that country.

Beginning in the fall of 1983, investigators monitored negotiations between Badalamenti and the Catalano joint venture members in New York. The conspirators encoded their drug conversations in language involving purchase and sale of garments, for example, "twenty-two containers" of "10 percent acrylic shirts," which the investigators interpreted to mean twenty-two kilos of a 90-percent-pure illicit drug, either cocaine or heroin, which would be shipped to the Fort Lauderdale area. As the deal developed, communication between the Illinois, Rio de Janeiro, and New York branches of the drug network intensified. In March 1984 the FBI sent a five-agent team to Brazil, while the New York office worked feverishly to identify the Rio pay phones used by Badalamenti. Though the traces were successful on several occasions, the agents were never quick enough to catch Badalamenti himself at a phone.

As the delivery date approached, the FBI was confronted with a dilemma: either to intercept the drugs, exposing the investigation, or to let the shipment through and wait, holding out for Badalamenti to surface. Frank Storey, head of the New York FBI's organized-crime division, balked at letting the drugs into the country but was overruled by Assistant United States Attorney Louis Freeh, United States Attorney Rudolph Giuliani, and FBI Director William Webster, who decided that apprehending Badalamenti and shutting down the whole narcotics pipeline was worth the harm that would be caused by permitting one more drug shipment to enter the country. The issue became moot, however, when the shipment was delayed. Shortly thereafter, through intercepted calls, the FBI learned that Badalamenti planned to meet with a coconspirator in Madrid and decided to arrest him in Spain.

DEA agents and Spanish police arrested Gaetano Badalamenti and his son Vito in Madrid on April 8, 1984. The next day, while officials from the FBI, DEA, Custom's Service, police, and the Manhattan United States Attorney's Office coordinated operations from the FBI command post in Manhattan, over four hundred federal and local law enforcement agents in Illinois, New Jersey, Philadelphia, Wisconsin, Michigan, and New York simultaneously raided the homes and businesses of the Pizza Connection conspirators. Incredibly, while agents discovered numerous illegal weapons and significant caches of money, they found virtually no drugs. Nonetheless, four years of investigation had provided massive evidence of international drug trafficking and money laundering.

The Trial

Of the thirty-five defendants named in the indictment, only twenty-two appeared for trial; the remainder either had fled, died, been prosecuted in Europe, pled guilty, or entered into cooperation agreements with the government. Of these twenty-two defendants, nineteen remained at the trial's end; Gaetano Mazzara was murdered in December 1986, while Vincenzo Randazzo and Lorenzo DeVardo pled guilty to lesser charges during the course of the trial.

Federal District Judge Pierre Leval presided; Assistant United States Attorneys Louis Freeh, Richard Martin, Robert Stewart, and Robert Bucknam represented the government. Selection of the trial's twenty-four anonymous jurors and alternates took one month; ultimately, the financial and personal hardship of serving on a seventeen-month trial whittled their number to sixteen.

Before trial, the defendants moved to sever the prosecution into several smaller conspiracy cases.[8] Judge Leval ruled that with the exception of one defendant, the government's indictment properly charged a single drug importation and RICO conspiracy. The result was a trial of staggering complexity for jurors and lawyers alike. It brought the term "megatrial" into American jurisprudence and sparked a debate on the fairness of such prosecutions.

Four rows of seating in the fifth-floor courtroom at the Southern District's Foley Square courthouse were converted into seating for the defendants and their attorneys. The courtroom had to be wired for simultaneous Italian translation. The trial also required three translators and a host of United States marshalls for security.

The Southern District had seen large RICO prosecutions before, but *Badalamenti* was Foley Square's longest criminal trial. It generated over forty thousand pages of transcript and occupied dozens of lawyers for the three years between indictment and verdict. The twenty opening defense statements urged differing and often contradictory interpretations of the case's complex facts upon the jury. The trial was similarly marked by multiple cross-examinations, motions, objections, and affirmative defenses from the disparate defense team. The jurors faced the herculean challenge of compartmentalizing the evidence against each of the defendants whose roles we sketched briefly above.[9]

Two dramatic incidents during the trial exacerbated the conflicts within the defense camp. The murder of Gaetano Mazzara in December 1986 and the shooting of Pietro Alfano in February 1987 both sparked speculation by journalists and law enforcement officials of conflict among the defendants. It was widely theorized that Mazzara's murder, which occurred the weekend before his defense was to begin, was ordered by codefendants afraid that he would implicate them. After the Alfano shooting, the Badalamenti family members requested that they be placed in protective custody. This caused tensions between the Catalano and Badalamenti defendants to rise to the point that Ivan Fisher, attorney for Salvatore Catalano, felt compelled to publicly deny that his client was involved in the Alfano shooting.

The Prosecution

The prosecution's challenge was to present a massively complex case, highly dependent upon tapes of intercepted coded conversations, in a way that would be comprehensible and plausible to the jury; this had to be done without the aid of piles of drugs that are usually put in evidence in trafficking trials. While the prosecution team needed thirteen months to present its case, it stressed over and over that, in essence, they were simply proving the existence of a narcotics-smuggling and money-laundering conspiracy. According to Assistant United States Attorney Robert Stewart's opening statement for the prosecution,

The basic story of what occurred in this case is not very complicated. It is, stated in its simplest terms, the buying and selling of a commodity year in and year out, over and over again. [The commodity] was massive amounts of contraband narcotic drugs, heroin and cocaine.[10]

The prosecution set the stage and established the existence of the enterprise through the testimony of prominent organized-crime turncoats, including Tommaso Buscetta, Salvatore Contorno, Luigi Ronsisvalle, and Salvatore Amendolito. Only Ronsisvalle and Amendolito were directly involved in the crimes charged in *Badalamenti*, but the others could fill in background about the Cosa Nostra figures and their operations. Hundreds of photographs of meetings among the defendants and hundreds of recordings of their often-cryptic conversations supported the testimony of these witnesses. Two hundred surveillance agents, financial analysts, and intelligence experts explained the photographic and audio surveillance. They presented a picture of clandestine meetings, coded conversations, and secretive transactions.

The prosecution devoted the first few months to establishing the cooperative relationship between the Sicilian and American organized-crime groups and their heroin-trafficking networks. The government's first witness, Tommaso Buscetta, described the history of the Sicilian Mafia, the Corleonese war that had resulted in Badalamenti's ouster, and the origins, codes, and practices that defined the American and Sicilian Mafias. Buscetta had long been an associate of Badalamenti's, though he denied knowledge of Badalamenti's drug trafficking, but his contact with the remainder of the defendants was limited. His testimony was most valuable to the prosecution for the chilling picture it painted of the Sicilian Mafia.

The testimony of Salvatore Contorno and Luigi Ronsisvalle, coconspirators who had agreed to testify for the government, was directly relevant to the proof of the drug conspiracy. A Mafia member driven to cooperate with the government when he was marked for death by the Corleonese family, Contorno identified five of the New York-New Jersey defendants as having been present at a 1980 drug transaction in Bagheria, and he related discussions he had held with Sicilian Mafia members concerning their drug distribution contacts in the New York Cosa Nostra. Ronsisvalle, a Cosa Nostra associate who admitted to thirteen murders, testified to a meeting in which Sal Catalano and Giuseppe Ganci discussed a "heroin pipeline" from Sicily. He further testified to having transported heroin for Catalano's organization from New York to Chicago for five thousand dollars a trip. The defense attorneys clashed over the question of impeaching Ronsisvalle. Some wanted all of his murderous past entered into evidence in order to discredit him. Others wanted to keep his murders out in order to avoid tainting all of the defendants with his Mafia violence. The murders, though not their details, were admitted.

The government's next witness was Salvatore Amendolito, who described a series of money-laundering ventures generated by the Pizza Connection conspiracy. He initially operated by converting cartons of small bills, delivered to him by defendant Sal Catalano, into money orders with values just below ten thousand dollars (the amount that triggers federal cash-transaction reporting requirements) through a dozen different New York bank accounts.

Amendolito would then wire the money through Credit Suisse, Citibank, or Lavoro Bank to various Swiss bank accounts, from where it would be transferred to Sicily. As the volume of money expanded to suitcases full of cash, sometimes in amounts exceeding five hundred thousand dollars per shipment, Amendolito started personally to transport money by plane to the Bahamas, where he deposited it with Bahamian branches of Swiss banks for wire transfer to Switzerland. Amendolito identified a number of defendants, particularly Ganci, Castronovo, and Catalano, as the sources of the cash.

Having established the organizational hierarchy, membership, and operations of the Sicilian Mafia and the Bonanno crime family, and the nature of their joint drug trafficking conspiracy, the government proceeded to demonstrate each defendant's role. This task was mainly accomplished with intercepted conversations, though some physical evidence provided crucial support for the prosecution's case. A pharmaceutical scale and a notebook recording what were apparently drug transactions were found at Salvatore Mazzurco's house, and fingerprint checks made while the trial was in progress connected Mazzurco, Gaetano Mazzara, and Sal Catalano to government-monitored drug and money shipments. [11]

The government's case relied upon nine volumes of transcribed intercepted conversations, seventy-seven volumes of telephone toll records, and the testimony of a host of FBI and local police agents who had spent years following, photographing, and listening to the defendants. To present the wiretaps to the jury, the government hired four actors, known in the court as the "pizza players," to read the intercepted phone calls. For months, the jury listened to the reenactions of translations of cryptic Sicilian conversations. The jury heard such passages as,

". . . I lost the line because the guy who sews is not around. Now we are waiting minute by minute . . . because the tailor went up from down there . . . therefore, he will seek to be able to come up here . . . to be able to unravel this thing, more than anything else because it is becoming moldy."

"Are you talking about the shirts that come from Italy? Or the shirts from over there, where they have come from before."

and,

"Tomorrow speak with the guy whom you gave me those suits that time . . . ask him 'What appetite do you have, what appetite don't you have? What are you going to do?' "

The government then had to call agents (in their role as expert witnesses) to interpret these cryptic conversations. FBI agent Frank Tarallo testified that the codes used by the defendants were typical of those used in the world of drug smuggling, and he translated such terms as "suits" and "shirts" into the vernacular of the drug trade. Naturally, the defense lawyers objected continuously to the agents' inculpatory interpretations.

The testimony against Gaetano Badalamenti depended upon six crucial phone conversations. According to the prosecutors, Badalamenti's reference to "the thing of four or five years ago" supported the government's contention that Badalamenti was involved in a drug conspiracy of some duration. Similarly, the prosecution contended that Badalamenti's statement to Sal Lamberti, "This way, this month of March we can go and collect a bunch of asparagus," referred to the prospective profits from their drug trafficking. Most incriminating, however, was a series of conversations between Badalamenti and the New York group, in which Badalamenti referred to a prospective drug shipment to Fort Lauderdale, "The thing where it is hot":

BADALAMENTI: . . . I think that by the beginning of next week . . . or they will come with twenty-two parcels or with eleven parcels, whatever you guys prefer. . . .

ALFANO: I don't know about the twenty-two.

BADALAMENTI: Now there's another thing. I met the guy with the shirts of four years ago . . . but there's a little problem. . . . There's another guy here that has, there's ten percent acrylic. I understand little about this.

ALFANO: But ten percent is not bad.

BADALAMENTI: The cost over here is about forty-five cents. And over there it will cost about sixty cents . . . and the price is good.

The government constructed an overwhelming case against the defendants with hundreds of encoded conversations like this one, plus the testimony of informants and surveillance agents.

The Defense

The defense attorneys, especially those representing the minor defendants, were confronted with the formidable task of maintaining distinct identities for their clients and preventing them from fading into a morass of conspiracy and guilt by association. Their strategies were diverse and sometimes contradictory. Gaetano Badalamenti and Mazzurco testified in their own defense; five defendants struggled to provide innocent explanations for the prosecution's evidence against them through the testimony of friends, relatives, and associates. The other defendants relied upon cross-examinations and defense summations to raise reasonable doubts about their guilt.

Gaetano Badalamenti's defense came first. When he took the stand, however, he refused to answer many questions put to him both in direct examination by his own lawyer, Michael Kennedy, and in cross-examination by Assistant United States Attorney Louis Freeh. Badalamenti claimed (albeit without foundation in United States law) that pending charges in Italy justified his selective refusal to answer questions. He denied that the government's recorded phone conversations concerned drugs, stating that he had never been involved in drug smuggling. Badalamenti would not respond, however, to his attorney's inquiry as to what the conversations did involve, answering, "Mr. Kennedy, I will not explain for two reasons. I have never betrayed and I will never betray my secrets. The other is that it would cause me harm in Italy." Similarly, on cross-examination Badalamenti said, "If I am the depository of a secret, there is no one who can get it out of me. So many have tried, all different ways, torture included. . . . It is not drugs. I cannot explain what it is." Badalamenti refused to answer many other government questions about his Mafia past, referring only evasively to his defeat in the Corleonese war in Sicily and refusing to answer questions that could implicate him as a Mafia member. In response to Freeh's question "Are you now or have you ever been a member of La Cosa Nostra?" Badalamenti answered, "You know, if I were to say yes, I would have big problems in Italy." Judge Leval instructed the jury that Badalamenti's silences could be held against him, as he had waived his Fifth Amendment rights by taking the stand. After the conclusion of the trial, Badalamenti was convicted of criminal contempt for his refusal to answer Freeh's questions.

Mazzurco, the only other defendant who testified, asserted that a ledger offered by the government as evidence of recorded drug transactions actually referred to precious stones, and that a balance beam scale of a type commonly used in drug transactions actually was a pasta scale. The remainder of his testimony was equally incredible, including his claims that he was not involved with a heroin package wrapped in tissue paper bearing his palm print and that he had no relationship with the drug dealer Emanuele Adamita, who had Mazzurco's phone number in his address book. Michael Kennedy got Mazzurco to admit, "It was a taboo for anyone to be in touch with Mr. Badalamenti." Kennedy advanced the theory that Mazzurco's contact with Badalamenti was not for the purpose of drug dealing, but was to further a Sicilian Mafia plot against his client.

Following these two disastrous appearances, no other defendants took the stand. Catalano's case was undermined by a witness who, when asked about the Mafia family in his home village, responded, "Mafia—What's that? I don't even know what it is! Is it something that one eats?" An accountant testified that Greco had been with him examining pizzeria properties in New Jersey rather than testing batches of heroin in Italy, as the government claimed. This alibi was completely discredited when several entries supporting it in the accountant's date book were shown to be fabricated.

The other defendants' affirmative defenses were similarly marred by implausible testimony or by witnesses with criminal records or immigration problems. The majority of the defendants relied on attacks on the credibility of the government witnesses, challenges to the government's interpretations of the thousands of cryptic phone conversations that provided the bulk of the evidence against them, and their lawyers' summations. Ultimately, none of these defense tactics proved successful.

The defense attorneys frequently clashed with one another. Their most extreme conflict occurred when Kennedy claimed in his closing statement that a series of encoded phone calls referred not to drug dealing but to a plot involving defendant Mazzurco to murder his client, a position that enraged Mazzurco and Joseph Benfante, his lawyer. Throughout the trial, the defendants hindered each other's cases with objections and contradictory arguments.

The Verdict and Sentencing

The jury retired to begin deliberations on February 25, 1987, accompanied by the 120-page indictment, 350 pages of charges and instructions, 410 pages of evidentiary charts and summaries prepared by the government, and the 59-page verdict sheet. The jury took only six days to arrive at its verdicts. Vito Badalamenti, Gaetano's son, was the only defendant acquitted of all charges. Fifteen defendants were convicted of all charges. Mazzurco and Salvatore Lamberti were convicted of drug trafficking and RICO conspiracies but cleared of the continuing criminal enterprise charges. Salamone was found not guilty of the RICO and narcotics conspiracy charges but was convicted of currency-reporting violations.

Judge Leval sentenced ten of the defendants to between twenty and thirty-five years, five to between twelve and fifteen years, and four to five years or less. He also imposed significant fines, including $125,000 for Badalamenti and $1.15 million for Salvatore Catalano. In addition, in a novel application of the Victim and Witness Protection Act, Judge Leval ordered eight defendants collectively to pay $3.3 million to a fund for the rehabilitation of drug addicts.

The Appeal

Fifteen of the eighteen convicted defendants appealed their convictions. The Second Circuit's consolidated opinion, *United States v. Casamento*,[12] addressed ten of the appellants' arguments in detail.[13] With the exception of the sufficiency of evidence appeals, on which Giuseppe Trupiano's convictions were completely overturned and Frank Castronovo's continuing criminal enterprise conviction was overturned, the court found that Judge Leval had either been correct in his rulings or had made harmless errors. Three of the Second Circuit's holdings will be examined below.

1. The atmosphere and size of the trial: The appellants argued that the courtroom atmosphere created by the mass joinder, by the media attention it attracted, and by the violence that occurred during the proceedings made a fair trial impossible. Rejecting this argument, the Second Circuit wrote, "We will presume the jury followed [Judge Leval's] admonitions and avoided exposure to news reports about the trial," and, in evaluation of the trial's violence, "Whether the sudden absences of Mazzara and Alfano from the courtroom may possibly have made the jury more inclined to believe that these two defendants, and by association, the rest of the defendants, led lives of violence is a matter of conjecture."[14]

The court further rejected the argument that the trial was so long and complex that the jurors, unable to assimilate the evidence, had no alternative but to rely uncritically on the government's summary book and charts. Despite the fact that the jurors reached their verdicts in only six days, the court found that the handful of not-guilty verdicts demonstrated the jury's ability to evaluate critically the evidence against each defendant. Further, the court determined that a "lengthy, multi-defendant narcotics conspiracy trial [is] not beyond the ken of the ordinary juror, since [the] purchase and sale of hard drugs is basically a simple operation."[15] Finally, the court found that the not-guilty verdicts disposed of the appellants' argument that spillover prejudice had tainted the jury results; if the jury could distinguish those charges where it failed to find guilt, this implied that its evaluations of each charge were unaffected by its analyses of the other charges.

Further, the court rejected the argument that conflicts among the defendants had exacerbated the spillover prejudice, concluding that "severance is not necessarily warranted even if the defendants are hostile or attempt to cast the blame on each other."[16] The court concluded, "Differences [in trial strategies] will almost inevitably occur in multi-defendant trials, and to hold that they require severance would effectively ban this type of trial; we decline to impose such a ban."[17]

Though the appellate panel declined to impose a ban on mass trials, it did set out guidelines to control the size of future trials. In the future, where the trial judge determines that the time for presentation of the government's case will exceed four months, the prosecutor must file a motion demonstrating that a joint trial is more conducive to a fair administration of justice than a series of smaller trials; in cases with more than ten defendants, the government's burden of justification is particularly heavy. The court's discussion concluded with a plea:

[T]he judge is to be commended for the fairness, patience, and sound judgement he displayed throughout the conduct of this most extraordinary proceeding. Nevertheless, we offer the guidance outlined in the preceding paragraphs in the hope that we will not soon be again presented with the transcript of a seventeen month trial in which more than thirty persons were named as defendants.[18]

2. Sufficiency of evidence: The sufficiency-of-evidence appeals achieved some success. Defendant Giuseppe Trupiano's convictions were completely overturned; the court held that the government's sole evidence against him, a conversation in which he considered Alfano's request to "take a walk" if Alfano could send his "daughter or someone to stay with my wife,"[19] was legally insufficient to prove beyond a reasonable doubt that Trupiano was aware of and participated in the conspiracy. The court also overturned Castronovo's conviction on the continuing criminal enterprise charge, holding that the evidence did not show that he had controlled the activities of five other members of the conspiracy.

3. The restitution penalties: The appellants' sole other success lay in the Second Circuit's overturning of the restitution penalties imposed on eight defendants. The court concluded that the Victim and Witness Protection Act limited restitution orders to victims whose damages could be attributed directly to actions of specific defendants. Consequently, defendants in drug cases could not be ordered to pay restitution to drug rehabilitation centers that serve the general public.

Conclusion

Ultimately, *Badalamenti* was most significant for laying to rest the longstanding debate over Cosa Nostra's involvement with drug trafficking, for demonstrating the drug-smuggling alliance between the Sicilian and American organized-crime families, and for illustrating the international scope of their operations. Students of Cosa Nostra and even former family members turned state's witnesses have time and again recounted the injunction against drug dealing. For example, former Los Angeles family underboss Jimmy Fratiano testified that the drug-dealing ban is one of the Cosa Nostra rules whose violation is punishable by death. Likewise, in the Commission case, Tommaso Buscetta confirmed the ban on drug dealing; as recently as 1993, Salvatore Gravano repeated this assertion.

It seems likely that differences of opinion about the propriety of trafficking in drugs have caused substantial conflict and disruption within Cosa Nostra since the late 1970s. Some observers believe, for example, that the civil war within the Bonanno family was sparked by commission sponsorship of Philip Rastelli, who had committed to shutting down the drug dealing established by boss Carmine Galante. Another theory holds that Paul Castellano was assassinated because he was intent on enforcing the drug ban within the Gambino family by imposing a death sentence upon John Gotti's brother, Gene, and close friend, Angelo Ruggiero.

Organized crime's involvement in drug dealing merits extensive study. If there is a Cosa Nostra ban on drugs, it clearly has been frequently violated over many years. In 1986, the President's Commission on Organized Crime concluded that drug dealing is the norm rather than the exception in the contemporary Mafia.[20] *Badalamenti* lends support to this conclusion.

The Pizza Connection case demonstrated the significant developments in the internationalization of both crime and law enforcement that have occurred in recent years. For the first time, the Sicilian Mafia was shown to be active in the United States; more broadly, the prosecution exposed the sort of sophisticated international structure that is required to sustain ongoing, large-scale drug trafficking. The investigation of this United States–Sicilian connection led to the forging of new international cooperation among law enforcement agencies. The investigation was truly multinational: police of three countries—the United States, Switzerland, and Italy—were integral to the operation, the Spanish police cooperated in the final seizure of Badalamenti, and the Turkish police provided United States investigators with background information on the Mediterranean morphine trade.

In monitoring and recording the communications of the *Badalamenti* defendants, these police agencies employed a wide range of sophisticated surveillance tools, such as concealed video cameras, pen registers, eavesdropping devices, and computer-aided telephone tracing systems. The conspirators showed astonishment that their international payphone-to-payphone calls had been tapped. Contemporary Cosa Nostra members must operate under the assumption that their cummunications are not secure against modern-day high-tech government eavesdropping.

More than any other case, *Badalamenti* demonstrates how formidable an opponent to organized crime law enforcement has become. Remarkable changes in law enforcement methods, commitments, and technology occurring over the last three decades will make it impossible for organized crime to operate in its traditional way.

Notes

1. *United States v Santana*, 503 F2d 710 (2d Cir 1974).

2. A later prosecution, *United States v Adamita*, 88 CR 217 (SDNY 1989) (known popularly as "Pizza Connection II"), charged fourteen additional individuals with participation in the Pizza Connection conspiracy. The trial, in which presiding judge Sprizzo harshly criticized the prosecution for the unsupported breadth of its charges, was a setback for the government. Seven of the defendants were acquitted by Judge Sprizzo at the conclusion of the government's case; two were acquitted by the jury; four were convicted of heroin distribution and conspiracy to distribute heroin, and one was convicted of conspiracy to distribute heroin.

3. The indictment contained sixteen counts: count one charged all the defendants with conspiring to import and distribute narcotics; counts two through eleven each charged single defendants with engaging in and managing a "continuing criminal enterprise"; count twelve charged fifteen defendants with conspiring to transport money out of the United States without filing currency transaction reports; count thirteen charged six defendants with causing false statements concerning various cash deposits to be made to the IRS; count fourteen charged fifteen defendants and count fifteen charged ten defendants with failure to file currency transaction reports and international currency transaction reports; and count sixteen charged thirty-one defendants with a RICO conspiracy, specifically, conspiring to conduct and participate in, through a pattern of racketeering activity, an enterprise that engaged in international drug trafficking and money laundering.

4. The *Continuing Criminal Enterprise Statute* (CCE), *United States Code*, vol. 21, sec. 848, prescribes severe penalties—up to twenty years' imprisonment and $2 million in fines for a first offense and thirty years and $4 million for subsequent offenses, plus forfeiture of any criminal proceeds—for any individual proven to have committed a continuing series of violations of federal drug law while (1) occupying a supervisory position with respect to five or more persons, and (2) deriving substantial income from the illegal activity. Along with the RICO statute, CCE has played an important role in the government's campaign against the upper echelons of organized crime.

5. For a history of Mafia politics, see Henner Hess, *Mafia and Mafiosi: The Structure of Power* (Heath, 1973).

6. This section draws heavily on Ralph Blumenthal's detailed account, *Last Days of the Sicilians: At War with the Mafia—The FBI Assault on the Pizza Connection* (Random House, 1988).

7. Giovanni Falcone, *Men of Honour: The Truth about the Mafia* (Fourth Estate, 1992).

8. For a day-by-day account of the trial, see Shana Alexander, *The Pizza Connection* (Weidenfeld, 1988).

9. See National Association of Criminal Defense Lawyers, *Report on RICO Megatrials* (1987); *Megatrials: A Report by the Committee on Criminal Advocacy of the Association of the Bar of the City of New York* (1988); ABA Criminal Justice Section on RICO Trials, *Draft Report* (1988); *United States v Gallo*, 668 F Supp 736 (EDNY 1987); Brendan Judge, *No Easy Solutions to the Problem of Criminal Megatrials*, 66 Notre Dame Law Review 211 (1990); Annual Judicial Conference Second Judicial Circuit of the United States, 125 FRD 197 (1989).

10. *United States v Badalamenti*, 84 CR 236 (SDNY 1987), trial transcript p. 30.

11. Salvatore Mazzurco's palm print was found on the tissue paper wrapping a kilo of heroin sold to an undercover agent through murdered conspirator Benny Zito: Gaetano Mazzara's prints were found on the paper bag that had contained a different Zito shipment. Sal Catalano's thumb print was found on a piece of paper bearing his phone number that money launderer Sal Amendolito claimed Catalano had given to him as he delivered a suitcase containing $1.54 million in cash.

12. *United States v Casamento*, 887 F2d 1141, 1154 (2d Cir 1989).

13. The major issues addressed on appeal were as follows: (1) Did the mass trial deprive the defendants of their constitutional right to due process? (2) Was the evidence sufficient to convict the defendants? (3) Should certain hearsay statements and foreign depositions have been admitted? (4) Should Mazzurco's postarrest statements have been admitted? (5) Should Casamento's severance request have been granted? (6) Were the government's characterizations in summation of wiretapped conversations as coded drug references proper? (7) Was Gaetano Badalamenti's criminal contempt citation authorized by law? (8) Were the restitution fines legally valid? (9) Did the government breach its plea agreement with Lorenzo DeVardo? and (10) Should Salvatore Greco have been permitted to introduce a request by the government for an alibi whose dates suggested that government witness Salvatore Contorno had changed his testimony?

14. *United States v Casamento* at 1155.

15. Id. at 1150 (quoting *United States v Moten*).

16. Id. at 1153 (quoting *United States v Becker*).

17. Id. at 1153.

18. Id. at 1152–53. For an application of the *Casamento* guidelines, see *United States v Gambino*, 729 F Supp 954 (SDNY 1990).

19. Id. at 1167.

20. The President's Commission on Organized Crime, *Report to the President and the Attorney General, America's Habit: Drug Abuse, Drug Trafficking, and Organized Crime* (Washington, D.C., 1986). See also Senate Committee on Governmental Affairs and Senate Committee on Foreign Relations, *Sicilian Connection: Southwest Asian Heroin en Route to United States*, September 1980, 96th Cong., 2d Sess.

Prosecution's Opening Statement, Assistant United States Attorney Robert Stewart

May it please the court, counsel, ladies and gentlemen of the jury:

As his Honor said a few minutes ago, my name is Robert Stewart and I am one of the attorneys for the government.

The indictment in this case charges 35 defendants, 22 of whom are here today, with conspiracy to violate the narcotics laws and related offenses involving the importation and distribution of narcotic drugs between the years 1975 and 1984. The case involves a number of individuals in addition to the 35 who are charged and the 22 who are actually here. You will hear a number of names during the course of this trial.

Certainly the case involves a number of events over a relatively long period of time. Yet the basic story of what occurred in this case is not very complicated. It is, stated in its simplest terms, the buying and selling of a commodity year in and year out, over and over again.

What I want to do in the next hour and perhaps 15 minutes is, first of all, to describe to you the basic nature of the business operation which is at the heart and the core of this case; secondly, to identify for you eleven individuals who are absolutely essential to this case and around whom all major events in this case occurred; thirdly, to go over the indictment with you in a bit more detail, identifying what all the charges are, identifying who all of the defendants are, some of the principal co-conspirators, and to describe for you what the role and what the function was of each of those defendants and co-conspirators in this particular narcotics operation; and finally, to review with you very briefly some of the evidence which you will be hearing during the coming weeks and months.

First, as to the basic elements of the business operation, the buying and selling of a commodity, a commodity which came from overseas. All that happened in this case was that a group of individuals in the New York-New Jersey metropolitan area formed a joint business venture. They got their friends and associates to come together as investors in the business venture and they called up some other friends and associates overseas and they said to those people overseas "Can you supply us with a commodity?" And the associate overseas called some of his friends and associates. Some they asked "Can you provide us with raw material?" Others, they said "Can you manufacture the raw material into the commodity?" And still others they asked to transport that commodity to America and to deliver it to the people who were the customers in America.

When the overseas supplier had done all those things, gotten the raw material, gotten it manufactured into the commodity and had it transported to the people in America, the people here sold the commodity at wholesale to their customers.

Now they had a big pile of money in front of them, 5's, 10's, 20's, 50's, $100 bills. No checks, no bank accounts. Just cash. And they did two things with that money. Part of it, a good part of it, they put into their pockets, because that was their profit, and it was a very, very handsome profit indeed. What remained they sent back to the overseas suppliers who had provided them with the commodity, because they had purchased that commodity almost always on credit or what in the trade is referred to as consignment.

When those dollars got back across the ocean into the hands of the overseas supplier he did four things with that money. Part of it he gave to the person or persons who provided the raw material, part of it he gave to the person or persons who manufactured that raw material into the final commodity, part of it he gave to the people who transported that commodity to the customers in America, and the rest of it he put in his pocket.

That was all that happened in this case, month in, month out, year in and year out, throughout the nine years that are charged in the indictment.

What makes this particular business operation unusual and unique and, indeed, the subject of this prosecution is that the commodity in question was massive amounts of contraband narcotic drugs, heroin and cocaine, and secondly, that the individuals, every one of the people who was involved in the process of buying and selling these commodities, were members or associates of the Mafia, the Mafia in Sicily or the Mafia in the United States.

Because they were members of the Mafia and because they were trafficking in a contraband drug they went to great lengths to conceal what it was that they were doing, and so you will not see one of these defendants pick up the telephone in his office—and all of the defendants had legitimate businesses and they all had telephones in their legitimate businesses—you will not see them pick up those telephones and call an overseas supplier and say "Send me 22 kilograms of cocaine next week."

What you are going to see instead are people standing on street corners in the dead of winter, shivering and shaking for an hour waiting for a pay telephone call to come from somebody in Sicily or somebody in Illinois or somebody in Brazil who is also going to be using a pay telephone.

And when the call finally comes you're not going to hear ordinary intelligible sentences of a person ordering a commodity on terms and price and conditions. What you will hear is people talking in codes about shirts and shoes and pants and the old pants and the new pants and the architect and the engineer and the work over there and plants and potatoes and cheese, anything but what they are really talking about, which is heroin and cocaine and kilograms and dollars and cents.

You will be in a unique position because you will hear these conversations over pay telephones and you will know what the codes are. As a matter of fact, by the end of this case you will know the codes better than many of the defendants, because they had great difficulties during the course of the conspiracy keeping the codes straight, and consequently not infrequently you will see a person standing out on a street corner and never getting the call because somebody has made a mistake in the code and the call is going to another telephone somewhere halfway around the world. But you will have the benefit of knowing what the codes are and of understanding exactly and precisely what it is that these people are doing in their telephone conversations and in their other movements.

The evidence will demonstrate that there are two basic themes to this case. One of those themes involves the dynamics of smuggling, the smuggling of massive quantities of heroin and cocaine into the United States on a protracted and systematic basis and the smuggling of massive amounts of United States currency out of the United States to the overseas suppliers. Indeed, during just part of 1982 and 1983 just one of the overseas operations located in Sicily earmarked over a ton and a half of pure heroin for consignment to the core group individuals who were importing the drugs and distributing the drugs here in the New York metropolitan area. That ton and a half of heroin, pure heroin, had a wholesale value of over $333 million, a third of a billion dollars, in the space of a little over a year.

Between the years 1980 and 1983 the evidence will demonstrate that over $40 million was smuggled out of the United States into Switzerland for distribution to some of the suppliers in Sicily, and that does not count money that was smuggled out of the United States to pay for other overseas suppliers in Brazil.

Smuggling, then, is one of the basic themes of this case. The second basic theme of this case involves the dynamics of the Mafia, a secret criminal organization both there and in the United States which provided the cement that held together the components of this conspiracy year in and year out throughout the nine years charged in this indictment.

It was the Mafia organization discipline and protocol and rules of order which enabled the co-conspirators in this case to deal with one another a third of the way around the world from each other, to enter into agreements which although having no ability to enforce their contracts in the law were nevertheless binding upon the members and associates of the secret society, agreements involving millions of dollars in cash and millions of dollars in product.

It was the Mafia discipline which enabled members to take a package containing a million dollars in cash or a million dollars in heroin and go in the dead of night and walk down a dark alley to meet with somebody confident that they would not be ambushed and robbed by the person that they were going to meet because there was a code of honor among these people that bound them to honor their obligations.

That was the discipline and the organization that made this conspiracy possible, that brought these people together and that held them together year in and year out and gave them a very, very distinct advantage over any other competitor that lacked that basic organization.

Testimony of Tommaso Buscetta

Q. Mr. Buscetta, did you come to have conversations with members of La Cosa Nostra?

A. Yes.

Q. In the course of those conversations did you learn about the structure and the function of La Cosa Nostra?

A. Yes.

Q. Can you tell us what that was?

A. The organization was divided up into families.

Q. What do you mean by "families," sir?

A. The group was called families because we are or we were brothers. These families adopted the name of the village where they were located or of a small town where the family was located. The family consisted of a capo or boss, sotto capo or deputy boss, consigliere or counselor, capodecine and soldato or soldier.

Q. Mr. Buscetta, in that structure, what position did you have when you first joined?

A. Soldier.

Q. You told us that the boss or capo was Gaetano Filippone?

A. Yes.

Q. Mr. Buscetta, you said that you were a soldier in this organization, is that correct?

A. Yes.

Q. As a soldier, did you come to learn what your duties and responsibilities were within the organization?

A. Yes.

Q. Can you tell us what duties and responsibilities you had as a soldier?

A. There is not a great deal of difference between a soldier and a boss. The only difference lies in knowing how to deal with people during a conversation, some people speak better and some people speak not so well and as in everything, there has to be a boss, but there is no difference between the boss and the soldier as to dignity or conduct of the man.

Q. As a soldier in the Mafia family you were part of, can you tell us what you understood your responsibilities and duties to be?

A. My responsibilities were limited. Even my very conduct.

A. (Continuing) And I had to wait until orders were given to me by the boss through my capo decine as to whether I was to cooperate or participate in any particular undertaking.

Q. What do you mean that your conduct was limited, Mr. Buscetta?

A. I'm sorry, I don't understand your question. You say "my conduct was limited." I didn't say my conduct was limited.

Q. I think you said that you had limited responsibilities and you had to wait for orders from your boss or capo decine?

A. That is correct.

Q. Now, as a soldier, did you receive instructions or information about the way in which you were to comport yourself as a member of the Mafia?

A. Yes.

Q. You received those after you became a member, shortly after you became a member?

A. As a matter of fact, these qualities were required also before becoming a member of the organization.

Q. Please continue.

A. I was reminded to behave in the appropriate manner, to be silent, not to look at other men's wives or women, not to steal and especially at all times when I was called I had to rush, leaving whatever I was doing.

Q. Mr. Buscetta, you said that you had to be silent, is that correct?

A. Yes.

Q. Is there a particular word that was used by the organization to describe that concept?

A. Omerta.

Q. Can you tell us whether omerta applied within the organization or as to people outside the organization?

A. Mainly within the organization, but it can be applied also outside the organization.

Q. What would happen so far as you know, Mr. Buscetta, so far as you were told, if you violated one of those principles that you just described?

A. Death.

* * *

Q. Mr. Buscetta, let me now return to the time shortly after you took the oath and became a member of La Cosa Nostra as you described. I would like to ask you, sir, if there came a time when someone more senior in the family than you told you what your obligations were as a member of that La Cosa Nostra.

A. Yes.

Q. And how was that information passed on to you?

A. By voice. Nothing is written in the Mafia.

Q. Can you tell us what that person told you about your obligations as a man of honor?

A. There are many such things. The main ones are the maximum silence, secrecy also between husband and wife or brothers, and no leak of information from the Mafia outside.

There was another thing. A person of the Mafia could abstain from talking but when he talked he had to tell the truth.

Q. Your last answer, can you tell us a little more fully what you were told concerning your obligation to tell the truth?

A. A man of honor must tell the truth to another man of honor. He may also abstain from talking. Should he not tell the truth, then he may be subject to expulsion or death.

Q. With respect to silence, omerta, as you described it, Mr. Buscetta, what were you told, if anything, that you could say to people who were outside the Mafia about the existence of the Mafia?

A. Nothing. One cannot say anything.

Q. Mr. Buscetta, were you told shortly after you became a member of the Mafia anything about the identity of other members of the Mafia and how you could be introduced to them?

A. Yes.

Q. Can you explain to us what you were told and what you understood?

A. It was explained to me that there were many families, families in the sense of Cosa Nostra or Mafia, in the area of Palermo and that if I were to meet some of their members I needed an introduction by somebody else, I could not introduce myself by myself to these people.

May I continue?

Q. Please continue.

A. To continue answering your question, I may have access to any family in the area of Palermo through an introduction by my boss, I can never introduce myself alone, and I shall always follow the directions of the capodecine.

Q. Mr. Buscetta, you said that you had to be introduced to another man of honor by another person, is that correct?

A. That is correct.

Q. And how would that introduction take place or how were you told that such an introduction must take place?

A. I was introduced as Cosa Nostra, or the same thing, Stesa Cosa.

Q. And what did those words mean when they were used for such an introduction?

A. That I belong to a family.

Q. And what did it mean with respect to the other persons who were present during the introduction?

A. If there were two or three men of honor and another person who was not a man of honor, for me, I was introduced as "This is our friend," for the other person, who was not a man of honor, the introduction was "This is my friend," and it was understood, therefore, who was and who wasn't.

Q. Who was and who wasn't what, sir?

A. Who was a man of honor and who was not a man of honor.

Q. You said that you learned these things shortly after you became a member of a particular family, is that correct, Mr. Buscetta?

A. That is correct.

Q. And were you told why these rules existed?

A. For the secrecy of Cosa Nostra, of Mafia.

Q. Mr. Buscetta, you said that you became a member of a family. Did that family have a name?

A. Yes, Porta Nuova.

* * *

Q. And what were you told about how the capo of your family was selected?

A. Through a vote.

Q. A vote of whom?

A. We voted, including himself. All the members of a family voted.

Q. And did you come to learn whether the same procedure for electing a capo applied in other families?

A. Wherever there is Cosa Nostra it is the same in every place.

Q. And how did you come to learn that information, Mr. Buscetta?

A. Within my own family and then through contacts with members of other families.

Q. Mr. Buscetta, can you tell us if during the course of your membership in the Porta Nuova family you came to learn what the functions and duties of the capo were?

A. Yes.

Q. Mr. Buscetta, can you tell us how it was that you came to acquire that information?

A. By the members of my own family.

Q. Can you also give us an approximate time, how soon after you became a member you became familiar with the duties and responsibilities of the capo?

A. Immediately after.

Q. Now, Mr. Buscetta, can you tell us what the duties and responsibilities of the head of the family were?

A. The duties were to deal with all matters pertaining to the various members of the family in the best possible way, to deal and interact with members of other families, with other families, and always to have a good word in respect to the weak.

Q. You told us about a position of the underboss, of the sotto capo.

A. Yes.

Q. Can you tell us if you came to learn how the underboss was selected?

A. The underboss is chosen by the boss and he is not elected.

Q. Can you tell us, Mr. Buscetta, how you came to come by that information?

A. Within the family. In the family there are the young and the old members and the old members instruct the young ones one day after the other.

Q. And in your case is that how you came to learn the information that you have disclosed to us today about the structure of La Cosa Nostra?

A. Yes.

Q. Mr. Buscetta, you described the position of consigliere or counselor.

A. Yes.

Q. I would like to ask you if there came a time when you received information about the duties and functions of the person who had that job in the family as consigliere.

A. Yes.

Q. And how did you obtain that information?

A. Always within the family.

Q. What was the function, so far as you understood it, of the consigliere within the family?

A. The word itself describes the function. Consigliere counselor, is somebody who gives advice. He is elected, just like the boss, and no boss will take the responsibility of a decision unless he has called in the consigliere.

Q. How many consigliere would there be or were there in your family?

A. Three.

Q. You also described the position of capodecine, is that correct, sir?

A. Yes.

Q. Did you come to learn what the function of the capodecine was within the family?

A. Yes.

Q. How did you come to learn that information?

A. From the capodecine himself.

Q. And what did the capodecine tell you about his job?

A. No man of honor has any particular task to carry out within a family. Only he is—there is no specific job that somebody must do. Only I am at his orders and I must carry them out when he gives them.

Testimony of Agent Frank Tarallo

MR. MARTIN: Your Honor, at this time the government offers Agent Tarallo as an expert in narcotics activities.

THE COURT: You may proceed in asking your questions. If there are objections I'll rule.

Q. In your 24 years with DEA, FBN [Federal Bureau of Narcotics] and the Los Angeles Police Department, sir, you've engaged in undercover negotiations to buy and sell narcotics, is that correct?

A. Yes, sir.

Q. You've engaged in such negotiations both face to face and on the telephone?

A. Yes, sir.

Q. Now, can you tell us if in your face to face negotiations in 24 years of your experience the persons who have been offering to sell or sell drugs to you or buy drugs from you have used certain terms or patterns of speech which you've observed to be common?

A. Yes, sir.

Q. And can you describe the pattern of speech which you've observed to be conducted while in those discussions?

A. Yes, the patterns are deceptive. Instead of using direct definitions of a drug, for instance, there would be another word used in its place.

Q. And in conversations you've had have you had occasion to yourself use the words "heroin" or "cocaine" or other drugs?

A. On a few occasions I forced that issue.

Q. What do you mean by that, sir?

A. That I would on purpose mention the word "heroin" or "cocaine" depending on what negotiation I'm in.

Q. And did you receive any instructions or advice on those occasions when you used those terms?

A. On those occasions I would receive some admonishment that I shouldn't use the word, it is dangerous, the police may be around, the police are listening so use these other words, these other codes.

Q. And that was in face to face negotiations?

A. Yes, sir.

Q. Now, you said that the pattern of speaking would be to use words other than the words for drugs?

A. That's correct.

Q. In the 24 years that you have been a law enforcement agent in conversations that you have had in undercover situations in which you were either purchasing drugs or selling drugs, did the parties with whom you were negotiating use other coded terms to describe substances or objects other than drugs?

A. Yes, sir.

Q. Can you tell us what those other items would be?

A. The other items were money.

Q. Instead of using a specific amount of money, you're saying that some other word would be used?

A. Some other word or some minimizing of the amount would be used.

Q. Could you give us an example of a minimized amount?

A. Well, I would say 100,000 and somebody would say 1.

Q. So that in your discussions that you've had in referring to $100,000, you would use the, or the other individual would use the word "one"?

A. That's correct.

Q. And you would understand what he was referring to?

A. Yes, sir.

Q. In these conversations, did you also use ambiguous words to refer to persons and places?

A. Yes, sir.

Q. Could you describe conversations you can recall in which persons or places were referred to in such a way?

The Court: Just a moment. You asked him whether he used ambiguous terms.
Mr. Martin: I'm sorry.

Q. I meant to ask you whether you heard narcotics dealers with whom you were negotiating use words to refer to persons or places other than naming those persons and places?

A. Yes, sir.

Q. Could you give us an example?

A. Yes. Instead of explaining, for instance: We're going to meet at MacDonalds, the person would say: We're going to meet over there by that place, do you remember? Instead of using the person's real name, nicknames were given to people. And these were, it went both ways. I would also be given a nickname and use the same type of code.

Q. Could you tell us what understanding you had of such terms when they were being used?

A. Well, in the face to face conversation, it would be explained: Meet me over here but call me beforehand. And when I called: Oh, yeah, remember I told you meet me over here. Yes, I do. I'll see you there. And that's the type of dialogue.

Q. These patterns of speaking, can you tell us approximately how many times in the

24 years you've been involved in undercover activity, you've heard conversations like that where codes are used?

A. I'd have to say well over 500.

Q. And can you tell us if based on your experience, when dealing with narcotics dealers it is common practice to use codes?

A. Very common practice.

Q. Now, I've been asking you in this last series of questions about conversations you had during undercover negotiations which you were involved in face to face. Let me ask you, sir, did you also engage in undercover activities while using the telephone?

A. Yes, sir.

Q. And did you observe the same pattern of conversations used by narcotics dealers on the telephone?

A. Yes. I heard the same patterns.

Q. Could you compare the degree to which such codes were used on the telephone as compared with face to face discussions?

A. The conversations on the phone were as deceptive as face to face.

Q. Were you ever admonished about being careful how you spoke on the phone?

A. On several occasions.

Q. Did you receive instructions about using pay telephones during the course of your undercover negotiations with those people who were offering to sell to you narcotics?

A. Yes, sir.

Q. And can you tell us what instructions you received?

A. I was told to be very guarded when I spoke to a person on the phone, to use other than the direct words involving drugs, not to divulge locations, not to divulge the person's identity.

Q. And were you also given instructions about using pay telephones?

A. Yes, I was.

Q. Can you tell us if it was a common practice among persons whom you were negotiating with to buy drugs or whom you were negotiating with to sell drugs to have them tell you to use the pay phone?

A. Yes, it was common.

Q. And in the 24 years you've been involved in narcotics investigations, have you observed persons who you were investigating for narcotics activity using pay telephones?

A. Yes, sir.

Q. Is that true in the United States as well as in Italy?

A. Yes, sir.

Q. And when you made—were you sometimes, in the course of undercover negotiations, given telephone numbers?

A. Yes, sir.

Q. And were you given instructions to make telephone calls to such a number?

A. Yes, sir.

Q. And when you made that telephone call, did you determine that that telephone number was located in a bar, a restaurant or was a pay phone?

A. Yes, sir.

Q. Can you tell us if that was a common way of communicating in the undercover negotiations you were involved in?

A. Yes, sir.

Q. Now, in the four years that you were assigned to Italy, did you also make observations of individuals who were the targets of your investigations using pay telephones?

A. Yes, sir.

Q. And in the wiretaps that you've listened to, both in Italy and the United States, have you heard the participants in those wiretap conversations making calls over pay phones?

A. Yes, sir.

Q. And have you heard quarters and other money being dropped into a phone?

A. Yes, sir.

Q. Now, let me ask you, sir, in the 24 years that you have been a law enforcement agent, both in terms of your undercover activities and negotiating with narcotics dealers and in terms of the wiretaps that you listened to in Italy and the United States, can you tell us if you have heard certain common words which are repeatedly commonly used to refer to narcotics?

A. Yes, sir.

Q. Would you tell us what some of those words are?

A. The majority of the words used in narcotics sales and transactions are "shirts," "shoes," "suits," "sweaters," "cars," "ovens," "pieces," "clothes," "things," "stuff."

* * *

Q. Good morning, Mr. Tarallo.

A. Good morning.

Q. When we broke yesterday for the day I had asked you a question about common terms which you had heard in the 24 years of narcotics enforcement in undercover activity, on Title III's in the United States and Italy and also on the 8 major cases which you reviewed in your position as a supervisor in New York between 1982 and 1984.

Do you recall that, sir?

A. Yes, sir.

Q. And when we broke, I was writing down some of those terms on a chart.

A. Yes, sir.

Q. Before I continue, let me just ask you if it would also be fair to say that the terms "boy" and "girl" are very commonly used in narcotics—

The Court: Don't lead. Please don't lead.

Q. Can you tell us any other terms that are commonly used?

A. Other common terms in the United States are the expression of "boy" or "girl" that would depict various types of narcotics.

Q. And in your experience does "boy" depict one type of narcotics and "girl" another?

A. Yes.

Q. Can you tell us which?

A. "Boy" depicts heroin. "Girl" depicts cocaine.

Q. Agent Tarallo, let me ask you whether or not in your experience as a narcotics agent, you have heard the word "pants" used to refer to narcotics commonly or frequently in your 24 years?

A. I've heard that expression, yes.

Q. Agent Tarallo, yesterday you described for us that in your experience as a narcotics agent in the United States and in Italy and overseas, you had also heard different words used to describe sums of money. Could you tell us, based on your experience in the United States and Italy in the wiretaps that you've heard in the United States and Italy and in the wiretaps you've supervised from '82 to '84 in the New York area, what terms are most commonly used to describe money?

A. Most common terms is the minimization of an amount, going from a large sum to a small sum. Instead of saying 100,000 you say 1. That is the most common. The others are less descriptive such as "paper," "documents," names of vegetables, "lettuce." These are the more common ones.

Q. And in terms of minimization, could you give us examples of terms used to describe amounts of money that you've heard, that have been minimized in the way you described?

A. Minimized in forms of 1's or 2's or in cents. 60 cents. 90 cents.

Q. Agent Tarallo, I've written on that chart next to you under the word "Money" 60 cents, 90 cents, one dollar, 1, 2, documents, paper, lettuce, vegetables. That chart is marked 3685-4. Those are the terms which you've most commonly heard?

A. Yes, sir.

Q. Yesterday you also described for us a common practice that you were familiar with of narcotics dealers and suppliers in their conversations or face to face or over the telephone to refer to persons and places by other types of words. Do you recall that, sir?

A. Yes, sir.

* * *

Q. Agent Tarallo, to be clear, can you tell us in the conversations that you've been involved in or overheard, when persons used the terms 60 cents or 90 cents, what monetary value were they actually referring to?

A. Usually in the thousands.

Q. So would 60 cents be 60,000?

A. That's correct.

Q. And 90 cents would be 90,000?

A. That's correct.

Q. And you told us that one dollar would often be $100,000?

A. That's correct.

Q. These are terms that you've personally heard?

A. Terms that I've heard throughout my career.

Q. On the chart, Agent Tarallo, I've written at the bottom X cents equals X thousand dollars and below that one dollar equals $100,000. Is that a correct interpretation of the codes that you've heard employed?

A. Including just unit numbers such as 1 or 2 without dollars or cents.

Q. And 1 or 2 would refer to 100,000 or 200,000?

A. Depending on the conversation and the undercover situation.

Q. A moment ago I asked you about descriptions of persons that you've heard employed in the course of your 24 years. Could you give us some descriptions of terms that you've heard that have been used to refer to people without using their names?

A. Nicknames are adopted, change of first names are used, referencing such as "him," "they," "those." These type of examples.

Q. And by nicknames, what type of nicknames have you heard?

A. If a person has red hair they said: Did you talk to red? A person is distinctive in his form of dress: Have you talked to the gentleman? These are just nicknames. And they depict, usually, some characteristic of the person.

*　　*　　*

Q. Agent Tarallo, with respect to descriptions that you have heard employed to indicate a place or location, can you tell us if you've observed a common practice among narcotics dealers when talking face to face or on telephones to describe a place without giving its specific name or identification?

A. Yes, sir.

Q. Based on your knowledge and experience, Agent Tarallo, can you tell us, first of all can you tell us what you mean by drug paraphernalia?

A. I'm talking about weighing scales, glassine bags, blenders. Things of that sort.

Q. Can you tell us based on your experience and knowledge as a narcotics agent at what level of narcotics distribution those articles are used?

A. At the distribution level from wholesale through the retail level.

Q. And at the importation level, are such narcotics paraphernalia used?

A. Very rarely.

Brief for Defendant-Appellant Giovanni Cangialosi, United States Court of Appeals for the Second Circuit, Gerald DiChiara, Attorney

Point I: Joint Trial Was Manifestly Prejudicial So As to Abridge Cangialosi's Right to a Fair Trial

As in the case of all co-defendants, all pre-trial and trial applications of CANGIALOSI requesting severance were denied.

There is something inherently wrong with a joinder of defendants so that in a government presentation of some 12 to 13 months on its direct case a mere 3 to 4 days are spent on evidence relating to an individual defendant. Yet this is the position that CANGIALOSI as well as a few other defendants were in.

CANGIALOSI is alleged to have been a messenger between the heroin suppliers in Sicily and the heroin receivers in America. He is only alleged to have filled this role once when he comes to America on March 15, 1984 and was arrested returning to Sicily on April 8, 1984.

The evidence consisted primarily of association and circumstantial type evidence from which it was argued by the government that CANGIALOSI was aiding in the fulfillment of some future planned shipment by acting as a messenger between the parties.

It is submitted that the evidence and the inferences to be drawn from evidence as it related to the question of guilt or innocence were very close and hotly contested.

An analysis of the jury's verdict shows that there was some division amongst the jurors regarding CANGIALOSI's role and involvement:

Racketeering Act:

	Proved	*Not Proved*
ITTA: G. Soresi call to MAZZURCO, S. LAMBERTI and CANGIALOSI on 3/30/84 at 11:57 a.m. (GX 8172)	X	
ITTA: G. Soresi call to GANCI, G. LAMBERTI, MAZZURCO, CANGIALOSI on 3/26/84 at 12:03 p.m. (GX 8183)		X

There is no logical way to account for the above two findings by the jury unless that there was a compromise in the jury room. The entirety of the conversations are reproduced in the Appellants' Joint Appendix and a study of them indicates they appear, for the most part, to deal with the same subject matter.

Both calls were received over a pay phone on the Southern State Parkway involving almost the identical parties. Either CANGIALOSI was involved in the narcotics transactions or he wasn't.

Although juries often compromise and this is an accepted fact in our jury system, it is important to note the closeness of the verdict when determining the effect of prejudice and whether it was harmless or not.

General Principles of Severance

It is clear that in order to demonstrate that a Trial Court's denial of severance was an abuse of discretion, a defendant must establish that a joint trial subjected him not only to some prejudice, but to compelling prejudice against which the District Court could not afford protection.

*   *   *

There is a strong argument that no one in a seventeen month trial covering all of the various acts of so many people could possibly receive a fair trial. The people who were particularly prejudiced in this situation were those who had very limited roles and against whom there was very little evidence.

In point, to have to be subjected to a trial where the Government is allowed to open on the Galante murder which was later found inadmissible; to be joined with some co-defendants who believed that it was in their best interest to bring to the attention of the jury evidence of numerous murders over and over again; to be on trial when PAUL CASTELLANO was murdered; to have a co-defendant, GAETANO MAZZARA, be brutally murdered after the jury had viewed him in Court for over a year; to have a co-defendant take the stand and then refuse to answer questions; to have massive amounts of arms recovered from co-defendants presented to the jury; and, finally, during summations to sequester the jury because another co-defendant, PIETRO ALFANO, was also gunned down, must weigh very heavily when determining if any defendant could possibly receive a verdict based upon the evidence alone.

In CANGIALOSI's case, the prejudice directly aimed at him so far outweighed the evidence against him that it is inconceivable that the resultant verdict can be claimed not to have been affected by it.

Direct Prejudice

CANGIALOSI was denied a fair trial because he was irreparably prejudiced by inflammatory and antagonistic arguments advanced in summation by Michael Kennedy, counsel for co-defendant, GAETANO BADALAMENTI.

After the shooting of ALFANO, the Court should have protected CANGIALOSI's right to a fair trial by pursuing CANGIALOSI's request to either sever his case from that of his co-defendants or to preclude the prejudicial unsupported argument of co-counsel. Even at that late date in this marathon of mega-trials and in spite of what would have been an enormous judicial waste, a man's right to a fair trial must be paramount to the Court's desire to avoid a mistrial.

Kennedy's argument during summation resulted in the labeling of CANGIALOSI as the "messenger of death," whom it was argued was carrying a death warrant for the defendant, GAETANO BADALAMENTI and his family.

This alleged death warrant consisted of a scrap of paper with the following words written in Italian on it:

THE INTERPRETER: The first word, dottore, means doctor. It is followed by the letter E capitalized. Above it there is a word that to this interpreter appears to be Francia which means France.

MR. STEWART: And below that word?

THE INTERPRETER: Anniza. This interpreter doesn't recognize that as an Italian word. Phonetically it probably means in Nizza, Nizza which would be Nice, the city.

MR. STEWART: In France?

THE INTERPRETER: Correct.

MR. STEWART: There is another group of words in the top right portion of the notepaper, is that correct?

THE INTERPRETER: Yes, Nipote, NIPOTE, means nephew, niece. It can also be grandson or granddaughter.

MR. STEWART: All right.

THE INTERPRETER: It is followed by the capital letter E, and the following word, again, the interpreter does not recognize this as an Italian word.

MR. STEWART: Excuse me. When you say the capital letter E, you're referring to the English E, not the Italian E?

THE INTERPRETER: Correct, the capital letter E, E in Italian. It could be the initial for a proper name, the name for a city, or something like that. And Azzurico phonetically for this interpreter may mean in Zurich, the City in Switzerland.

MR. STEWART: In the bottom left-hand portion of the same slip of paper there are two more words, is that correct?

THE INTERPRETER: Nipoti, NIPOTI. This is the plural of nephew, niece. That would be nephews, nieces, grandchildren, grandsons, granddaughters. It may mean one of all those. And then the word America. (Tr. 27010, 27011, 27012.)

Based upon this counsel for GAETANO BADALAMENTI argued not only that this was a warrant for the death of GAETANO BADALAMENTI and his family but without any factual support he identified the sender of the note as GUISEPPE GANCI, a prime mover in the Government's presentation of the evidence and one of the few people involved in the case who had direct contact with a drug transaction which was videotaped by the Government, presented to the jury and included another non-present defendant, BENNY ZITO.

The simple fact is that this argument was not supported by the evidence presented including the so-called non-testimony of GAETANO BADALAMENTI nor can its impact be minimized by Kennedy's disclaimer that CANGIALOSI may have not known the contents or intent of the note.

The prejudice suffered by CANGIALOSI as a result of Kennedy's argument to the jury was underscored by the very real fact that it was made on the heels of the PIETRO ALFANO shooting.

During summations, PIETRO ALFANO, a co-defendant and relative of GAETANO BADALAMENTI, was gunned down in Manhattan, not very far from the Courthouse, itself. This fact and occurrence was known by a substantial part if not all of the jury.

The same jury that for seventeen months had viewed GAETANO BADALAMENTI and his co-defendant relatives seated as a group in the Courtroom and referred to repeatedly as the "BADALAMENTI GROUP" (Tr. 40773).

The members included in this group were GAETANO BADALAMENTI, SAM EVOLA, VINCENZO RANDAZZO, EMANUELE PALAZZOLO, VITO BADALAMENTI, GUISEPPE TRUPIANO, GUISEPPE VITALE AND PIETRO ALFANO (Tr. 39617). (Emphasis Added)

The common thread running throughout the BADALAMENTI GROUP's defense was that they were being hunted by the Sicilian Mafia. Unfortunately, for CANGIA-LOSI, he apparently was viewed as an expendable pawn to hammer home this theory.

In Kennedy's summation, CANGIALOSI, who was not even mentioned or referred to until the twelfth month of trial, was transformed from a bit player with a very limited alleged role by the Government and who seemed to blend with the woodwork of the Courtroom, into a representative of the Sicilian Mafia and a focal point of the BADALAMENTI defense.

Kennedy's argument about CANGIALOSI and the note was not supported by the evidence, prejudicial and denied CANGIALOSI the right to a fair trial. The Government in its rebuttal in a backhanded fashion while appearing to attack the baselessness and prejudicial impact and smear effect of Kennedy's argument maintained its theme in order to discredit CANGIALOSI's defense (Tr. 40916).

What was so tragic about the problem was that it was avoidable. If the District Court had intervened when requested to do so by CANGIALOSI's counsel, the resultant prejudice to Cangialosi would not have occurred.

The morning after the ALFANO shooting, CANGIALOSI's counsel having gotten wind of Kennedy's intention and anticipating that Kennedy would seek to capitalize on the ALFANO shooting to further the BADALAMENTI Theory at the expense of CANGIALOSI, moved for an Order severing CANGIALOSI's case or, in the alternative, precluding argument that was unsupported by the record regarding the scrap of paper found on CANGIALOSI (Tr. 39324).

Prior to, during and after Kennedy's argument, numerous mistrial applications and requests for severance were denied. Although co-counsel's right to comment on the evidence generally should be broadly interpreted and permitted in fairness the

Court must utilize its discretion and temper argument which is so obviously unsupported by the evidence and so prejudicial to a co-defendant's rights.

*   *   *

Kennedy's Summation

KENNEDY: . . . But there are people out to kill him. There are Sicilian heroin dealers, the winners of the war, who are looking all over the world for him. . . .

So began the argument that would lead to the antagonistic description of CANGIA-LOSI as the Messenger of Death.

Initially, Kennedy's tone and argument appeared soft but as the summation progressed and grew in fever and pitch so did the resultant prejudice to CANGIALOSI.

KENNEDY: What's Ganci's agenda? We don't learn that until Mr. CANGIALOSI, the messenger, appears on the scene and Mr. CANGIALOSI, the messenger, is given a message, I suggest, by GANCI.

Let me tell you something about the messenger. I am not suggesting to you that this messenger understands anything about this sinister message. I am suggesting to you as a matter of fact he probably does not know anything about this sinister message, otherwise he wouldn't have had to write it down. Also, you wouldn't want your messenger to know.

What does GANCI tell in this message to the Sicilian heroin dealers? The doctor is in Nice. The nephew is in Zurich. The nieces and nephews are in America.

*   *   *

MR. DICHIARA: Your Honor, once again I renew my application for a mistrial which I made at the time that PIETRO ALFANO was shot and I requested the Court to prohibit Mr. Kennedy from arguing what he just argued to the jury about the contents of the message and the intent of that message because now my client has suddenly been tranformed into a messenger of death and whether he knows it or not, the prejudice to my client, I think is insurmountable in this type of a case considering the fact that two of the defendants in this case are no longer present and we know the reason. I believe the jury knows the reason.

THE COURT: Your Motion is denied.

*   *   *

MR. KENNEDY: . . .

Let me get back to the dangerous dance. *This Government Exhibit 778H was gotten off the person of Mr.* CANGIALOSI *when he was arrested in April.* I suggest it came out of a meeting that he attended on the 30th day of March. *It was given to him by Mr.* GANCI. *And it is a death warrant, calling to the attention of the Sicilian heroin dealers that the doctor,* GAETANO BADALAMENTI, *is in Nice—thank God, at that time he wasn't,* their information was several months dated—that ENZO RANDAZZO, the nephew, was in Zurich, and the nieces and nephews are in America.

. . . There wasn't any deal. They wanted a meeting. GANCI wanted to find out where GAETANO BADALAMENTI was so he could execute this death warrant. I wish it were not so.

In late February—that was the last call from GAETANO BADALAMENTI, the last call to New York; he is still in touch with PIETRO ALFANO—we know from the telephone calls, particularly the midwestern calls, but we know that AUGUSTINO BADALAMENTI *has been killed in Germany, another one of* BADALAMENTI's *relatives killed in this dreadful war.* GAETANO BADALAMENTI is out of touch then. No more contact.

We know there's that meeting on the 30th with PIETRO ALFANO. *PIETRO ALFANO does not leave with* CANGIALOSI. *He's picked up at the airport with* CANGIALOSI, *but there is no evidence that they had a meeting. As a matter of fact, the evidence is that* MAZZURCO *went off with* CANGIALOSI, *trying to talk* CANGIALOSI *into a meeting with* PIETRO ALFANO. That didn't happen. (Tr. 40599, 40600.) (Emphasis Added)

*   *   *

PIETRO ALFANO is the only one who keeps in touch. The next thing that happens is in March and in March GANCI sends what I say is the death warrant to the Sicilian heroin dealers.

GANCI has somehow gotten information the doctor is in Nice. The nephew—this is how they called him on the calls—the nephew is in Zurich and the nieces and the nephews are in America. It is all in Sicilian—it is this bottom, one down here—but this has been translated formally for us by the translators and that's what it says.

This is the most sinister of all because it proves that GAETANO BADALAMENTI was right. All he could do was probe. He couldn't tell them where he was and he had to lie about it and, if he hadn't, he wouldn't be on trial here today. (Tr. 40651, 40652.)

The implications of Kennedy's argument are clear. PIETRO ALFANO is a casualty of the BADALAMENTI Mafia War and CANGIALOSI was tied directly into this war since he was cast in the roll of the messenger carrying the death warrant for the BADALAMENTI family. No number of disclaimers about whether CANGIALOSI did or did not have knowledge could erase the prejudice and antagonism of this argument made eight days after the shooting of PIETRO ALFANO.

5

Teamsters International:
United States v. International Brotherhood of Teamsters

(Complaint filed June 1988; Settlement signed March 1989)

Introduction

United States v. International Brotherhood of Teamsters is the Department of Justice's most ambitious labor racketeering suit and perhaps the most far-reaching effort at institutional reform through litigation ever attempted. The civil RICO suit charged Cosa Nostra members and the Teamsters' general executive board (GEB) with running the nation's largest union as a racketeering enterprise in which union officials obtained mob support for their union careers and the mob obtained all kinds of opportunities for siphoning money out of the union and its employers. Ultimately, the suit was settled, with the Teamsters agreeing to a three-person trusteeship that, over the course of three years, purged almost two hundred corrupt officials from the union and, in 1991, supervised the first direct GEB election. After the election, an independent review board (IRB) was established to continue investigating and monitoring the union.

Background

Charges that the International Brotherhood of Teamsters Union (IBT) was tied to organized crime were made as early as the 1940s and 1950s. The

1958 report of the Senate Select Committee on Improper Activities in the Labor Management Field ("McClellan Committee") revealed widespread contacts with organized crime by union president Jimmy Hoffa. The sharp exchanges between the committee's chief counsel, Robert Kennedy, and union president Jimmy Hoffa drew national attention.[1] Less well remembered is the 1958–1960 three-person Board of Monitors that was imposed on the union via a consent agreement which resulted from a lawsuit filed by thirteen rank-and-file Teamsters from the New York area who alleged that Hoffa had stacked the 1956 union convention with illegal delegates in order to guarantee his election as president.[2] In the end, due to union stonewalling, this trusteeship failed. Hoffa and the GEB continually frustrated the board by refusing to bring charges against corrupt union officials and litigating virtually every Board of Monitors decision. These tactics, combined with in-fighting on the board itself, resulted in the collapse of the trusteeship in early 1961. Shortly thereafter, the union reelected Jimmy Hoffa as president.

When Robert Kennedy became attorney general of the United States, he made convicting Hoffa a top Justice Department priority. In 1964, Hoffa was finally convicted of pension fraud and jury tampering and sentenced to prison. The presidency passed to Hoffa's hand-picked successor, Frank Fitzsimmons. Several years later, after his release from prison, Hoffa began campaigning to regain control of the union on a platform of freeing the union from mob domination. He disappeared in 1975, the presumed victim of a mob assassination.

Throughout the 1960s and 1970s, leading Teamster officials joined with mob figures to devise ways to defraud the IBT. Some of these methods were related to the multibillion-dollar Central States Pension Funds, managed by mob associate Allen Dorfman. The funds, in effect, functioned as a "mob bank," providing organized crime with extensive loans for ventures in Las Vegas and for other criminal activities.[3]

In 1981, after Frank Fitzsimmons died of cancer, Roy Williams assumed the union presidency. In 1982, the Senate Permanent Subcommittee on Investigations heard testimony about widespread corruption, racketeering, and violence in the Teamsters Union. Charles Allen, a self-confessed killer and enforcer who worked for Teamster local officials as well as for important Cosa Nostra figures such as Russell Buffalino and Tony Provenzano, explained his role to Senator Warren Rudman:

SENATOR RUDMAN: What was your job, your responsibility, what were you supposed to do?

MR. ALLEN: I actually did anything that I was told to do, from murder to selling drugs, from extortion to beating up people, hijacking. Whatever they told me to do, I did.[4]

These hearings also revealed how the Teamsters attempted to bribe Nevada Senator Howard Cannon to oppose the trucking deregulation bill.[5]

Roy Williams was convicted of attempting to bribe Senator Cannon and sentenced to a long prison term. Facing the prospect of spending the rest of his life in jail, he decided to cooperate with the government. He provided valuable testimony to the President's Commission on Organized Crime and in an extraordinary deposition in the civil RICO suit that is the subject of this chapter. In his deposition, Williams explained how his career in the Teamsters was orchestrated all the way to the presidency by Nicholas Civella, head of the Kansas City Cosa Nostra crime family. In 1981, Williams became president only with the consent of other Cosa Nostra leaders, including the "commission."[6] In 1982, Williams was convicted of attempting to bribe a United States senator and resigned the presidency.

Williams' successor, Jackie Presser, was the son of Big Bill Presser, an associate of the Cleveland Cosa Nostra crime family. Jackie Presser himself was allegedly involved with organized crime. Unlike Williams, Presser refused on Fifth Amendment grounds to answer any questions when he was deposed by the President's Commission on Organized Crime. While the civil RICO suit was pending, Presser was indicted for arranging a no-show job for his friend and sometime bodyguard, Tony Hughes. In July 1988, before either criminal or civil charges were resolved against him, Presser died of a heart attack.[7]

In *United States v. Salerno* (the Commission case), former Cleveland underboss Angelo Lonardo testified that the Cosa Nostra commission approved and insured the elections of Williams and Presser to the Teamsters presidency. In 1986, the President's Commission on Organized Crime, drawing on Roy Williams's testimony, branded the Teamsters the union "most controlled" by organized crime and called for a civil RICO suit to be brought against the union's general executive board.[8] As the President's Commission found,

The leaders of the nation's largest union, the International Brotherhood of Teamsters (IBT), have been firmly under the influence of organized crime since the 1950s. Although many of the hundreds of IBT locals and joint councils operating throughout the country are not criminally infiltrated, organized crime influences at least 38 of the largest locals and a joint council in Chicago, Cleveland, New Jersey, New York,

Philadelphia, St. Louis, and other major cities. Former Teamster President Roy L. Williams told the Commission, "Every big [Teamster] local union . . . had some connection with organized crime.

Criticism also came from within the union from Teamsters for a Democratic Union (TDU). Begun in 1976 as a rank-and-file reform movement, TDU initially focused on the need for better contracts, safer working conditions, and more union democracy. Soon, its energies also included exposing corruption and demanding an end to mob ties with the union.

As rumors flew around Washington that the Justice Department was contemplating a RICO suit against the Teamsters' general executive board, more than two hundred congressmen sent a petition to the Justice Department urging that no such suit be brought. This formal appeal by so many members of Congress to the Justice Department was unprecedented. After the suit was filed, many labor leaders denounced it as a sinister attempt by the Reagan administration to destroy the labor movement—by attacking the Teamsters, who ironically had endorsed Reagan's candidacies in 1980 and 1984.

The Lawsuit and Settlement

Despite intense political opposition, the government did move forward with a civil RICO suit against the IBT. A jurisdictional dispute between Rudolph Giuliani, the United States attorney for the Southern District of New York, and Dave Margolis, the head of the organized crime and racketeering section of the Department of Justice, was resolved in favor of Giuliani. Randy Mastro, an assistant United States attorney working for Giuliani, drafted the complaint, which was filed in June 1988.

The Complaint

The complaint named as defendants (1) the International Brotherhood of Teamsters; (2) the Cosa Nostra commission; (3) twenty-six Cosa Nostra members and associates (including Anthony Salerno, Matthew Ianiello, and Anthony Provenzano); (4) the IBT's general executive board; and (5) eighteen present and former members of the IBT's general executive board (including the president, Jackie Presser, and the general secretary-treasurer, Weldon Mathis). The RICO enterprise, labeled "the Teamsters International Enterprise," was defined as "the Teamsters International Union and various of its area conferences, joint councils, locals and benefit funds." The first RICO count charged that the organized-crime defendants, aided and abetted by the union defendants, "unlawfully, wilfully, and knowingly acquired and maintained, directly and indirectly, an interest in and control of the Teamsters International Enterprise through a pattern of racketeering activity." The second RICO count alleged a conspiracy (i.e., an agreement) to do what was alleged in the first RICO count.

The racketeering activities allegedly committed by the mob and aided and abetted by the union defendants were (1) defrauding the union members' intangible rights to select their own leaders, to their benefit from leaders' fair and honest performance of their duties, and to be informed about the Cosa Nostra control over their leaders; and (2) depriving the union and the union members of money that was unlawfully diverted from the unions and its members to the defendants.

The complaint further alleged that the defendants' racketeering activity involved extorting union members' democratic rights by creating a climate of intimidation and fear. In support of that allegation, the government recounted Teamsters violence, beginning with the 1961 Provenzano assassination of a union rival, Anthony Castellitto, and including the "disappearance" of Jimmy Hoffa. According to the complaint, the climate of intimidation and fear was reinforced by the union defendants' repeated appointments of persons with known criminal histories and/or criminal records to union offices and union employment and to the defendants' open association with persons with known criminal histories and/or records.

In addition to creating and/or tolerating a climate of fear and intimidation, the union defendants were charged with creating or tolerating pervasive corruption:

The Teamster International Union officer defendants have consistently failed to take action to rid the Teamsters International Union and various of its affiliated Area Conferences, Joint Councils, Locals and Benefit Funds of corruption. These defendants have repeatedly allowed corrupt union officials to remain in office, failed to investigate charges of union corruption, and failed to redress demonstrated instances of pervasive and long-standing corruption.

From the government's perspective, the advantage of the civil RICO suit was that no new FBI investigations were necessary. The entire case was constructed from the record of past convictions and government reports. Since this was a civil suit, once the complaint was filed the historical record could be supplemented with depositions obtained from Angelo Lonardo, Roy Williams, and others.

As a remedy, the government asked for the removal of any IBT general executive board members found to have committed RICO violations, the appointment of a trustee to oversee the union's executive, collective-bargaining, and/or political activities, and new elections designed to protect against the possibility of corruption. The IBT moved to dismiss the complaint on three grounds: (1) the complaint violated IBT members' First Amendment rights to free association; (2) federal labor law preempted RICO; and (3) the complaint failed to state a RICO claim. In the alternative, the defendants sought to have all IBT-affiliated local unions and councils joined as defendants. Judge David Edelstein denied these motions, as well as the government's motion for summary judgment against certain defendants, and set the case for trial.[9]

Many of the mob defendants, already in jail on related criminal charges, signed settlement agreements, promising not to have anything to do with the union. Since most of them were facing long jail terms, as a result of the Commission case and other prosecutions, and since they could not claim to have any legitimate role in the union's affairs, there was no point in contesting the suit. Mounting legal fees and poor prospects of ultimate success also led a number of the union defendants to sign agreements with the government promising to be bound by whatever final relief the court entered.

The Consent Decree

On March 13, 1989, the government and the remaining defendants (including the GEB) entered into a consent decree. The defendants admitted "that there have been allegations, sworn testimony and judicial findings of past problems with La Cosa Nostra corruption of various elements of the IBT."[10] They agreed "that there should be no criminal element or Cosa Nostra corruption of any part of the IBT." They accepted the principle that "it is imperative that the IBT, as the largest trade union in the free world, be maintained democratically, with integrity and for the sole benefit of its members without unlawful outside influence."

The consent decree provided for three court-appointed officers to oversee union operations: an independent administrator, an investigations officer, and an elections officer. Judge Edelstein filled these positions with former federal judge Frederick Lacey, former assistant United States attorney Charles Carberry, and labor lawyer Michael Holland. The independent administrator (Lacey) was empowered to take disciplinary action, including suspension or termination of membership rights, against any corrupt union officials (including the general president) and to veto appointments of union officials and expenditures of any union funds used to further racketeering activity. He was invested with all the disciplinary powers of the general president. The investigations officer (Carberry) was given broad power to investigate corruption and bring disciplinary charges before Administrator Lacey. The decree authorized the elections officer (Holland) to supervise a direct, rank-and-file, secret-ballot election for the union's top officers.

Resistance to the Suit

Jackie Presser's death in July 1988 triggered a scramble for the presidency among various Teamster vice-presidents. The GEB eventually elected William McCarthy, a long-time union official from Boston.

Almost before the ink was dry on the consent decree, the union, especially President McCarthy, began a campaign of resistance to the court-appointed officers. Various IBT locals were encouraged to attack the consent order by filing lawsuits in Chicago, Cleveland, New Jersey, and elsewhere.[11] The suits sought to force the government to defend the jurisdiction of the consent decree over Teamster locals all over the country. In response, the government moved to have all matters pertaining to the IBT case brought before the District Court for the Southern District of New York. Judge Edelstein granted that motion, concluding that nationwide jurisdiction in the Southern District would promote judicial economy and avoid possible inconsistent interpretations of the consent decree.[12] This crucial decision kept the government from having to contest a multitude of lawsuits around the country. It meant that the court-appointed officers would not be paralyzed by litigation, as their predecessors had been in the late 1950s.

The union opposed all sorts of expenditures by the officers (whose salaries and expenses the union was paying) and tried to limit their authority at every turn. For example, the IBT refused to pay for office space for the investigations officer in New York City, arguing that the decree only provided for office space in Washington, D.C. Lacey applied to the court to force the IBT to provide the office space. Judge Edelstein held that proper investigative efforts implied a broad reading of the investigations officer's authority and approved the Manhattan office. Subsequently, Lacey had to petition the court to force the IBT to fund the elections officer's staffing requests; once again, Judge Edelstein ruled in his favor.

Lacey also faced resistance with respect to communications between the court-appointed officers and the membership. In order to disrupt the flow of information to the rank and file about the independent administrator's findings and sanctions for corruption, the GEB threatened to discontinue the

International Teamster, a monthly newsletter. Siding with the administrator, the court found that the consent decree mandated continuation of the monthly publication. In order to educate the membership and promote union democracy, Judge Edelstein also ordered that the court's decisions and the independent administrator's reports be made available to union members.

Electoral Reform

The consent decree provided for the first direct, rank-and-file secret-ballot election of the IBT's president and GEB. The federal prosecutors believed that, ultimately, the mob could only be purged from the union if the rank and file had the opportunity to participate in free and fair elections of their representatives. They concluded that this goal could best be achieved by a direct and secret election of national officers (as opposed to the highly controllable "delegate system"). TDU had been campaigning for just such a direct election since the mid-1970s.

Trustee Holland initiated a three-step process. First, the IBT locals would hold secret-ballot elections for delegates to the IBT convention. Second, the delegates would nominate candidates for office. Third, the rank and file would vote in a nationwide direct, secret-ballot election.[13]

This electoral reform generated much controversy and conflict. The government and the IBT disagreed on the election officer's authority to supervise the IBT election. The IBT argued that the term "supervise" in the consent decree merely meant monitoring the IBT electoral process for fraud and, in the event of any fraud, suggesting remedial action. The Teamsters took the position that the election officer had no authority to propose rules for the upcoming election. As for the rules that were proposed, the IBT objected to Holland's plan for alternate delegates, widespread dissemination of campaign literature through the *International Teamster,* and secret ballots.

The Association for Union Democracy (AUD), a civil rights organization, also criticized the proposed election rules. The AUD objected to Holland's proposal that the local unions maintain control over such election matters as printing ballots, deciding the eligibility of potential candidates, running the election, and storing and counting the ballots. In its amicus brief, the AUD argued that local officials were just as influenced by Cosa Nostra as the GEB and could not be trusted to conduct fair elections. In a rare decision overruling one of his appointees, Judge Edelstein agreed with the AUD and amended the proposed election rules to provide for more stringent supervision by the elections officer.

The 1991 election was vigorously contested by three serious candidates and a few minor ones.[14] At the union nominating convention, Ron Carey, who carried the reform banner, obtained the support of only 15 percent of the delegates (who were mostly established office holders of the more than six hundred locals); 85 percent voted for one or the other of the two old-guard candidates. Moreover, the delegates voted not to make some of the changes in the union constitution required by the consent decree. Judge Edelstein held this vote to be void and declared the consent decree binding on the IBT via its own constitution.

Despite widespread apprehensions about intimidation and voter fraud, Carey, who ran with TDU support, was elected president, drawing almost 50 percent of the vote in the direct secret-ballot election.[15] The lock on the union held by a ruling elite allied with Cosa Nostra appeared to be broken.[16]

Carey immediately took the following reformative steps: (1) he removed thirty-nine union officials who were earning multiple salaries from the union's payroll; (2) he sold the union's jets and allocated the proceeds to a union organizing fund; (3) he created the Ethical Practices Committee and a Human Relations Commission; and (4) he imposed trusteeships over a number of corrupt locals. However, ultimate reform is far from guaranteed since many local unions remain in the hands of the old guard.

Investigative Efforts

Under the consent decree, the investigations officer was authorized to investigate corruption and bring disciplinary actions before the administrator. The charges resulted from information supplied by the FBI, investigations of books and records of the various locals, interviews of union officers, sworn testimony, previous information supplied by IBT members, and a systematic review of old criminal cases.[17]

Judge Lacey served as the trier of fact and sentencing authority on almost two hundred charges brought by Carberry against Teamster members and officials.[18] These included having an association with, and membership in, Cosa Nostra,[19] failure to investigate corruption,[20] embezzlement,[21] assault,[22] and refusal to testify at the disciplinary hearings.[23]

In most cases, Lacey found that the investigations officer had met his "just cause" burden in proving the charges.[24] Some union members and officers sought and obtained settlement agreements; others resigned. Lacey's punishments varied according to the seriousness of the misconduct. He expelled some officers from the union for associating with Cosa Nostra members. Lacey stated, "There is only one just and reasonable penalty to be imposed when a Union Officer . . . sees fit to hobnob with mob bosses and underlings—permanent debarment from the very union that he has tainted."[25] Officials who failed to meet their responsibility to investigate corruption were also expelled.[26] Some officials who refused to testify in response to the investigations officer's request for information were suspended for varying periods.[27] In addition, Lacey placed nine locals under trusteeship.

One of the more important confrontations between Judge Lacey and the GEB concerned the administrator's authority to interpret the IBT constitution. At the behest of then–IBT Vice-President Theodore Cozza, who faced disciplinary charges for knowingly associating with members of organized crime, the board, asserting that the consent decree did not give the administrator authority to interpret the IBT constitution, passed a resolution that limited the type of conduct that could be disciplined, in effect circumscribing the authority of the court's appointed officers. Judge Edelstein rejected the resolution, ruling that the consent decree gave the administrator the same disciplinary powers as the general president and GEB, including the power to interpret the IBT constitution.[28]

Some years later, Judge Edelstein would reflect that the "IBT [has] embarked on a fierce campaign to avoid the reforms that it agreed to in the Consent Decree. In over three years of constant litigation in this Court and the Court of Appeals, the IBT repeatedly has sought to advance its cause by arguing for a narrow, restrictive interpretation of the Consent Decree."[29]

Independent Review Board

With the certification of the 1991 election results and the accession of Ron Carey to the IBT presidency, the reform process entered a new phase. The terms of the independent administrator and the investigations officer expired; they were replaced by an independent review board (IRB), designed to continue supervision of the IBT. (The elections officer's authority extends to the 1996 election. Holland has been replaced by Amy Goldstein, a labor lawyer from New York City.) Under the consent decree, the IRB consists of three members, one appointed by the government, one by the IBT, and the third by both parties. The government chose Lacey, while the IBT picked E. Harold Burke, Carey's former campaign manager. Burke has since been replaced by Grant Crandall, a labor lawyer from West Virginia. The two parties could not agree on the third member and thus Judge Edelstein confirmed the administrator's recommendation of William H. Webster, former director of both the FBI and the CIA and a former federal judge.[30]

The IRB has the same investigative duties and responsibilities as the general president and the GEB. It can investigate corruption, issue written reports, and hold adjudicatory hearings in which binding decisions are rendered. One important difference between the IRB and the court-appointed officers, however, is the scope of the IRB's involvement. While the independent administrator had the power to veto major contracts and appointments, the IRB is not authorized to oversee the day-to-day operations of the IBT. Also, the IRB must give the GEB an opportunity to act before it holds a hearing.

Conclusion

For decades, the IBT served as a Cosa Nostra power base, providing mob leaders with money, jobs, and political clout. The Cosa Nostra commission and other leaders controlled many locals and played a major role in choosing the IBT presidents. Influence in the IBT was used to control the massive Central States Pension Fund and to obtain favored positions in locals throughout the country. Teamster affiliation gave some Cosa Nostra members a legitimate status that they could parlay into political power. The marriage between the mob and the Teamsters was the subject of many commissions, hearings, books, and exposés, but until the mid-1980s this relationship seemed indissoluble.

The construction of the civil RICO suit demonstrates the enormous power and flexibility that the RICO statute provides the government. The Department of Justice converted criminal convictions into a followup civil RICO. The Department of Justice was able to bring about an extensive purge of mobsters and their allies under the speedy procedures used by the court-appointed officers, who could exercise extensive powers to review IBT records and compel testimony. Moreover, under the extraordinary authority granted to the court-appointed officers, consorting with mobsters became an "offense" punishable by expulsion or suspension. Most importantly, the government was able to break organized crime's lock on the GEB and presidency through election reform.

The civil RICO suit against the IBT may well constitute the most ambitious institutional reform litigation in American history. The challenge of purging Cosa Nostra and its allies from central headquarters and its six hundred far-flung locals, with 1.6 million members, is truly mind boggling. Given the ambition of the suit, it is not surprising that no one is yet ready to declare complete success.

It would be naive to think that Cosa Nostra will simply cede its power and prerogatives in the IBT. Many locals remain under the influence of organized crime. It will take continuing effort and a major commitment by the

Carey regime to purge the mob from all these power bases. The Local 560 case demonstrates all too clearly how entrenched the mob is in some union locals and how hard it is to dislodge, even with the assistance of a court-appointed trustee who has been on the job for years. Although Carey has set up an ethical practices committee and has placed at least two locals into trusteeship, he has drawn criticism for not working quickly or aggressively enough.[31] Unlike the court-appointed officers, the Carey administration has many priorities other than purging organized crime. The danger is that, over time, the goal of ridding the IBT of all organized-crime influence will be abandoned before the job is done.

The RICO suit and Ron Carey's election offer the *possibility* that the decades-old alliance between the Teamsters and Cosa Nostra may be broken, but whether that possibility becomes a reality will not be clear for years.

Chronology of the United States v. IBT *Litigation: Partial List of Most Important Reported Decisions*

United States v IBT, 708 F Supp 1388 (SDNY 1989). (The district court denied the defendants' motion to dismiss the complaint as well as the government's motion for summary judgment.

United States v IBT, 88 Cir 4486 (DNE 14 March 1989) (Consent Order).

United States v IBT (Election Officer Order), 723 F Supp 203 (SDNY 1989) stay and certification denied, 728 F Supp 920 [SDNY 1989], aff'd 931 F2d 177 [2d Cir 1991]. (The district court approved broad supervisory powers for the elections officer, granted the election officer's staffing requests, and created a $100,000 fund for the operating expenses of the court-appointed officers.)

United States v IBT, 728 F Supp 1032 (SDNY 1990), aff'd 907 F2d 277 (2d Cir 1990). (The district court granted the government's request to exercise its powers under the All Writs Act to preclude collateral suits by subordinate entities of the IBT in any other forum.)

United States v IBT, 905 F2d 610 (2d Cir 1990). (The appeals court affirmed one-year suspensions of certain union officials and recognized the independent administrator's ability to disregard a GEB resolution limiting his powers.)

United States v IBT, 742 F Supp 94 (SDNY 1990). (The district court approved the promulgation of campaign literature in the union magazine, provided candidates with access to membership lists, applied final election rules to Canadian locals, and mandated that the elections officer supervise every facet of the union election.)

United States v IBT, 745 F Supp 908 (SDNY 1990), aff'd, 941 F2d 1292 (2d Cir 1991). (The district court determined that the union's interest in ridding all organized-crime influence outweighed a union official's right to associate freely

United States v IBT, 754 F Supp 333 (SDNY 1990). (The district court affirmed the two-year suspensions of certain union officials and held that a preponderance of evidence standard to sustain charges, rather than a clear and convincing standard, was not arbitrary and that the officials' failure to investigate alleged misuse of union funds could provide evidence of intent to defraud the union of its funds.)

United States v IBT, 777 F Supp 1133 (SDNY 1991), *aff'd*, 970 F2d 1132 (2d Cir 1992). (The district court affirmed the independent administrator's suspension of a union official and allowed the administrator's determination that an official brought reproach upon the union by invoking the Fifth Amendment during a deposition.)

United States v IBT, 787 F Supp 345 (SDNY 1992). (The district court affirmed the lifetime suspension of a union business agent on assault and embezzlement charges.)

United States v IBT, 803 F Supp 761 (SDNY 1992). (The government's motion seeking the promulgation of rules for the operation of the IRB was granted.)

United States v IBT, 803 F Supp 806 (SDNY 1992), aff'd 12 F3d 360 (2d Cir 1993). (The district court approved the choice of William Webster as the third member of the IRB, over the objections of the IBT.)

Notes

1. See Robert Kennedy, *The Enemy Within* (Harper, 1960); Dan E. Moldea, *The Hoffa Wars: Teamsters, Rebels, Politicians, and the Mob* (Paddington Press, 1978); Steven Brill, *The Teamsters* (Simon and Schuster, 1978).

2. See Michael Goldberg, *Cleaning Labor's House: Institutional Reform Litigation in the Labor Movement* 1989, Duke Law Journal 903. See also *Cunningham v English*, 175 F Supp 764 (DDC 1958) *decree modified*, 269 F2d 517 (DC Cir), *cert. denied*, 361 US 897 (1959).

3. Dorfman was the son of Paul Dorfman, a powerful associate of the Chicago crime family that backed Hoffa's rise to the IBT presidency. Hoffa rewarded this support by arranging for Allen Dorfman to control the Central States Pension Fund. Dorfman was later convicted of conspiracy to influence an employee benefit plan by accepting a bribe, wire fraud and conspiracy to commit wire fraud. See *United States v Dorfman*, 470 F2d 246 (2d Cir 1972), *cert. dismissed*, 411 US 923 (1973).

4. Allen was a member of Teamsters Local 326 in Wilmington, Delaware, and acted at the direction of Frank Sherran (a defendant in the Teamsters case).

5. See *United States v Dorfman, et al.*, 81 CR 269 (ND Ill 1981), *aff'd sub nom United States v Williams*, 737 F2d 594 (7th Cir 1984), *cert. denied*, 470 US 1003 (1985) (Roy Williams, Allen Dorfman, Joseph Lombardo, Andrew Massa, and Thomas O'Malley were convicted of attempting to bribe a U.S. senator in this case.)

6. Depositions by Lonardo and Williams indicate that, upon a vacancy in the union presidency, the commission met to choose the next president and then

manipulated the delegate system through its control over many key locals to assure that individual's victory.

7. James Neff, *Mobbed Up: Jackie Presser's High-Wire Life in the Teamsters, the Mafia, and the FBI* (Atlantic Monthly Press, 1989).

8. President's Commission on Organized Crime, *Report to the President and Attorney General: The Edge—Organized Crime, Business, and Labor Unions* (Washington, D.C., 1986), 136.

9. *United States v IBT*, 708 F Supp 1388 (SDNY 1989).

10. See Frederick Lacey, *The Independent Administrator's Memorandum on the Handling and Disposition of Disciplinary Matters*, report to Judge Edelstein (hereinafter "The Report"), 7 October 1992, 1.

11. The Report, 5–6.

12. *United States v IBT*, 728 F Supp 1032, 1047–48 (SDNY), *aff'd*, 907 F2d 277, 280 (2d Cir 1990).

13. *United States v IBT*, 803 F Supp 761, 770 (SDNY 1992), *aff'd in part, rev'd in part*, 998 F2d 1101 (2d Cir 1993).

14. By the 1991 Teamsters convention and elections, McCarthy's support had deteriorated severely; the evaporation of political support, plus a stroke, convinced him not to seek reelection.

15. See Kenneth C. Crowe, *Collision: How the Rank and File Took Back the Teamsters* (Scribners, 1993).

16. In the fall of 1993, however, rumors surfaced regarding Carey himself. Alfonse "Little Al" D'Arco, former acting boss of the Lucchese crime family and currently a cooperating government witness, charged that Carey was tied to Cosa Nostra through a former Teamster vice-president. After the investigation, however, the IRB found no support for these accusations.

17. *United States v IBT*, 803 F Supp 767.

18. Although the independent administrator had the same investigatory powers as the investigations officer, Judge Lacey decided that, in order to avoid conflicts of interest and to give the proceedings a stamp of impartiality, he would refrain from exercising this power too often.

19. *Investigations Officer v Senese, et al.*, Decision of the Independent Administrator (12 July 1990), *aff'd*, *United States v IBT*, 745 F Supp 908 (SDNY 1990), *aff'd*, 941 F2d 1292 (2d Cir 1991), *cert. denied*, *Senese v United States*, 112 SCt 1161 (1992).

20. *Investigations Officer v Calagna, Sr., et al.*, Decision of the Independent Administrator (14 June 1991), *aff'd*, *United States v IBT*, 1991 WL 161084 (SDNY 1991).

21. *Investigations Officer v Salvatore*, Decision of the Independent Administrator (2 October 1990), *aff'd*, *United States v IBT*, 754 F Supp 333 (SDNY 1990).

22. *Investigations Officer v Wilson, et al.*, Decision of the Independent Administrator (23 Dec. 1991), *aff'd*, *United States v IBT*, 787 F Supp 345 (SDNY), *aff'd in part, vacated in part*, 978 F2d 68 (2d Cir 1992).

23. See *Investigations Officer v Calagna*.

24. "The Investigations Officer must establish just cause at disciplinary hearings by a fair preponderance of the evidence." *United States v IBT*, 754 F Supp 333, 337–38 (SDNY 1990), *aff'd, Investigations Officer v Salvatore*.

25. *Investigations Officer v Cozza*, Decision of the Independent Administrator (January 4, 1991), *aff'd, United States v IBT*, 764 F Supp 797 (SDNY 1991), *aff'd*, 956 F2d 1161 (2d Cir 1992).

26. Judge Lacey defined the standard for adequate investigation in *Investigations Officer v Crapanzano and Lanza*, Decision of the Independent Administrator (30 March 1992), *aff'd, United States v IBT*, 803 F Supp 740 (SDNY 1992). This standard required that union officers make all reasonable efforts to discern the truth of any allegations of corruption. Therefore, failure to investigate corruption meant anything from endorsing corruption to sitting idly by and ignoring blatant criminal activity.

27. *Investigations Officer v Parise*, Decision of the Independent Administrator (29 July 1991), *aff'd, United States v IBT*, 777 F Supp 1133 (SDNY 1991), *aff'd*, 970 F2d 1132 (2d Cir 1992) (24-month suspension).

28. *United States v International Brotherhood of Teamsters*, 725 F Supp 162 (SDNY 1989), *aff'd*, 905 F2d 610 (2d Cir 1990).

29. *United States v IBT*, 803 F Supp 769.

30. The IBT has unsuccessfully appealed this appointment, arguing that Webster's selection was premature (i.e., before the government and the IBT had reached an impasse). The appeal also asserted that Webster has a conflict of interest due to the fact that he presently serves on the boards of directors of two corporations, one of which is a Teamsters employer and the other of which has a reputation for strikebreaking. See 803 F Supp 806 (SDNY 1992), aff'd, 12 F3d 360 (2d Cir 1993).

31. See New York Times, 28 June 1993, A1.

Congressional Petition to Justice Department

Congress of the United States
Washington, DC 20515

December 10, 1987

The Honorable Edwin Meese, III
Attorney General
U.S. Department of Justice
Main Justice Building
Room 5111
Washington, D.C. 20530

Dear Attorney General Meese:

Numerous press articles have stated that the Department of Justice is preparing civil suits under the Racketeer Influenced and Corrupt Organizations Act (RICO) with the intention of imposing federal trusteeships over the International Brotherhood of Teamsters, the Laborers' International Union of North America, the Hotel Employees and Restaurant Employees International Union and the International Longshoremen's Association. We are concerned over the accuracy of these reports and seek clarification of the Department's efforts thus far and information regarding its future intentions. We are also writing to express our serious reservations regarding both the utility and equity of imposing federal control over private institutions. This concern is intensified in these circumstances since the historic position of this government is one of minimal intervention in the internal affairs of labor organizations.

Congress has enacted numerous laws which ensure that unions function as democratic institutions. In addition to the full panoply of criminal statutes, laws including the Labor-Management Relations Act, the Labor-Management Reporting and Disclosure Act and the Labor-Management Racketeering Act ensure both that unions function as democratic institutions and that those who abuse union office may be effectively prosecuted and promptly removed from positions of trust.

This legislation has been carefully drafted to deal with specific problems within the labor movement without unduly intruding into the operation of private organizations. Thus, we are very troubled by reports that the Department of Justice has chosen a broad and unprecedented enforcement strategy that must, of necessity, undermine the ability of a union to perform its statutory functions as the collective bargaining representative of its members. Labor unions in this society serve as a counter-balance to the institutions of government and corporations and afford workers a vehicle for exercising a voice in the determination of national policy as well as their wages and working conditions. To function properly, unions must be independent of government or corporate control in order to reflect and represent the interests of their members. The imposition of trustees to administer an international union by the government is, on its face, inherently destructive of the ability of workers to represent and speak for themselves through their unions. The exercise of such authority by the government to essentially remove one of the major participants in the democratic process, establishes a precedent which strikes at the very foundation of our democracy.

We strongly and wholeheartedly support enforcement of the law to rid unions of those individuals who misuse their positions. We cannot support, however, the abandonment of the carefully constructed network of law which achieves the desired goals with limited government intervention in favor of a broad effort which sweeps out the fundamental rights of the rank-and-file union member as well as the wrongdoers.

In conclusion, we would appreciate such information as you may appropriately share regarding the efforts of your agency in this area. Further, we would urge the Department to consider carefully the options available to it and to reject those that are inconsistent with the overall national goal of fostering an independent and democratic union movement. [Signed by 264 members of Congress]

Association for Union Democracy, Letter to Members of Congress

Association for Union Democracy, Inc.
YWCA Building
30 Third Avenue
Brooklyn, N.Y. 11217
(718) 855-6650

August 4, 1988

Dear Congressman———

You were listed as a signator on a letter signed by 264 members of Congress criticizing in advance the recent RICO suit filed by the Department of Justice against officials of the Teamsters union and members of La Cosa Nostra. Intervention by the government in this instance, you insist, "is inherently destructive of the ability of workers to represent and speak for themselves through their unions." The actuality is quite different in my opinion. Existing law has proven inadequate to assist members of unions dominated by organized crime. The government suit aims to take power out of the hands of racketeers and their abettors and restore the right of members to control their own unions. From this standpoint, the action of Justice should be applauded as a welcome, even overdue, action by government to end racketeer infiltration of a major union.

I am not writing, however, to argue the merits of the government's case. Choices are admittedly difficult, and differences of opinion are inevitable even among partisans of a strong, democratic, free labor movement. As a private citizen I can only express an opinion, hoping that my views can somehow affect events. As a member of Congress, you, however, are endowed with enormous power to determine the policies our country will follow. If you are convinced that the Department of Justice is acting improperly in its method of addressing racketeering and anti-democracy in the Teamsters unions, you have a moral and political responsibility to go beyond expressing an opinion and to take action that will help to combat racketeering in unions effectively and properly.

I pose two questions: 1) In exercising your legislative powers, how do *you* propose to eradicate the racketeer combine in the Teamsters union? It is apparent that past law enforcement efforts have resulted in this or that individual corrupt union official being sent to jail, only to be replaced by a twin. In the meantime, the members' democratic rights are continually violated by a powerful and ruthless criminal enterprise operating on a national scale.

2) How do *you* propose to defend the rights of those courageous members of the Teamsters union who have been fighting against organized crime control of their union and who have been victimized for their efforts? In this connection, I call attention to the enclosed letter of John Kuebler, a member of Teamsters Local 282 here in New York. He fought against a corrupt local officialdom; he impelled law enforcement authorities to act and send a crooked official to jail. But Kuebler himself, after this service to his union and to the public, lost his job because of fraudulent actions of his union's officials. He appealed to the National Labor Relations Board which upheld his claim, and vindicated his charges. It ordered the offending union to pay him his lost wages.

Ten years have passed. The NLRB has failed to enforce its own decision; Kuebler has not collected one single cent.

John Kuebler is only one example of the hundreds of union members who have turned to the NLRB for help after suffering retaliation for their reform activity. The NLRB has proven impotent to provide defense and recourse for union reformers who face racketeers. Legislative oversight of NLRB policies and correction of remedial deficiencies are obviously essential. You were moved to speak out on behalf of the rights of the Teamster establishment. What do you have to say for those who have been victimized by the union's officials?

Reformers like John Kuebler have little money to donate to campaigns backed by PAC's; they have no political clout. But in their unions they do carry on the battle for American democracy that we all cherish. Don't you think that now is the time to come to their assistance?

Sincerely yours,

Herman Benson
Executive Director
Association for Union Democracy

Deposition of Roy Williams

Q. Mr. Williams: Did you know a man named Nick Civella?

A. Yes.

Q. When did you first meet Nick Civella?

A. 1952. Late in '52 or early '53

Q. What were the circumstances?

A. Kansas City operated with an eastern judge, a western judge, and a central—I
mean a presiding judge. During that time there was—I know seven and there
could be eight different democratic clubs because at that time Kansas City and
Jackson County was basically democrat. I was the head of the Teamsters Club.
Civella was the head of the North End Political Club. Bill Cirman, who was the
mayor of Independence, was the chairman of the Eastern Democratic Club. And
a man by the name of Moran, Tim, I believe, Moran, was the head of the Central
Club. And every time there was an election come up, you wouldn't want your
man to run for auditor. You'd want him to run here. This club would want his
man to run. And anyway, you could have as many as seven or eight people.

I was appointed by our group as the chairman of our club. Nick Civella was
the chairman of his club. If there was an argument as to who we thought we could
win with, it came to our committee, the four of us, and we determined who we
thought we could win with. And we had the authority to direct the clubs to
withdraw their particular candidate for the particular political job and put the one
in that we suggested.

Q. After you first met Mr. Civella in connection with this political club, how long
did you know him?

A. I knew him starting in 1952 or early '53, and I knew him till he died sometime in
'81 or early '82. I'm not sure.

Q. After you met Nick Civella in 1952, did there come a time later when you
learned what position, if any, he had in organized crime?

A. Well, there again, you're calling my attention to dates, and I'm not sure. The first
time that I thought that he was mixed up with some group was after the Apalachin
meeting, and I believe the Apalachin was in New York. I'm not sure. He and a
man by the name of Falardo were arrested at that Apalachin meeting, and the
papers in Kansas City played it up big. That was my first impression that he might
be a head of an undesirable group.

Q. Was that Apalachin meeting in the late 1950s?

A. Yes.

Q. After that Apalachin meeting, did you meet with Mr. Civella and discuss the Apalachin meeting?

A. Not to—well, I met with him, but it wasn't solely to discuss the Apalachin.

Q. At the time you met him after the Apalachin meeting, did he tell you anything about what happened at the Apalachin meeting?

A. Civella told me that, among other things, territory and cooperation was discussed.

Q. What did he tell you about territory and cooperation?

A. Civella said that he had Kansas City as his territory. He had working relations with other areas. He had friends in Wisconsin, he had friends in Chicago, he had friends in Cleveland, and he had friends in New Orleans.

Q. Did he say he had friends in New York?

A. No, he never mentioned New York.

Q. Did he say anything about how they had divided up the territories?

A. No, he did not, other than just what I said that Nick told me. He didn't tell me about anybody else.

Q. How did he refer to these other people with whom he had met at the Apalachin conference?

A. My people are my friends.

Q. Did you learn whether or not Nick Civella had been arrested at this Apalachin meeting?

A. That's what the papers said.

Q. Did you discuss that with Mr. Civella?

A. No, I did not.

Q. Was there anyone else present at the time you had this conversation with Mr. Civella?

A. No, sir.

Q. Did Mr. Civella say anything to you about how you could benefit from his friends?

A. No.

Q. Did Mr. Civella say anything to you about how his friends might be of help to you?

A. Later but not at that meeting.

Q. Did Mr. Civella say anything to you about helping you if you went into other areas of the country?

A. Yes.

Q. What did he tell you in that regard in his conversation?

A. He told me if I went into areas that I thought there would be some problems, to get ahold of him and he would get ahold of his friends.

Q. Did there later come a time when you did contact Mr. Civella and ask for his help?

A. Twice.

Q. Can you describe those?

A. Once was in San Francisco at a bad strike. I didn't know anybody in San Francisco. I was sent in there by Mr. Hoffa, and when I got to this meeting, I had kind of a hostile president of that union. I always went in alone. I started to meet him, and Hoffa told me to break up the strike. I started the meeting. I noticed some people standing around the room with topcoats on, never sat down. Plenty of seats but didn't sit down. The meeting was over. I got a vote on the strike to where it ended and the meeting broke up and everybody left, including the people with the trench coats.

Q. Before you went to San Francisco, had you gone to Mr. Civella to tell him about your trip?

A. I just said yes, I contacted him and told him I was going, and he said he'd get ahold of his friends.

Q. What was the second occasion in which you asked for Mr. Civella's help with his friends?

A. In New Orleans, Louisiana. Hoffa called me and wanted me to meet him in New Orleans at the hotel across from the airport. I went to New Orleans. I told Nick that I was going to New Orleans with Hoffa, and the oil workers was wanting to go into the Teamsters Union. When they found out—when the city fathers or whoever it is—they had already rented a hall. When they found out it was James R. Hoffa that wanted to rent the rooms or meeting hall, they refused to give it to him. There was quite a few Teamster members there that had no place to meet. I'm a veteran. I contacted the Veteran's Administration, and they let us use their hall just outside of New Orleans.

Hoffa conducted the meeting. The weather was warm. There again, there was other chairs to sit in, but there was maybe five or six people standing around the outside. They didn't have trench coats. They said nothing, nor neither did they sit down, and there was no problems at that particular meeting except one man that kept coming to the front and arguing and so forth. And he got hit in the head with a mallet, and Jimmy Hoffa said, "Sergeant of arms, please remove this object on the floor so we can continue the meeting." The sergeant of arms come and got him, took him outside. About 20 minutes he was back in, and I have to say he acted like a gentleman when he came back in.

Q. When approximately did this meeting in New Orleans take place, if you recall?

A. I don't recall.

Q. Do you know whether these men who were in the back of the room in the meeting hall in New Orleans were Teamsters?

A. No, sir. I think he was an oil worker and was probably sent there by the oil workers' people.

Q. Mr. Williams, I wasn't referring to the man who was removed.

A. I thought that's what you said.

Q. The men in the back of the room, sir, do you know whether or not they were Teamsters?

A. No, I do not.

Q. Did you recognize them to be Teamsters?

A. I didn't even pay any attention whether they were Teamsters, oil workers, or who they were. I just know they stood up in the back of the room like they did— certain people done in San Francisco.

Q. Were there any seats in the meeting hall?

A. Lots of them.

Q. Were there seats in the meeting hall in San Francisco?

A. Yes.

Q. When approximately was this meeting in San Francisco, if you recall?

A. I don't recall.

Q. Mr. Williams, directing your attention to the period after this discussion you had with Nick Civella about the Apalachin meeting, did there come a time when you received a threat from two men who identified themselves as friends of Nick Civella?

A. Well, first I have to go back just a little bit.

Q. Certainly.

A. As I said earlier, the pension fund was instituted in '55. We started paying small pensions in '57. I started getting a lot of conversation from Nick that he wanted to support particular loans.

Q. When was this, sir?

A. Sir?

Q. When was this that you got those requests?

A. Sometime later in the later part of '58 when the pensions started getting a few dollars, and I put up with that and refused to do any of these things that he was asking me to do regarding the pension fund. I told him how it was set up and how it was to be operated and so forth, about the A and O committee and so forth.

One night when I'm coming out of a meeting—we were in the old building. 116 West Linwood is where our office was, and we kind of shared with McGilley Funeral Home. On Sundays if we had big meetings and they had no funerals, we used their lot and vice versa.

Q. What city was this in?

A. Kansas City.

Q. What happened next?

A. When I come out to get in my car, there was two men standing, one on each side. They said, "Get in, Mr. Williams, and park your car over in the other lot. Take the keys because we intend to bring you back." They shoved me in a big car, in the middle, between the two of them. About a half a block they put a blindfold on me. It seemed like about 20 minutes we stopped. They took me inside of a building. They sat me on a chair. The place was dark. At least it was to me. I couldn't see nothing. And they took the blindfold off.

There was a great big light over my head that showed around about ten feet of my stool that I was sitting on. They told me that I was brought there for a reason.

That I was going to have to cooperate closer with Nick Civella. I didn't recognize any of them. I knew none of them. I didn't know how many was in the room. The acoustics in the ceiling sounded similar to a basketball court or something. I don't know how many people was in the room because I couldn't see nobody.

They threatened my family, named my two children. They were both young at that time. My oldest daughter was twelve. My youngest daughter was six. They said if I didn't cooperate, they were going to kill my children, my wife, and you will be the last to go. Do you understand what we're talking to you about? I said yes. They asked me if I was going to cooperate with Nick closer, and I said I'll have to think about it. They put the blindfold back on me, took me back to my car. I got in my car and went home.

And I don't know—I can't describe the feeling I had. I mean, it just never happened to me. I come from a family of 13 on a farm. I had a sixth grade education, and I never knew there was these kinds of people in the world. So I didn't say nothing to my family because I didn't want to excite them. I went looking for help.

Q. The room where these two men took you, could you see anything in the room?

A. Nothing.

Q. Why was that, sir?

A. Because it was dark. There was no lights on other than the one over my head.

Q. Was the light over your head a bright light?

A. Real bright. It looked like it was sort of a spotlight, and I only presume that it covered about ten feet around my stool that I was sitting on.

Q. When you say you went for help after you received this threat, who did you go speak to?

A. I went to talk to Tom Flynn first.

Q. Who was Tom Flynn at that time?

A. Tom Flynn at that time was an assistant to Van Tobin—no, excuse me. He was a director of the central conference—I mean the eastern conference at that time because he left as assistant to Tobin in 1952 so I had forgotten that. But anyway, I went to him because I knew him real well. He sent me to Jimmy Hoffa.

Q. First, what did Mr. Flynn say to you when you went to speak to him?

A. He said, "I think you should go talk to Jimmy." He didn't want to make any comments at that time.

Q. Did you then go see Mr. Hoffa?

A. Yes.

Q. What happened when you went to see Mr. Hoffa?

A. I told Mr. Hoffa what happened, and he said, "Roy, it's a bad situation." He said, "You can run, but you can't hide. You could quit. You still can't hide. My advice to you is to cooperate or get your family killed."

Q. Did Mr. Hoffa say anything to you about whether he was aware of Nick Civella and his friends?

A. Mr. Hoffa said, "Roy, there are bad people. And they were here a long time before you and I come, and they'll be here a long time after we're gone." He said, "They're either infiltrated into every local union, big local union, every conference, pension funds, even the AFL-CIO." And he says, "They're bad and certainly I think you should go cooperate with them." He says, "I'm tied tight as I can be."

* * *

Q. Subsequently did Mr. Civella tell you what kind of cooperation he wanted from you?

A. He wanted me to vote for some loans that he was interested in in Las Vegas. He told me on one particular loan that he wanted me—I believe it was Argent. He told me that he wanted me to follow Plug's lead. That was the nickname for Bill Presser who had taken over the chairmanship with Fitzsimmons of the health and welfare and pension—excuse me. Not health and welfare. Pension.

Q. In addition to the Argent loan, did Mr. Civella tell you he wanted you to support other loans?

A. I don't know whether he wanted me to do that other than to follow The Plug or Fitzsimmons. He didn't want any—me to oppose any of the loans that Fitzsimmons or The Plug or Bill Presser recommended.

Q. What were some of the loans that were recommended in this manner?

A. Well, we had an executive committee by that time. The executive committee was attended by Frank Ranney, Fitzsimmons, Bill Presser, and I believe Joe Morgan. And anybody requiring a loan of any description went to see this particular executive committee. The auditors were there, the lawyers were in there, the actuaries. All of them including the asset manager was all in these meetings. They'd give us a book. We met every three months, and they'd give us a book so thick. On the first page it identified the fact that they had looked at it. They recommended approval, recommended hold, or recommended that it be denied. 98 percent of the time we went along with the recommendations of the committee.

Q. Mr. Williams, after you received this threat, how would you characterize Nick Civella's influence, if any, over you within the Teamsters?

A. Well, to be right frank about it, if I didn't want to get killed, I was his boy. And I characterized the fact that I cooperated with him, but I never had to oppose any of these loans because they were recommended by the executive committee after they had all met.

* * *

Q. How did it come about that Nick Civella gave you money in 1974?

A. I think he had just gotten the Argent loan or something to that effect. I don't know what else it would have been. He just told me this was my share. Now, I believe it was the Argent Corporation and the Hacienda owned by—I forget his name now. A little lawyer.

Q. Was that Allen Glick who was the owner of Argent?

A. Allen Glick, yeah.

Q. Had the Argent Corporation sought a loan for the Stardust Casino?

A. I think it was for the Stardust and possibly for the Hacienda. I'm not sure.

Q. How big a loan had the Argent Corporation sought?

A. I believe it was something around 60 million dollars.

Q. Had you voted in favor of that loan?

A. Yes.

Q. Had you had any discussions prior to your vote on that loan application with Mr. Civella about whether Mr. Civella wanted you to support that loan application?

A. He told me to follow The Plug's lead on that application.

Q. Again, who was The Plug that you just referred to?

A. Bill Presser.

Q. Did you follow Bill Presser's lead on that application?

A. Yes.

Q. Did you vote in favor of that application?

A. Yes.

Q. When did you start to receive money from Mr. Civella?

A. Sometime in 1974.

Q. What was the first occasion on which you received money from Mr. Civella?

A. I don't know, sir.

Q. Who gave you the money on this first occasion?

A. Nick Civella. Other times it was delivered by Sam Ancona.

Q. How much money did you receive on the first occasion?

A. Fifteen hundred as I stated a while ago.

Q. How long did you continue to receive money each month?

A. Right after I was elected general president, I came back home in June and resigned my position as president of Local 41 and president of the Teamsters counsel. Met Nick out at the ballpark. It was at a motel there close to the ballpark, and I told him that—and Nick was very sick at that time. The fact of the matter, I think he died that year. I'm not sure. But I told him I didn't want to take the money anymore. I was going to take over the Teamsters International Union and I didn't need the money and I would rather not have it. And I never received anymore from him, and he died shortly after that.

Q. How often did you receive this money after this first $1500 payment in 1974?

A. I thought I said earlier every month.

Q. How much money did you receive each month?

A. 1500 sometimes, 1200 sometimes, 1300 sometimes, 1,000 sometimes, but it was made up later so it averaged out 1500 a month.

Q. Mr. Williams, I'd like to refer you to your testimony at the deposition in the

Salerno case starting on Page 129 and going on to Page 130, starting at Line 18 on Page 129 and continuing until Page 130.

Q. Mr. Williams, I ask you to read beginning at Line 18 on Page 129 continuing on to Page 130 down to Line 6.

THE WITNESS: On 18 the prosecutor at the hearing—Line 18 now I'm talking about—where he asked me, "As International vice president, members of the executive board, did you become aware that other members of the board knew of your ties to Nick Civella?" My answer is this. I said, "Yes." "How did you become aware?" "Because I made no bones about it."

Q. And the answer continues doesn't it, Mr. Williams?

A. Yes.

Q. What's the rest of the answer after "because I made no bones about it"?

A. "I was controlled by Nick, and I think everybody knew it because Hoffa told me that Nick was in the hierarchy of the so-called organized crime group. And when he threatened me, why that's when I became his boy."

Q. Now, at the deposition in the Salerno case do you recall being asked those questions and giving those answers about being controlled by Nick Civella?

A. I saw it on the tape that I said I became his boy.

Q. You do recall giving that testimony; correct, sir?

A. Yes, I do.

Deposition of Angelo Lonardo

Q. You testified earlier about Milton Rockman. Directing your attention to Mr. Rockman, what role if any did he have with the Cleveland La Cosa Nostra family?

A. Well, he was an associate of ours. He was not a member.

Q. As an associate what activities was he involved in?

A. Mostly the unions, Teamsters union.

Q. Was there anyone in particular in the Teamsters union that Mr. Rockman dealt with?

A. Well, he dealt with Bill Presser and Jackie Presser.

Q. Did Mr. Rockman ever tell you what type of relationship he had with Bill Presser and Jackie Presser?

A. They were very very close and he could control them.

Q. Mr. Lonardo, have you ever heard of a man named Frank Fitzsimmons?

A. Yes.

Q. Do you know what position if any he held with the Teamsters union?

A. He was president of the union.

Q. Of the international union?

A. Of the whole thing, yeah.

Q. Did there come a point in time when he ceased to be president of the international union of the Teamsters?

A. Yes, he died.

Q. Directing your attention to the period a few months before Mr. Fitzsimmons' death. Did you have any conversations with Milton Rockman about Mr. Fitzsimmons?

A. Yes, we did.

Q. Can you describe those conversations please?

A. Well, Mr. Rockman said it looks likes Fitzsimmons is going. He says don't look like he'll last too much longer. He says it looks like we better start getting ready. He said Nick Civella had already talked to him about Roy Williams in case Fitzsimmons dies and that Nick Civella, who happened to be the boss of the Kansas City LCN, says that Roy Williams was his man and that he could control him.

And Maishe said "Well, I'll talk to the Pressers in Cleveland and we'll get together later, you know." And Jackie agreed, and I believe Bill Presser was still living at the time—he was—and he agreed that Roy Williams would be all right.

Q. After you had these conversations with Maishe Rockman, what did you do next?

A. Well, we thought best was to get ready and talk to people in Chicago and the people in New York. We went to Chicago first and met with Joey Aiuppa, the boss of Chicago, and Jack Cerone who was the underboss.

Q. Who went to Chicago?

A. Jack Licavoli, I and Maishe Rockman, Milton Rockman.

Q. How soon after these conversations you had with Maishe Rockman did you go to Chicago?

A. It wasn't too long.

Q. Who arranged for the trip to Chicago?

A. I think Jack White had somebody from Cleveland call Jackie Cerone's son to tell him that we were coming in to see him, to see Jackie Cerone and Joey Aiuppa and what day would be best for us to come there.

And Jackie Cerone's son, he made the appointment with his dad, and he got word back to this fellow in Cleveland and he told Jack about it. We went, we got a car and the next day or two, whenever it was, and we went to a suburb of Chicago.

Q. When you say that you said you should "get ready" what did you mean by that?

A. To get ready so we could have the delegates ready to vote for Roy Williams.

Q. When you went to the suburb of Chicago where did you go?

A. We went to a restaurant there. I don't remember the name of it. It was in the outskirts of Chicago, and we met with Joey Aiuppa and Jackie Cerone there.

Q. At that point in time what position if any did Jackie Cerone hold in La Cosa Nostra?

A. He was the underboss.

Q. Of what family?

A. In the Chicago family.

Q. And at that time what position if any did Joey Aiuppa hold in La Cosa Nostra?

A. He was the boss.

Q. Of what family?

A. Chicago family.

Q. When you got to the restaurant did you have discussions with Aiuppa and Cerone?

A. Yes, we did, but before we started to talk, Joey Aiuppa, he thought we were there to talk about family business. And he knew Maishe wasn't Italian and he was not a member. He asked Maishe, you know, if he would excuse himself and walk out for a little bit and come back.

Q. And did Rockman leave at that point?

A. Yes, he did.

Q. After Rockman left the meeting did you have discussions with Aiuppa and Cerone?

A. Yes, I did.

Q. What was discussed?

A. I says to Joey Aiuppa and Jack Cerone, I says "What we are here for mostly is to talk about Fitzsimmons is dying and talking about getting Roy Williams to run."

We told them that Maishe Rockman knew more about this union stuff than any one of us did, and we thought he should have stayed, you know. He said, well, Joey Aiuppa apologized for excusing Maishe, he says he didn't know what we were there for, and he says "I'll apologize to Maishe when he comes back in." He says "I thought it was for something else concerning family matters."

So we said no, it was about Roy Williams, if it would be all right with you fellows after Fitzsimmons dies if you go along with Roy Williams.

Q. Did you tell Aiuppa and Cerone anything about Nick Civella?

A. We told him that Nick Civella was interested in Roy Williams running because he controlled Roy Williams and he knew him very well, that he would listen to him.

Q. What position if any did Nick Civella hold in La Cosa Nostra at that time?

A. He was the boss of the Kansas City LCN.

Q. Did you tell Aiuppa and Cerone anything about Jackie Presser during this conversation?

A. Yeah, we also told him that Roy Williams promised to Jackie Presser that he would have control of the central states.

Q. What did Aiuppa and Cerone tell you in this conversation?

A. Well, they said that they would go along with Roy Williams; they were satisfied with everything.

Q. Did they tell you what they would do for Roy Williams?

A. That they would line up the delegates, whatever they had to do they would have everybody ready.

Q. After this conversation, did there come a point in time when Maishe Rockman returned to the table?

A. He did.

Q. When Maishe Rockman returned to the table was there any further discussion?

A. Yeah, well, Joey Aiuppa apologized to Maishe for excusing him and Maishe told him, he says, "after all, I knew more about this than either one or Jack" and he says "I could have explained it better" but he says "as long as everything is straightened out, no use talking about it any more."

Q. When Maishe Rockman returned to the table was he informed of what had been discussed?

A. He was.

Q. What was he told?

A. He was told that we discussed about Roy Williams running for the president, presidency. And we told him everything else and he was satisfied with what went on.

* * *

Q. Did there come a time when you went to New York?

A. Yes, there was.

Q. Who went to New York?

A. Milton Rockman, I, and John Tronolone met us at the airport. He arrived about—well, we arrived there about five minutes before he did.

Q. How long after the meet you'd had outside Chicago was your arrival in New York?

A. About a week later.

Q. Where did you go?

A. 116th Street to the social club.

Q. Who did you see there?

A. Tony Salerno.

Q. Was there anyone else there at the time?

A. Well, Fish was there, Fish Cafaro, he was around there. Pepe was there.

Q. Did you have a meeting at that point?

A. We did.

Q. Who did you meet with?

A. Tony Salerno.

Q. Did you have any discussions at that point with Mr. Salerno?

A. Well, we had told him that since Fitzsimmons was dying we were getting ready.

Q. What did you say to him, Mr. Salerno?

A. That we were getting ready and we'd—we had talked—Maishe had talked to Roy Civella and Roy Civella was interested in getting—Carl Civella was interested in getting Roy Williams in there and we had told him—I told him we had talked to Chicago and Chicago was well satisfied with Roy Williams and they were getting ready with their delegates if he would be interested.

He said that would be all right. He said Nick knows him and he could control him, it's all right with us. And we also told him that about Jackie Presser getting the central states and Roy Williams.

Q. When you just mentioned Nick, to whom were you referring?

A. Nick Civella.

Q. And when you just said Chicago, to whom were you referring?

A. Joey Aiuppa and Jackie Cerone.

Q. What, if anything, did Tony Salerno say to you after you told him this?

A. He said that he would get ahold of Sammy Provenzano and that he would talk to him in lining up the delegates.

Q. In support of whom?

A. Roy Williams.

Q. What position if any did Sammy Provenzano hold at that time in the Teamsters union?

A. I think he was president of his local there, something. He was also international vice-president.

Q. Are you familiar with a man named Tony Provenzano?

A. I know of him or heard of him. I didn't know him.

Q. What position if any did Tony Provenzano hold in La Cosa Nostra at that time?

A. He was a capo, had been a capo in the Genovese family.

Q. Do you know if there was any familial relationship between Sammy Provenzano and Tony Provenzano?

A. They were brothers.

Q. What was your understanding of what Tony Salerno meant when he said that he would contact Sammy Provenzano to line up the delegates?

A. He said that he would talk to him and get ready with the delegates.

Q. After this meeting in New York with Tony Salerno did you return to Cleveland?

A. Yes, we did.

Q. Did there come a time thereafter when Frank Fitzsimmons died?

A. There was.

Q. Do you know who then became president of the Teamsters?

A. Right after that Roy Williams ran and he got elected.

Q. After Roy Williams became president of the Teamsters international did something happen to him?

A. Well, Roy Williams got indicted and a couple of months after that we says, well, looks like maybe he might get convicted, better start getting ready for the next president.

*   *   *

Q. Did you meet with Tony Salerno?

A. Yes, we did.

Q. Did you have discussions during this meeting?

A. We did.

Q. What did you discuss at this meeting?

A. Well, we told him what we came there for, to see how he felt about Jackie Presser running for president of the Teamsters union, and we told him that we already had been to Chicago and first they objected to him and then they agreed that they would go along.

And Tony says "well, why did they object to Jackie Presser first?" So we told him that Jackie Cerone had said that they heard that he was an informant.

And he didn't tell us where they heard it from but that's what he heard, and it come from a reliable source and at first they didn't go along with it, but the next day Maishe got the call and he agreed to go along with Jackie Presser.

Q. In this conversation with Tony Salerno did you say anything about Milton Rockman's relationship with Jackie Presser?

A. Yeah, we did. We told him that Maishe controlled Jackie Presser and Jackie would listen to anything he would tell him to do.

Q. What did Tony Salerno say to you in this conversation?

A. Well, at first, when we started to talk, he said "if you have any trouble in Chicago," he says, "let me know, I'll talk with them."

But we told him that they agreed and that they would go along with Jackie

Presser. He says, "Well, as far as I'm concerned, I'll go along with it too. I'll start doing the same thing I did for Roy Williams. I will get hold of Sammy Pro, Sammy Provenzano and tell him to get ready with the delegates."

Q. After the meeting did you go back to Cleveland?

A. Yes, we did.

Q. Did there come a point thereafter when something happened to Roy Williams?

A. Well, Roy Williams got convicted.

Q. Who succeeded Roy Williams as Teamsters president, if you know?

A. Jackie Presser.

Q. After you returned to Cleveland, did you have any conversations with Maishe Rockman about Jackie Presser?

A. Oh, we talked about Jackie Presser a few times. I know one time he told Jackie Presser—Jackie Presser said to him "thanks for all the help I'm getting from you." He said "Don't thank me," he said "thank Chicago and New York and Angelo, if you get elected, he would be responsible for you getting the job."

Q. By "the job" to what are you referring?

A. President of the Teamsters union.

*   *   *

Q. Returning for a moment and directing your attention to the discussions that you had about Roy Williams and Jackie Presser becoming president of the Teamsters. Why were you interested in who became president of the Teamsters?

A. So we'd have somebody there in case we needed any favors with the central states or we also used to get favors putting men to work in the union.

Q. What kind of favors would you get from the Teamsters union?

A. Well, putting different men to work there and if we needed any loans from the Central States' Pension Fund, something big, you had control of it.

Q. What about union charters?

A. Charters.

Q. Can you recall any example of when a La Cosa Nostra member wanted a union charter from the Teamsters?

A. Well, Tony Salerno had said to Maishe, he said "Maishe, when you get back will you talk to Jackie Presser if you could get a friend of mine a charter here in New York in the Teamsters local?" So Maishe said yeah, and he gave Maishe the name I guess and Maishe took care of [it] with Jackie.

Q. When was that in time, when did that conversation occur?

A. During one of the trips we had made to see Tony.

Q. When was that approximately?

A. 1981 or early '82, something like that.

Q. Did you ever have any conversations with Milton Rockman about Harold Friedman?

A. Well, after Jackie Presser took his dad's place Maishe was thinking of putting

Harold Friedman with Jackie. So he went down to see Jackie Presser and he told him, he says "I think you should put Harold Friedman on that job."

He said "I already did. I know you were going to tell me to do it and I got Harold Friedman in there with him."

Q. Did Milton Rockman tell you why he wanted Harold Friedman in that position?

A. Well, that he knew him and he knew him very well to talk to and could handle him and get favors done over him, too.

Q. What position was it that Harold Friedman got that you were just describing?

A. He was vice-president of that local, joint council 41.

Q. Was that in Cleveland?

A. In Cleveland.

Q. In terms of favors from the Teamsters union, in addition to charters, union jobs and loans from the Central States' Pension Fund, were there any other kinds of favors that you got from the Teamsters union?

A. I didn't, no.

Q. Did you ever get any favors in terms of vending or skimming in connection with the Teamsters union? Not you personally. La Cosa Nostra members or associates.

A. Well, we got the loan for Allen Glick at the Stardust Hotel in Las Vegas.

＊　　＊　　＊

Q. I'd like to direct your attention to the period just after you became underboss of the Cleveland La Cosa Nostra family in 1976. Did you have any discussions with Maishe Rockman at that point about the Stardust?

A. Yes, I did.

Q. Can you tell me the substance of the conversations?

A. Well, he told me how the money was coming from Vegas and how it got started.

Q. What did he tell you on that subject?

A. He says that Allen Glick had gone to see Frank Balistrieri from Milwaukee who was the boss there and Allen Glick had asked Frank Balistrieri if he could do him a favor and he said "Well, if I could I will."

He said "Could you get some other people in that pension fund to go along for a loan for the Stardust for me?" And he said "I'll see that you get something out of it."

Q. When you say "in that pension fund" to what are you referring to?

A. From the Teamsters pension fund, to get money to loan. So Frank Balistrieri says "well, I got Frank Ranny on there as a trustee." He says "he's my man, he says I could talk to him." He says "I'll get ahold of Nick Civella to get ahold of Roy Williams" and he says "I'll get Nick Civella to talk to Cleveland where he knows the people in Cleveland to talk to Bill Presser."

And he went over and see Nick Civella about it and he said, Yeah, I could talk to Roy and get ahold of Maishe and meet with Maishe and Maishe—Nick Civella had talked to Maishe about talking to Bill Presser, and he says OK, he says, as soon as I get back to Cleveland I'll talk to my brother-in-law and I'll get back to you.

Q. What position if any did Frank Balistrieri hold in La Cosa Nostra at that time?

A. He was the boss of the Milwaukee family.

Q. What position if any did Nick Civella hold in La Cosa Nostra at that time?

A. Boss of Kansas City.

Q. What position if any did Roy Williams hold in regard to the Teamsters Central States' Pension Fund at that time?

A. He was a trustee.

Q. What position if any did William Presser hold in connection with the Teamsters Central States' Pension Fund at that time?

A. He was a trustee.

Q. What position if any did Frank Ranney hold in connection with the Teamsters Central States' pension fund at that time?

A. Trustee.

Q. The Maishe who you were just referring, who was that?

A. Milton Rockman.

Q. What did Milton Rockman tell you if anything about the contacts made with Roy Williams and Bill Presser?

A. Well, after Maishe had talked to Civella he come back to Cleveland, he talked to Johnny Scalish about it and Johnny says to him, he says "how much money do them guys need? How much do they want to make?" He says "why don't you mind your own business, leave it alone?"

So Maishe told him "Johnny, we could make money there." And [Johnny] said "I don't care what you could make."

So finally Maishe finally convinced him. So Johnny says, "listen, you go ahead do what you have to, in case you get into any trouble over that, don't you come to me for help because I'm not going to give you no help."

And he said OK. And from there he went down and talked to Bill Presser and naturally Bill Presser went along with Maishe and he took care of the loan, and they got it.

Q. When you say "they got it" what do you mean?

A. Allen Glick, got the money for the Stardust from the pension fund.

Q. What pension fund?

A. The Teamsters' pension fund.

Q. What position if any did Johnny Scalish hold with La Cosa Nostra at that time?

A. At that time he was the boss of the Cleveland LCN.

Q. And these conversations with Milton Rockman, was there any discussion of why Bill Presser or Roy Williams approved the loan?

A. Well, they knew that we would get a piece of—at the time I didn't. This was told to me later on. After I got to be underboss—that we would get 10 percent of the Stardust, each member, plus the skim money.

Q. Who would get 10 percent of the Stardust?

A. Cleveland would get 10, Chicago would get 10 I think. I think they got 10, I don't know.

Q. When you say Cleveland and Chicago, to whom are you referring?

A. And Kansas City also. I mean Milwaukee, too.

Q. When you say Cleveland, Chicago, Kansas City and Milwaukee, to whom are you referring?

A. To the LCN.

Q. In these conversations you had with Maishe Rockman after you became the underboss of the Cleveland La Cosa Nostra family in 1976, was there any discussion of whether any Teamsters officials had received payoffs in connection with this loan?

A. Well, Roy Williams was getting $1500 a month and Bill Presser was getting something.

Q. Did Milton Rockman tell you this?

A. Yeah. He also told Jack Licavoli, too.

Q. Did Milton Rockman tell you who was paying Roy Williams $1500 a month?

A. Nick Civella.

Q. And Milton Rockman told you that?

A. Yeah.

Q. Did Milton Rockman tell you who was paying off Bill Presser?

A. He was taking care of it.

Q. Who?

A. Maishe was.

Q. Taking care of Bill Presser? You have to answer yes or no.

A. Yes, he did.

Q. What interest did the Cleveland La Cosa Nostra family get in connection with the Stardust after this loan was approved for Allen Glick?

A. Well, we were supposed to have 10 percent of the Stardust, and we got the skim money.

Q. How much skim money—how often did you get skim money?

A. Monthly, every month.

Q. How much skim money did you get every month?

A. It was an average of $40,000 a month for each city, for Milwaukee, Kansas City and Cleveland.

Q. Each city got a separate 40,000?

A. Yeah.

Q. Did the Cleveland La Cosa Nostra family continue to get this skim money after Roy Williams was elected president of the Teamsters?

A. Yes, we did.

✻　　✻　　✻

Q. Mr. Lonardo, before the break I was asking you questions about skim money from the Stardust casino. Do you recall that questioning?

A. Yes, I do.

Q. Who among the La Cosa Nostra families collected the skim money?

A. You mean who got it?

Q. Yes.

A. Who split it up?

Q. Yes.

A. It was Kansas City first. Kansas City, Milwaukee and Cleveland.

Q. Who if anyone collected the skim money for the Cleveland La Cosa Nostra family?

A. Milton Rockman.

* * *

Q. Now, I direct your attention to your testimony yesterday about the Cleveland La Cosa Nostra family helping certain individuals get Teamsters' jobs. Do you recall that testimony?

A. Yes.

Q. Besides the testimony you've already given about Harold Friedman, Nick Nardi, Roy Williams and Jackie Presser, do you know anyone who obtained a job with the Teamsters through the Cleveland La Cosa Nostra family?

A. Yes, I do.

Q. Who?

A. Besides what I said yesterday, it was Carmine Parise.

Q. Who is Carmine Parise?

A. He's the business agent for the truck drivers union that works with the Plain Dealer.

Q. Is that a Teamsters union?

A. Yes, it is, Local 436.

Q. How did Mr. Parise obtain that job, if you know?

A. Well, there was a fellow by the name of DePalma, he passed away, who was the business agent, and Carmine Parise went to Jack Licavoli and asked Licavoli if he could talk for him in regards to getting DePalma's job.

And Jack says, "Well, I'll see what I could do for you." And he talk to Maishe and Maishe talked up for Carmine Parise and he got the job as business agent to replace DePalma.

Q. How did you learn that?

A. Through Jack and through Milton Rockman.

Q. Have you ever heard of an individual named Babe Triscaro?

A. Yes.

Q. Who is Babe Triscaro?

A. He was president of the Local 436.

Q. Did there come a time when Babe Triscaro ceased to be president of Local 436?

A. Yeah, he died.

Q. Who succeeded Babe Triscaro, if anyone?

A. His son-in-law, Sam Busacca.

Q. What role if any did the Cleveland La Cosa Nostra family play in Sam Busacca becoming the president of Teamsters Local 436?

A. Well, Johnny Scalish had told Maishe to talk for Sam Busacca to get that job so Sam Busacca could keep on taking care of Babe Triscaro's wife financially.

Q. Was there any familial relationship between Sam Pistol and Babe Triscaro?

A. Sam Pistol was Babe's son-in-law.

Q. What steps if any did Johnny Scalish take on Sam Pistol's behalf?

A. Well, he talked to Maishe to see that Sam Busacca would get Babe's job.

Q. What was the result?

A. He got it.

Q. How do you know that?

A. Oh, I know it.

Q. From whom?

A. Well, I know it personally and I know it through Maishe and everybody else.

Q. What position if any did John Scalish hold in La Cosa Nostra at that time?

A. He was the boss.

Q. Of what family?

A. Cleveland family.

Q. When did this occur, approximately?

A. Well, it was just right after Babe died. I don't know what year Babe died, around 1975. Somewhere around there. I don't quite remember.

Q. Was there a Teamsters local that Sam Busacca became the president of?

A. Yes, it was.

Q. Who was it from the Cleveland La Cosa Nostra family if any who dealt with Jackie Presser?

A. Milton Rockman.

United States v. International Brotherhood of Teamsters, Appeal of Disciplinary Actions
(July 30, 1992)

MCLAUGHLIN, Circuit Judge:

Appellant ("Parise") is the former Secretary-Treasurer of International Brotherhood of Teamsters ("IBT") Local 473, and the former President of Joint Council 41, an IBT affiliate. Both organizations are headquartered in Cleveland, Ohio. He asks us to review an order of the United States District Court for the Southern District of New York (David N. Edelstein, *Judge*), upholding disciplinary sanctions imposed on him.

For the reasons set forth below, we affirm the order of the district court.

Background

The case law within our circuit swells with decisions emanating from the Teamsters Litigation. Our earlier decisions exhaustively discuss the genesis of the Consent Decree settling the government's charges against the IBT and its officials. *See United States v. International Bhd. of Teamsters*, 931 F.2d 177, 180–81 (2d Cir.1991); *United States v. International Bhd. of Teamsters*, 905 F.2d 610, 612–13 (2d Cir.1990) [hereafter *Friedman & Hughes*]. Accordingly, we need recount only those provisions of the Consent Decree that are necessary to understand the current dispute.

Pursuant to the Consent Decree, the Investigations Officer served charges on Parise on July 30, 1990. The charges accused Parise of bringing reproach upon the IBT, in violation of the IBT constitution, by (1) assaulting, threatening and harassing Jerry Jones, a Local 473 member; and (2) refusing to testify about his involvement in a beating Jones suffered at the hands of Frank Costanzo, another Local 473 member.

The Independent Administrator scheduled a hearing on the charges for December 18, 1990. Before the hearing began, however, Parise and the Investigations Officer signed a settlement agreement to resolve the charges (the "Proposed Agreement"). Under the Proposed Agreement, Parise would be suspended from the IBT for three months, beginning on January 8, 1991.

In the Proposed Agreement, Parise stated, in two paragraphs that lie at the heart of this appeal, his understanding of the authority of the Independent Administrator and the district court:

7. I agree that this agreement will be submitted to the Independent Administrator for his review and approval. If approved by the Independent Administrator, I understand he will submit it to the district court for that court to enter as an order.

8. I understand the Investigations Officer makes no representation as to the determination of the Independent Administrator or the court with respect to this agreement.

Without holding a hearing or making any factual findings, the Independent Administrator approved the Proposed Agreement. He then submitted the Agreement to the district court for its approval. The court refused to do so, advising the Independent Administrator that "In light of the severity of the charges against Mr. Parise, I find the terms of the . . . agreement unacceptable. I am returning the . . . agreement unapproved."

With the agreement thus unravelled, the Independent Administrator scheduled a hearing.

The scheduled hearing went forward on April 9, and the Investigations Officer presented a compelling case against Parise. Perhaps the most damaging evidence on the first charge were the tape and transcript of a conversation between Parise and fellow union member Jerry Jones. Upset with Jones' alleged attempts to steer an upcoming IBT election free from his influence, Parise fired a verbal fusillade at Jones. In various diatribes laced with colorful, macho expletives, Parise threatened to "bust [Jones'] head" and "have somebody give [Jones] a . . . beating." He further told Jones that he would "never work again," and would not "get a . . . job anyplace Teamsters are at." Parise concluded "[T]he day after [the election] win, lose, or draw you're fucked and I want you to know it."

The Investigations Officer presented convincing evidence on the second charge as well. Specifically, he introduced the transcript of a deposition in which Parise had relied on his Fifth Amendment privilege against self-incrimination to refuse to testify about Frank Costanzo's assault on Jones.

Beginning his defense case, Parise's counsel moved to suspend the hearing, arguing that, despite the district court's disapproval of the Proposed Agreement, an associate of the Independent Administrator told him that the Agreement had resolved all charges against Parise. Counsel claimed that the associate told him that the district court's approval would only be required if the court sought to impose contempt sanctions when Parise later failed to comply with the Agreement. The Independent Administrator expressly rejected this claim:

It has never been my position that Judge Edelstein's signature was not necessary for approval of any agreements that have been entered into by the investigations officer and counsel for the respondent in any charge and there have been many of them. That's why I forward them automatically to Judge Edelstein.

Accordingly, the Independent Administrator denied counsel's motion and ordered the hearing to continue.

Parise then testified. Unable to challenge the tape and transcript of his phil-
ippic against Jones, he delivered *ad hominem* attacks on Jones, claiming
that he had "urinated off the docks" in Cleveland, "antagonized people" and "spen[t]
a great deal of . . . time in saloons and coming back from lunch half tanked
and just bothering everybody and anybody." Parise also attempted to down-
play his failure to testify at the deposition, claiming that this decision was made
"against [his] better judgment [because he] listened to [his] lawyers." He also testified that he did not know about Costanzo's attack on Jones until the day after
the incident.

The Independent Administrator determined that the Investigations Officer's evidence "conclusively proved" that Parise had "violently threatened" Jones, and that
Parise would likely have carried out the threats had Jones not recorded them. He
further found that Parise's invocation of his Fifth Amendment privilege against self-
incrimination at his deposition "precluded the Investigations Officer's authorized
scrutiny into possible corrupt and dishonest activities in Parise's local." He ordered
Parise suspended for twenty-four months from the IBT and its affiliates, but allowed
Parise credit for his self-imposed three-month suspension. Finally, he determined that
because Parise had committed acts of union misconduct, Local 478 could not pay his
legal fees to defend the charges.

Parise sought review of the Independent Administrator's decision in the district
court. On October 24, 1991, the district court issued an order finding that there was
"overwhelming evidence" to support the charges against Parise, and an "ample basis"
to impose a twenty-four month suspension. The court, therefore, affirmed the Independent Administrator's decision, and Parise now appeals.

Parise renews his claim that the Proposed Agreement took effect despite the district
court's explicit rejection of it. Alternatively, he contends that the district court erred
in refusing to approve the Proposed Agreement. Finally, he argues that the district
court erred in affirming the Independent Administrator's decision suspending him
from IBT membership for twenty-four months, and preventing Local 473 from paying
his attorney's fees.

Discussion

I. The Effect of the Proposed Agreement

Parise claims that, because of his settlement with the Investigations Officer, the
district court was not empowered to reject the Proposed Agreement. In his view, the
Proposed Agreement became effective when the Independent Administrator signed it;
and it was thereafter submitted to the district court for the sole purpose of being
"so ordered."

[1] Parise relies upon Paragraph 7 of the Proposed Agreement:

I agree that this agreement will be submitted to the Independent Administrator for his *review and approval*. If approved by the Independent Administrator, I understand *he will submit it to the District Court for that court to enter as an order.* (emphasis added).

Parise interprets this paragraph to mean that while the Independent Administrator could review the Proposed Agreement, the district court's role was to "rubber stamp" it. We disagree.

Paragraph 8 of the Proposed Agreement explodes Parise's argument:

I understand the Investigations Officer makes no representation as to the determination of the Independent Administrator or the court with respect to this agreement.

II. The District Court's Review of the Proposed Agreement

[2] A court must scrutinize a proposed settlement before giving it a judicial imprimatur. . . . The district court must ensure that the agreement "does not put the court's sanction on and power behind a decree that violates Constitution, statute, or jurisprudence." We hold that the district court appropriately exercised its authority in refusing to approve the Proposed Agreement.

[3] The Investigations Officer's charges against Parise were serious. They accused Parise of assaulting, harassing, and threatening to beat Jones, and refusing to testify about Costanzo's attack on Jones. Judge Edelstein, who has scrupulously overseen the Teamsters Litigation since its inception and has ruled on scores of the Independent Administrator's applications of the Consent Decree, was in the best position to determine whether the Proposed Agreement imposed a punishment commensurate with the charges against Parise. We see no reason to disturb the district court's decision that the severity of the charges against Parise required a suspension greater than the three months envisioned in the Proposed Agreement.

Parise also contends that, in reviewing the Proposed Agreement, the court failed to defer to the "findings" of the Independent Administrator, as required by our decision in *Friedman & Hughes*. The difficulty with this argument, however, is that it rests on the false premise that the Independent Administrator actually made "findings" when he approved the Proposed Agreement. There are no such findings in the record. The Proposed Agreement itself does not refer to any "findings." Nor did Parise make any admissions in the Proposed Agreement that could be construed as findings. Thus, because the Independent Administrator did not make any findings in conjunction with the Proposed Agreement, the district court owed no deference to the Administrator's decision to approve the Agreement.

III. *The Decision of the Independent Administrator*

[4] The Independent Administrator concluded that the evidence against Parise warranted a twenty-four month suspension from the IBT. He further ruled that Local 478 could not pay Parise's attorney's fees for his defense. The district court affirmed the Independent Administrator's decision in its entirety. On appeal, Parise claims that the evidence against him did not warrant such a severe punishment. Once again, we are not persuaded.

The district court must give "great deference" to the decisions of the Independent Administrator. Consistent with *Friedman & Hughes*, the district court reviewed the Independent Administrator's decision to determine whether it was arbitrary or capricious, and concluded that it was not.

Our standard of review is not so clearly defined. *Friedman & Hughes* permitted us to affirm a district court decision that is supportable under "any reasonable standard of review." The district court's decision here certainly fell within the realm of reason. Thus, we again leave the question of the precise standard of appellate review to another day.

Parise's threats of physical and economic harm resonated throughout his conversation with Jones. And, as the Independent Administrator noted after listening to Parise testify at the April 9 hearing, Parise was not a man given to idle threats, and would likely have harmed Jones if the conversation were not taped. Moreover, prior to the April 9 hearing, Parise had refused to testify about Costanzo's assault on Jones. Parise did not contest any of the Investigations Officer's evidence against him. In sum, there was a plethora of evidence to support the charges against Parise, and a sufficient basis to suspend him from the IBT for twenty-four months.

In challenging his suspension, Parise contends that the Independent Administrator should have imposed a punishment closer to the three-month suspension provided in the Proposed Agreement. We disagree. The Independent Administrator based his approval of the Proposed Agreement on factors different from those that led him to determine that Parise deserved a suspension of twenty-four months. The Independent Administrator did not review the evidence against Parise before the April 9 hearing. He was not given the tape and transcript of Parise's threats against Jones until the very morning of the April 9 hearing. After considering the damning evidence against Parise, the Independent Administrator determined that a harsher sanction was warranted than that delineated in the Proposed Agreement.

[5] Finally, the Independent Administrator did not err in ordering Local 478 not to pay Parise's attorney's fees. A union official may obtain reimbursement of his legal expenses only when his actions inure to the benefit of the union. Here, the Independent Administrator found that Parise had brought reproach upon the IBT, and thus had violated the IBT constitution. In so doing, Parise obviously acted in a manner that did not inure to the benefit of the IBT.

Conclusion

We hold that the district court (1) had the authority to review the Proposed Agreement, and (2) did not err in withholding approval. We also hold that the district court did not err in (3) affirming the Independent Administrator's decision suspending Parise from IBT membership for twenty-four months, and (4) preventing Local 473 from paying Parise's attorney's fees.

AFFIRMED.

6

The Dapper Don:
United States v. Gotti

(Trial: February 1992)

Introduction

United States v. Gotti was the culmination of a determined government effort to convict a mob boss who, in the public mind, had come to symbolize the power and persistence of organized crime. The prosecution's success depended in part, however, upon the cooperation of a mob defector who, on the basis of his record, warranted the most serious government attention and societal condemnation. The Gotti conviction was attributable to many other important, and yet controversial, decisions, including the trial judge's disqualification of the defense lawyers who had represented Gotti (with great success) and other members of his crime family for years and the decision by the judge to sequester the jury from the beginning of the trial and to keep their identities anonymous.

Background

In the late 1980s, with the Cosa Nostra crime families around the country decimated and most of the visible family bosses convicted or killed, John Gotti stood out as the most visible boss still in power. His personal style seemed calculated to call attention to himself.[1] Flamboyant and vocal, Gotti enjoyed the stature of a folk hero in his neighborhood, the Howard Beach section of Queens, New York, and was featured in the national media. Thus, it is not surprising that the FBI and the Justice Department sought to prosecute Gotti for a fourth time in less than a decade.

Prior to the case discussed in this chapter, Gotti had been prosecuted three previous times during the 1980s, but had escaped conviction on each occasion. In 1984, the Queens district attorney charged Gotti, then a Gambino crime family soldier, with violently attacking and beating a man who had honked his horn at him. Because of the victim's positive identification and testimony before the grand jury, the case seemed very strong. In the interim between the indictment and the trial (a little over one year), however, Gotti had become boss of the Gambino crime family. After the victim read about Gotti in the papers and received threatening phone calls, he stated that he no longer wished to testify at trial, no doubt fearing retaliation from the Gambino family more than punishment for contempt. The Queens district attorney continued the prosecution despite the victim's recalcitrance. During the trial, the victim first invoked the Fifth Amendment when questioned about the alleged assault. After receiving immunity (for any possible perjury), he nevertheless stated that he could not identify his attackers. Not surprisingly, the judge granted a defense motion to dismiss the charges in March 1986.

In 1985, the United States attorney for the Eastern District of New York charged Anniello Dellacroce (Gambino family underboss), Gotti, and eight members and associates of the Gambino family with violations of RICO. Gotti was charged with seven predicate offenses, three of which were for crimes for which he had already been convicted: two hijackings and attempted manslaughter.[2]

The prosecution faced problems throughout this trial. Bruce Cutler, Gotti's defense lawyer, used the government witnesses' criminal backgrounds and lack of direct knowledge of Gotti's crimes to effectively impeach them. Moreover, at least one of the jurors was bribed to vote in Gotti's favor (and was successfully prosecuted in 1992). In any event, all the defendants were acquitted.[3]

Four years later, the Manhattan district attorney charged Gotti with conspiracy to assault and with assault (by shooting) of a Carpenter's Union vicepresident who, according to the district attorney, was being punished for setting fire to a restaurant that was owned by a Gambino soldier. The district attorney had built a strong case based on tape-recorded conversations from the Gotti headquarters, the Queens Bergen Hunt and Fish Club. James McElroy, a defector from the Westies (an Irish gang associated with the

Gambino family), testified for the government that Gotti had hired them to carry out the attack. However, once again the victim was unwilling to testify against Gotti. In fact, he elected to testify in Gotti's behalf! The defense team of Gerald Shargell and Cutler successfully focused on McElroy's criminal record and forced him into many inconsistencies. In addition, the audiotapes were difficult to understand. Gotti was again acquitted.

The Investigation

These three setbacks did not discourage law enforcement agencies, which continued to concentrate on Gotti. The FBI, which had formed a Gambino crime family squad in 1979, placed Gotti under intense open and covert electronic surveillance.[4] Despite his elaborate security precautions, the FBI successfully bugged the main room of Gotti's headquarters, the Ravenite Social Club in Manhattan's Little Italy. The FBI planted its most fruitful bug, however, in an apartment two flights upstairs from the social club, where Gotti conducted his most confidential and important business. The surveillance also involved the use of telephoto lenses and videotapes to record numerous "walk-talks" among Gambino members (walks around the neighborhood to avoid government eavesdropping). Altogether, almost five hundred hours of taped conversations were intercepted, recorded, and analyzed.

The Indictment

Andrew Maloney, the U.S. attorney for the Eastern District of New York, brought the next prosecution against Gotti. The initial indictment charged John Gotti (boss), Frank Locascio (*consigliere*), Salvatore Gravano (underboss)[5] and Thomas Gambino (capo) with thirteen counts of racketeering, murder, illegal gambling, loansharking, and obstruction of justice. In the fall of 1991, however, the trial of Thomas Gambino was severed and Salvatore Gravano decided to become a government witness.

Thereafter, Gotti and Locascio were charged with conducting the affairs of an enterprise (the Gambino crime family) through a pattern of racketeering activity (murders and other crimes). The new indictment laid out the table of organization of the Gambino crime family and alleged that it operated through crews who reported to capos who, in turn, reported to the bosses. The indictment charged that the "methods and means by which the members of the enterprise furthered its criminal activities were the actual and threatened use of violence, including murder."

The core of the thirteen counts in the superseding indictment was a RICO charge based on twelve predicate acts, including conspiracies to murder and the murders of Paul Castellano, Thomas Bilotti, Robert DiBernardo, Liborio Milito, and Louis DiBono; conspiracy to murder Gaetano Vastola; and illegal gambling, loansharking, and obstruction of justice. The indictment also included bribery and tax charges.

Pretrial Developments

Before trial, the government achieved three major successes: the disqualification of Gotti's long-time defense attorneys, the conversion of Salvatore Gravano into a government witness, and the sequestration of the jury. While a variety of factors contributed to Gotti's conviction, these victories provided the prosecution with significant advantages as the trial commenced.

Defense Attorney Disqualifications

Immediately following the indictment, the government moved to disqualify three of the Gambino crime family's long-standing defense lawyers—Bruce Cutler, John Pollok, and Gerald Shargell—on the grounds that because of serious conflicts of interest, they could not function as defense counsel without prejudicing the defendants' case, the government's case, or both. In an important pretrial ruling, Judge Glasser granted the government's motion.[6] Later, the government also succeeded in disqualifying George Santangelo, another attorney on the defense team.

The prosecutors argued that the attorneys had a disqualifying and nonwaivable conflict of interest in that (1) their receipt of under-the-table payments would make them wary of vigorously defending their clients for fear that the government would retaliate against them,[7] (2) their acceptance of benefactor payments from the leaders of the Gambino family to represent lower-level members would be offered as proof of the existence of an enterprise, making the lawyers witnesses against their clients,[8] and (3) Cutler's previous representation of a potential government witness would compromise the range of his cross-examination. In addition, the government urged that allowing these lawyers to remain in the case would unfairly disadvantage the government, because, as participants in several intercepted conversations, the lawyers would become unsworn witnesses able to rebut the government's interpretations of those conversations during the course of the trial.

Judge Leo I. Glasser granted the government's motion, rejecting the defense contentions that (1) there was no conflict of interest, (2) if there was a conflict of interest, it could be edited out of the evidence, and (3) in any event, the conflict was waivable.

The counsel disqualification may be more important for its symbolic significance than for its impact on the quality of Gotti's and Locascio's defense. Albert Krieger and Anthony Cardinale, the two lawyers who replaced the original team, were highly qualified and represented their clients vigorously. Nevertheless, in its successful motions to disqualify the original defense attorneys, the government displayed a new level of aggressiveness in dealing with organized crime.

Gravano Plea Agreement

The most extraordinary event in the Gotti case was Salvatore Gravano's decision to become a witness for the government. Gravano was the highest-ranking member of a New York Cosa Nostra family to become a turncoat. The defection of Gotti's most trusted aide dealt a major blow to the defense and further undermined the edifice of Cosa Nostra solidarity.

Gravano was charged with three murders. Under the plea agreement, he admitted to *sixteen* additional murders and to participating in extortion, robberies, burglaries, loansharking, fraud, assaults, and kickback schemes, though he emphatically denied ever being a drug dealer.[9]

Ironically, Gravano's success in organized crime enabled him to negotiate an extremely favorable plea bargain. In exchange for his agreement to testify against Gotti, Locascio, and others, the U.S. attorney agreed to recommend him for the Witness Security Program and to allow him to plead guilty to a single RICO count, carrying a maximum sentence of twenty years.[10] Sentencing would be delayed until he had finished testifying as a government witness.[11]

Cooperation agreements like this one raise questions about the witness's reliability. In effect, through the cooperation agreement, the government "purchases" a defendant's testimony by granting the defendant/witness substantial leniency or even immunity. If the defendant takes the offer, he must testify fully and truthfully. If he does not, the government reserves the right to cancel the bargain. Such agreements raise the possibility that defendants will provide the testimony that the government desires. Of course, the defendants facing such a witness can expose the cooperation agreement (which federal prosecutors disclose as a matter of course) and subject the witness to grueling cross-examination with respect to his deal. Whether that will always be enough to protect against the possibility of perjured or shaded testimony can be debated.[12] Moreover, the fact that the judge will ultimately sentence the witness arguably creates an incentive for the witness to testify truthfully.

Though the prosecutors clearly had a strong interest in Gotti's and Locascio's convictions, Gravano's stature in organized crime and record of ruthless violence raise ethical questions about the plea agreement. Are some defendants so evil that the government should not grant them substantial leniency in order to convict other criminals? Does the decision to grant substantial leniency turn on how critical the cooperating witness's testimony is? If so, how valuable must the testimony be, and how can that be determined before the fact?

Jury Anonymity and Sequestration

Arguing that the Gambino family, and Gotti in particular, had been involved in jury tampering in the past and that they therefore posed a risk to the safety of the jurors and to the government's interest in a tamper-proof jury, the government moved for an anonymous jury. The defendants unsuccessfully argued that the jury would be disposed to convict them if it believed the men on trial posed a threat to their lives. Jurors were only referred to by number. Neither the trial judge, the prosecutors, the defense lawyers, the defendants, nor the U.S. marshals knew the jurors' names. Furthermore, the trial judge prohibited the press from sketching or photographing the jurors.

Judge Glasser also granted the prosecution's motion, over defense objections, to sequester the jury throughout the trial. In order to counteract possible prejudice against the defendants, the jurors were told that sequestration was necessary to guard against the jury's possible contamination by publicity. Consequently, the jurors were housed at a secret location to which they were escorted by armed U.S. marshals driving buses with tinted windows.

The U.S. marshals controlled access to the jurors. They did not permit the jurors to see visitors and only occasionally allowed them to take escorted trips out of their secret hotel. Marshals monitored calls to and from family members and examined all incoming and outgoing mail.[13]

The Trial

The six-week trial began in February 1992. U.S. attorney Andrew Maloney headed the prosecution team, but he actually only made the opening statement and a portion of the rebuttal summation. Assistant U.S. Attorney John

Gleeson carried the lion's share of the government's responsibilities. Anthony Cardinale and Albert Krieger represented the defendants. Leo Glasser, an experienced district court judge, presided over the trial.

The Prosecution's Case

The prosecution primarily based its case on recordings of Gotti's conversations and on Gravano's testimony. However, in order to prove the existence of the RICO enterprise, the government (over defense objection) also called FBI agents to give "expert testimony" on the organization, rules, and activities of Cosa Nostra generally and the Gambino crime family specifically.

The government introduced tape recordings from four different locations that had been intercepted over an eight-year period. These tape recordings linked Gotti and Locascio to the Gambino crime family and to a range of predicate crimes, including the murders of Liborio Milito and Robert DiBernardo.

The jury also heard Gotti pronouncing a death sentence on DiBono:

Louie DiBono . . . I sat with this guy. I saw the papers and everything. He didn't rob nothin'. You know why he's dying? He's gonna die because he refused to come in when I called. He didn't do nothing else wrong. . . . He's gonna get killed because he, he disobeyed coming.

Gravano proved to be an extremely effective witness. His nine days of testimony covered the nature, organization, and goals of the Gambino crime family and the roles that he and the defendants had played in perpetrating crimes to further the interests of the enterprise, and he gave an account of his and Gotti's on-the-scene orchestration of Paul Castellano's assassination.

Gravano told his story with impressive command over facts and details. He described the secret rituals that initiated him into Cosa Nostra. He testified about the structure of the Gambino crime family, and its operations. According to Gravano, John Gotti headed the family and carried the title "boss"; Gravano served as the underboss; Joe "Piney" Armone functioned as *consigliere*, and while Armone was in jail, Gotti's codefendant, Frank Locascio, acted as *consigliere*. Gravano identified the twenty-one capos who supervised the soldiers and associates and outlined the organization of the Gambino family's four hundred made members. He testified as to how cash moved up the chain of command from "crews" to the "boss." Gravano stated that he himself provided Gotti with approximately $1.2 million per year, mostly from his manipulations of the construction industry.

Gravano emphasized the importance of murder as a disciplinary mechanism in the Gambino family. The routine nature of capital punishment for family members is indicated by the language used to describe a murder contract—"a piece of work." Gravano recounted Gotti's order to kill Louis DiBono ("Di B") and described the murder itself:

[Di B] came downstairs. He said hello. He sat down. Then old man Paruta got up and I told him to get Di B a cup of coffee. He got up. In the cabinet there was a .380 with a silencer. He took the gun out, walked over to Di B, and shot him twice in the back of the head. Me and Eddie picked him up and put him in the back room, locked it up. We left the office. We locked the office up and I went and met with Angelo and I told him it was done.

The Defense

Not surprisingly, neither Locascio nor Gotti chose to testify, considering the certainty that they would be impeached with their prior criminal activities. The defendants attempted to call several peripheral witnesses, including Gravano's personal trainer and his hypnotist, but Judge Glasser rejected them as irrelevant to the charges in the case. Ultimately, the defendants only called a single witness, a tax lawyer who claimed to have advised Gotti that since he was under indictment, he did not have to file a tax return!

The defendants' major defense strategy was thus to discredit Gravano and the other witnesses. Gravano was subjected to days of intense cross-examination, but he proved unflappable. The defense attempted to show that Gravano was lying about the conspiracy to kill Castellano in order to enhance his value as a government witness, and they unsuccessfully tried to reveal inconsistencies in his account of the Castellano assassination. The defense sought to simplify the case by arguing to the jury that the prosecution should stand or fall on the credibility of its account of the Castellano murder, but it was successful neither in this effort nor in its attacks on the testimony about Castellano's assassination.

Judgment, Sentence, and Appeal

The jury convicted Gotti and Locascio of substantive and conspiracy violations of RICO and various predicate acts. Judge Glasser sentenced each defendant to life imprisonment and other prison terms, to run concurrently, and to $250,000 in fines.

The defendants raised many issues on appeal to the Second Circuit, including (1) disqualification of defense counsel; (2) admission of expert

testimony; (3) jury instructions; (4) prosecutorial misconduct; (5) jury sequestration; (6) failure to sever Locascio, and (6) new trial motion based on
nondisclosure of additional crimes committed by Gravano. The appeals court
rejected all of their arguments.[14] Here we summarize four appellate issues.

Attorney Disqualification

The appeals court first dealt with the argument that by disqualifying
their attorneys of choice, Judge Glasser had violated the defendants' Sixth
Amendment rights to be represented by the counsel of their choice. Following well-settled precedent, the court was of the opinion that

[t]he accused does not have an absolute right to counsel of her own choosing. . . . In
deciding a motion for disqualification, the district court recognizes a presumption in
favor of the accused's chosen counsel, although this presumption can be overcome
by a showing of an actual conflict [of interest] or potentially serious conflict.

The court next found that more than the defendant's rights to a fair trial
are at stake in guaranteeing that the defendant's lawyer does not have a
conflict of interest. The court has "an independent interest in ensuring that
criminal trials are conducted within the ethical standards of the profession
and that legal proceedings appear fair to all who observe them."

Turning to the facts of the case, the Second Circuit panel held that Judge
Glasser had not abused his discretion in disqualifying Cutler because Cutler's
acceptance of benefactor payments could have been used as evidence of the
existence of the Gambino enterprise. In language highly critical of Cutler's
legal ethics, the court noted that Cutler had functioned as house counsel to
the Gambino crime family, having accepted fees from Gotti for the representation of other members of the family, and that this practice raised serious
ethical questions.

Although we are cognizant of the right of the accused to obtain representation, we
are also conscious of the institutional interest in protecting the integrity of the judicial
process. If an attorney will not perform his ethical duty, it is up to the courts to
perform it for him. Bruce Cutler had no place representing John Gotti in this case,
and the district court properly determined that he should be disqualified.

Admissibility of FBI Agent's Expert Testimony

The defendants claimed that they were unfairly and unconstitutionally
prejudiced by the testimony of FBI agent Lewis Schiliro, who testified as an
expert witness on the nature and function of the organized-crime families.
The defense argued that the existence and nature of Cosa Nostra and the
Gambino crime family and the alleged crimality of its members were issues

of fact and not subjects on which expert testimony was appropriate. Moreover, the defense argued that Agent Schiliro was no "expert" in the legal sense of the term and that by qualifying him as an expert, Judge Glasser enabled the government to introduce the theory of its case to the jury through the mouth of one of its own operatives, thereby subjecting the defendants to extreme prejudice.

Under the Federal Rule of Evidence 702 (advisory committee note), expert testimony is permissible when "the untrained layman would [not] be qualified to determine intelligently and to the best possible degree the particular issue without enlightenment from those having a specialized understanding of the subject involved in the dispute." The court found that while popular images of organized crime abound in our society, "jurors are not well versed in the structure and methods of the organized crime families." Therefore, the subject matter of the structure and organization of Cosa Nostra is appropriate for expert testimony. Having cleared that hurdle, the court had no difficulty holding that Agent Schiliro, with seventeen years in the FBI and five in organized-crime control, qualified as an expert.

Jury Instructions—The RICO Pattern Requirement

RICO makes it a crime to conduct the affairs of an enterprise through a pattern of racketeering activity. The statute defines a pattern of racketeering activity as any two federal or state predicate offenses committed within a ten-year period. Over the years, all of the federal circuit courts have been asked to consider whether the two predicate acts have to further the affairs of the enterprise or merely be "related" to the affairs of the enterprise. The defense lawyers argued that Judge Glasser should have instructed the jury that it could not find the defendants guilty if it found that the racketeering acts were committed solely for the individual's own purposes, not to further the affairs of the enterprise. The appeals court made short work of this argument, reaffirming its interpretation of RICO as requiring only that the offenses were made possible by virtue of the defendant's position in the enterprise or were related to the activities of the enterprise.

Gotti also argued that the trial judge should have instructed the jury that RICO requires the two racketeering acts to be related to one another. The Second Circuit, again looking to its own precedents, rejected this interpretation of RICO, instead taking the looser view that the predicate acts upon which a RICO violation rests need not be directly related to one another so long as both are related to the RICO enterprise in such a way that they become indirectly connected to each other.

Prosecutorial Misconduct

The appellate court judges were clearly concerned with U.S. Attorney Maloney's rebuttal summation, in which he stated,

Let me conclude with this. I may be insulting some of you. I hope I'm not. If you accept the proof of what you are dealing with here, the boss of a murderous and treacherous crime family, and his underboss, you would be less than human, if you didn't feel some personal concern.

At that point, Judge Glasser sustained the defendants' objection but rejected their motion for mistrial. The appellate court labeled Maloney's comment indefensible but held that it was harmless error in light of both Judge Glasser's striking of the comment and the overwhelming evidence against the defendants.

Postscript

The government's attack on the Gambino crime family did not end with the conclusion of the Gotti trial.[15] In the prosecution against Thomas Gambino, which was severed from the original Gotti indictment, Gambino was convicted of racketeering charges. The Manhattan District Attorney's Office brought a criminal restraint-of-trade suit against Thomas and Joseph Gambino and their trucking companies, which for decades had dominated the New York City garment industry. The case ended with a plea bargain in which the Gambino brothers agreed to sell off a substantial portion of their trucking interests and pay fines of $12 million. In a subsequent criminal case, Thomas Gambino was convicted of managing racketeering activities in Connecticut for the Gambino family and sentenced to five years' imprisonment. A drug-smuggling and racketeering case in which Gravano testified against Joseph and John Gambino resulted in a deadlocked jury (except for a conviction for a single count of bail jumping) in June 1993; they subsequently agreed to a plea bargain.

Conclusion

Though the campaign against the Gambino family continues, *U.S. v. Gotti* was undoubtedly its highlight. It pitted Cosa Nostra's arrogant, vibrant, cocky strongman against the government's tenacious crime control apparatus. As long as Gotti was on the scene, playing to adoring audiences in his neighborhoods and attracting national headlines as "the Dapper Don," all of the successes of the 1980s might have been undermined. Organized crime might still have maintained its indestructible image. Gotti's conviction and life sentence must be seen as an immensely important psychological victory for law enforcement. The public may now be convinced that Cosa Nostra is neither invincible nor inevitable .

The defection of Salvatore Gravano bears special comment. While there were a string of mob turncoats in the 1980s, as we have noted throughout this book, Gravano's defection, like Gotti's conviction, captured the public's attention and impressed the message that organized crime is unraveling. The combination of more effective law enforcement, better prosecution, and draconian penalties, coupled perhaps with changes in attitudes and values among members of the mob, has brought about the collapse of the code of loyalty that for decades had enabled Cosa Nostra to flourish. Gravano was one of the pillars of the Gambino crime family, the most powerful Cosa Nostra organization in the country. His defection from the very core of Cosa Nostra cannot be dismissed as an aberration, but rather must be understood as a symptom of fundamental change.

Reality often follows belief. As the public perception of organized crime changes, so will the reality. As long as businesspeople and other citizens believed that Cosa Nostra was omnipotent, they would not cooperate with law enforcement but would instead accede to organized crime's demands. If they come to believe that Cosa Nostra is vulnerable to government attack, they will be more willing to resist its demands and avoid making corrupt accommodations.[16]

Notes

1. There has been a steady stream of popular literature on John Gotti. See John M. Cummings, Goombata: The Improbable Rise and Fall of John Gotti and His Gang. (Brown, 1990); Douglas Fieden, Sleeping the Good Sleep: The Life and Times of John Gotti (Random House, 1990); Gene Mustain and Gerry Capeci, Mob Star: The Story of John Gotti (Dell, 1989); John H. Davis, Mafia Dynasty: The Rise and Fall of the Gambino Crime Family (Harper Collins, 1993); Howard Blum, Gangland: How the FBI Broke the Mob (Simon and Schuster, 1993).

2. Gotti had served prison time before the cases considered in this chapter. In the late 1970s, he was convicted of attempted manslaughter, and in the 1960s he was convicted of hijacking.

3. In addition to these problems, the FBI became outraged when an assistant U.S. attorney identified Willie Boy Johnson, a long-time associate and friend of Gotti's, as an FBI informant. Despite the fact that Johnson refused to testify for the government, the FBI feared for his life. He was murdered in August 1988.

4. In the past, Gotti was able to find out about law enforcement surveillance from a corrupt New York City police officer, William Peist. Peist's cousin, Peter Maris, was an associate of the Gambino family (more specifically, of the crew captained by Joseph "Butch" Corrao). Peist received periodic payments for his services to the Gambino crime family. He recently pled guilty to racketeering charges and was sentenced to eight years in prison along with Joseph Corrao.

5. The superseding indictment stated that Frank Locascio became acting underboss after the death of Frank Deciccio and the incarceration of Joseph Armone in 1987. It also alleged that Gravano became *consigliere* following the incarceration of Joseph N. Gallo in 1989. By 1991, however, electronic surveillance revealed that Gravano and Locascio had switched places. Throughout this chapter, we will refer to Gravano as the underboss and Locascio as the *consigliere*.

6. *United States v Gotti*, 771 F Supp 552 (EDNY 1991).

7. In an intercepted conversation, Gotti himself noted his lawyers' conflicts of interest:

LOCASCIO: And, they [Cutler and other defense lawyers] ain't got the balls to do what they supposed to do.

GOTTI: They can't come in. Right.

LOCASCIO: They ain't got the balls with doing what they're supposed to be—

GOTTI: Don't you know why? . . . You don't wanna do it because, you cocksucker, you know and I know that they know that you're taking the money under the table. Every time you take a client, another one, one of us on, you're breaking the law.

8. The following quotation was offered as proof of Gotti's benefactor payments to lawyers on behalf of his subordinates:

I paid a hundred thirty-five thousand for their appeal. For Joe Gallo and "Joe Piney's" appeal, I paid thousands of dollars to [attorney] Pollock. That was not for me. . . . I gave [lawyers] three hundred thousand in one year [and they] didn't defend me. I wasn't even mentioned in none of these fucking [indictments]. I had nothing to do with none of these fucking people.

9. After the trial, the prosecutors were told that Gravano had committed several other murders and they passed this information along to the defense team. The government argued that this information was unreliable; in fact, two of Gravano's alleged victims were still alive! The defense's motion for a new trial was denied, and the denial was upheld on appeal. After Gambino was convicted in a subsequent trial, information about Gravano's drug dealing surfaced, despite his testimony that he had never dealt in drugs. The judge in the *Gambino* trial also denied the motion for a new trial.

10. Under Rule 11 of the Federal Rules of Criminal Procedure, the plea agreement between Gravano and the government needed the approval of the trial court before taking effect.

11. As of February 1994, Gravano had testified in at least four cases, and he still had not been sentenced.

12. For an excellent discussion of this problem and cooperation agreements generally, see Graham Hughes, *Agreements for Cooperation in Criminal Cases*, 45 *Vanderbilt Law Review* 1–69 (1992).

13. These security precautions paid off when a routine search of a package that Juror Number 3 was sending to her husband revealed several pieces of paper listing the names, addresses, and telephone numbers of five of the sitting jurors and a note stating her belief that an FBI agent was coaching a government witness on the stand. Judge Glasser dismissed the juror.

14. *United Stated v Locascio and Gotti*, 6 F3d 924 (2d Cir 1993), cert. denied, 114 S.Ct. 1645 (1994).

15. See John H. Davis, *Mafia Dynasty: The Rise and Fall of the Gambino Crime Family* (HarperCollins, 1993).

16. On April 27, 1994, the U.S. Supreme Court turned down John Gotti's final appeal. On September 26, 1994, Judge Glasser sentenced Sammy "the Bull" Gravano to five years in prison.

United States v. John Gotti et al., Indictment

Introduction to All Counts

The Enterprise

1. The members and associates of the Gambino Organized Crime Family of La Cosa Nostra ("the Gambino Family") constituted an "enterprise," that is, a group of individuals associated in fact. The Gambino Family was an organized criminal group that operated in the Eastern District of New York and other parts of the United States. It engaged in, and its activities affected, interstate commerce. The Gambino Family was referred to by its members in various ways, including as a "borgata," a "cosa nostra," a "family" and "this thing of ours."

2. The Gambino Family operated through groups of individuals headed by "captains," who were also referred to as "skippers," "caporegimes" and "capodecinas." These groups, which were referred to as "crews," "regimes" and "decinas," consisted of "made" members of the Gambino Family, who were also referred to as "soldiers," "friends of ours" and "good fellows," and associates of the Gambino Family.

3. Each captain was responsible for supervising the criminal activities of his crew, and provided crew members and associates with support and protection. In return, the captain received a share of the earnings of each of the crew's members and associates.

4. Above the captains were the three highest-ranking members of the Gambino Family. The head of the Gambino Family was known as the "Boss." He was assisted by an "Underboss" and a counselor, who was known as the "Consigliere." With their assistance, the Boss was responsible for setting policy, resolving disputes among members of the Gambino Family, resolving disputes between members of the Gambino Family and members of other criminal organizations, and approving all significant actions by members of the Gambino Family, including murders.

5. The Boss, Underboss and Consigliere of the Gambino Family, who were sometimes referred to collectively as the "administration," supervised, supported,

protected and disciplined the captains, soldiers and associates, and regularly received reports regarding their various activities. In return for their supervision and protection, the Boss, Underboss and Consigliere received part of the illegal earnings of each crew.

6. The Gambino Family was part of a nationwide criminal organization known by various names, including the "Mafia" and "La Cosa Nostra," which operated through entities known as "Families." The ruling body of this nationwide organization was known as the "Commission," the members of which included the Bosses of the five New York–based Families, including the Boss of the Gambino Family.

7. From time to time, the Gambino Family would propose a list of associates to be "made," that is, to become members of the Gambino Family. This list would be circulated to the other Families based in the City of New York. Upon becoming "made," each member would take an oath of "omerta," vowing never to reveal any information about the Gambino Family, its members or its associates.

The Defendants

8. The defendant JOHN GOTTI was a captain in the Gambino Family until December 16, 1985, when the Boss of the Gambino Family, Paul Castellano, was murdered. After the murder of Castellano, JOHN GOTTI became the Boss of the Gambino Family.

9. The defendant FRANK LOCASCIO, also known as "Frankie Loc," has been a member of the Gambino Family for approximately 35 years. After the death of Frank DeCicco on April 13, 1986, and the incarceration of Joseph "Piney" Armone on December 22, 1987, LOCASCIO became the Acting Underboss of the Gambino Family.

10. The defendant SALVATORE GRAVANO, also known as "Sammy" and "Sammy Bull," has been a member of the Gambino Family for approximately 13 years. Following the incarceration of Joseph N. Gallo on May 30, 1989, GRAVANO became the Consigliere of the Gambino Family.

11. The defendant THOMAS GAMBINO has been a captain in the Gambino Family since at least as early as 1985.

The Purposes, Methods and Means of the Enterprise

12. The principal purpose of the enterprise was to generate money for its members and associates. This purpose was effected through various criminal activities, including the operation of illegal gambling businesses, the extortionate extensions and collections of credit, and the generation of income from various businesses through illegal means, including the exploitation of the Gambino Family's corrupt control of union officials. Among the methods and means by which the members of the

enterprise furthered its criminal activities were the threatened and actual use of violence, including murder.

13. The members and associates of the enterprise engaged in conduct designed to prevent government detection of their identities, their illegal activities and the proceeds of those activities. That conduct included the cultivation of corrupt sources of confidential law enforcement information and a commitment to murdering persons, particularly other members or associates of organized crime families, who were perceived as potential witnesses against members of the enterprise. The members and associates of the enterprise also took steps to obstruct ongoing investigations into and prosecutions arising out of the criminal activities of the members of the enterprise.

14. The Gambino Family provided lawyers for members and associates who became involved in criminal prosecutions. Significant decisions in such prosecutions, including a decision to plead guilty, required the approval of the Gambino Family.

Count One: Racketeering

*　　*　　*

16. From in or about January 1985 up to and including the date of the filing of this Indictment, the defendants JOHN GOTTI, FRANK LOCASCIO, SALVATORE GRAVANO and THOMAS GAMBINO, together with others, comprising the leadership of and being employed by and associated with the Gambino Family, which enterprise engaged in, and the activities of which affected, interstate commerce, unlawfully, wilfully and knowingly conducted and participated, directly and indirectly, in the conduct of the affairs of that enterprise through a pattern of racketeering activity. Each of the defendants participated in the affairs of the enterprise through the commission of multiple racketeering acts, as set forth below.

Introduction to Racketeering Acts One and Two

17. The members of the Gambino Family were constantly concerned that their fellow members and associates might become informants or witnesses against them if faced with long prison sentences. As a result, from at least as early as April 1982 through and including December 1985, there was a rule imposed by Paul Castellano, the Boss of the Gambino Family, that any member or associate of the Gambino Family who was found to be involved in narcotics trafficking would be murdered.

18. During April, May and June of 1982, court-authorized electronic surveillance was conducted in the home of Angelo Ruggiero, a member of the Gambino Family and JOHN GOTTI's close associate. Conversations intercepted during that period revealed extensive narcotics trafficking by members of JOHN GOTTI's crew, including

Angelo Ruggiero, Gene Gotti and John Carneglia. In September of 1983, those three individuals and other members of JOHN GOTTI's crew were indicted for various offenses, including heroin trafficking. In May of 1984, pursuant to court order, copies of the narcotics-related conversations intercepted in Ruggiero's home (the "tapes" or the "Ruggerio tapes") were provided to Ruggiero and his co-defendants.

19. After the copies of the tapes were provided to Ruggiero, Paul Castellano repeatedly demanded that Ruggiero provide copies to him.

20. During 1985, Aniello "Neil" Dellacroce was the Underboss of the Gambino Family. He took steps to protect Ruggiero from having to provide the tapes to Castellano. Dellacroce, Ruggiero and JOHN GOTTI were concerned about turning the tapes over to Castellano because they included conversations about narcotics trafficking and references to Commission meetings.

21. In or about late 1985, Paul Castellano obtained copies of the Ruggiero tapes.

22. On December 2, 1985, Aniello "Neil" Dellacroce died of natural causes. Between that date and December 16, 1985, Paul Castellano informed JOHN GOTTI of Castellano's intention to break up GOTTI's crew and to reassign its members to other crews in the Gambino Family.

Racketeering Act One: Conspiracy to Murder and Murder—Paul Castellano

A. Conspiracy to Murder

23. Between December 2, 1985 and December 16, 1985, JOHN GOTTI and others conspired to murder Paul Castellano.

24. In furtherance of the conspiracy, and in order to accomplish its objectives, the defendant JOHN GOTTI and his coconspirators committed and caused to be committed the following overt acts:

a. On December 16, 1985, arrangements were made for a meeting with Paul Castellano at Sparks Steakhouse, 210 East 46th Street, New York, New York.

b. On December 16, 1985, the defendant JOHN GOTTI went to the vicinity of Sparks Steakhouse.

c. On December 16, 1985, Anthony Rampino went to the vicinity of Sparks Steakhouse.

d. On December 16, 1985, Paul Castellano was murdered as he arrived at Sparks Steakhouse.

B. Murder

25. On or about December 16, 1985, the defendant JOHN GOTTI, together with others, knowingly, wilfully and intentionally murdered Paul Castellano.

Racketeering Act Two: Murder—Thomas Bilotti

26. On or about December 16, 1985, JOHN GOTTI, together with others, knowingly, wilfully and intentionally murdered Thomas Bilotti.

Racketeering Act Three: Conspiracy to Murder and Murder—Robert DiBernardo

A. Conspiracy to Murder

27. Between December 16, 1985 and June 5, 1986, JOHN GOTTI and SALVATORE GRAVANO, together with others, conspired to murder Robert DiBernardo.

* * *

B. Murder

29. On or about June 5, 1986, JOHN GOTTI and SALVATORE GRAVANO together with others, knowingly, wilfully and intentionally murdered Robert DiBernardo.

Racketeering Act Four: Conspiracy to Murder and Murder—Liborio "Louie" Milito

A. Conspiracy to Murder

30. Between January of 1988 and March 8, 1988, JOHN GOTTI and SALVATORE GRAVANO, together with others, conspired to murder Liborio "Louie" Milito.

* * *

B. Murder

32. On or about March 8, 1988, JOHN GOTTI and SALVATORE GRAVANO, together with others, knowingly, wilfully and intentionally murdered Liborio "Louie" Milito.

Racketeering Act Five: Solicitation of Murder— Louis DiBono

33. In or about late 1989, the defendant SALVATORE GRAVANO, with the intent that John Gotti authorize and direct the murder of Louis DiBono, solicited, requested, importuned and otherwise attempted to cause John Gotti to engage in such conduct.

Racketeering Act Six: Conspiracy to Murder and Murder—Louis DiBono

A. Conspiracy to Murder

34. Between February 1989 and October 4, 1990, JOHN GOTTI, FRANK LOCAS-CIO and SALVATORE GRAVANO, together with others, conspired to murder Louis DiBono.

35. In furtherance of the conspiracy, and in order to accomplish its objectives, the aforesaid defendants and their coconspirators committed and caused to be committed the following overt acts:

a. In or about late 1989, SALVATORE GRAVANO asked JOHN GOTTI for permission to murder Louis DiBono.

b. In or about late 1989, JOHN GOTTI authorized the murder of Louis DiBono.

c. On or about October 4, 1990, Louis DiBono was murdered.

*   *   *

Racketeering Act Seven: Conspiracy to Murder— Gaetano "Corky" Vastola

37. Between April 28, 1989 and April 26, 1990, JOHN GOTTI, FRANK LOCASCIO and SALVATORE GRAVANO, together with others, conspired to murder Gaetano "Corky" Vastola.

Racketeering Act Eight: Illegal Gambling Business— New York

39. From in or about January 1985 through December 1990, JOHN GOTTI, FRANK LOCASCIO and SALVATORE GRAVANO knowingly and wilfully conducted, financed, managed, supervised, directed and owned an illegal gambling business, in violation of the laws of the State of New York, which business involved five or more persons who conducted, financed, managed, supervised, directed and owned all or part of the business and remained in substantially continuous operation for in excess of thirty days and had gross revenues of $2,000 or more in a single day.

Racketeering Act Nine: Illegal Gambling Business— Connecticut

40. From in or about December 1985 through December 1990, JOHN GOTTI, FRANK LOCASCIO, SALVATORE GRAVANO and THOMAS GAMBINO knowingly and

wilfully conducted, financed, managed, supervised, directed and owned an illegal gambling business, in violation of the laws of the State of Connecticut, which business involved five or more persons who conducted, financed, managed, supervised, directed and owned all or part of the business and remained in substantially continuous operation for in excess of thirty days and had gross revenues of $2,000 or more in a single day, in violation of Title 18, United States Code, Sections 1955 and 2.

Racketeering Act Ten: Loansharking Conspiracy

A. Extortionate Extensions of Credit

41. From in or about December 1985 through December 1990, JOHN GOTTI, FRANK LOCASCIO, SALVATORE GRAVANO and THOMAS GAMBINO, together with others, conspired to make extortionate extensions of credit.

B. Extortionate Collections of Credit

42. From in or about December 1985 through December 1990, JOHN GOTTI, FRANK LOCASCIO, SALVATORE GRAVANO and THOMAS GAMBINO, together with others, conspired to use extortionate means to collect and attempt to collect extensions of credit.

Racketeering Act Eleven: Obstruction of Justice— The Thomas Gambino Trial

43. Between June 22, 1989 and November 30, 1989, the case *United States* v. *Thomas Gambino*, 89 CR 431 (JBW) (the "*Gambino* case"), was an official proceeding pending in the United States District Court for the Eastern District of New York.

44. Between November 8, 1989 and November 30, 1989, JOHN GOTTI, together with others, knowingly and wilfully intimidated and corruptly persuaded other persons with intent to prevent the testimony of such other persons in the *Gambino* case.

Racketeering Act Twelve: Obstruction of Justice— The Castellano Murder Investigation

45. From in or about October 1988 through and including May 1990, a grand jury was conducting an investigation into the murders of Paul Castellano and Thomas Bilotti (the "Castellano murder investigation").

46. Between November 1989 and May 1990, JOHN GOTTI, FRANK LOCASCIO and SALVATORE GRAVANO, together with others, knowingly, wilfully and corruptly

endeavored to influence, obstruct and impede the due administration of justice with respect to the Castellano murder investigation.

Count Two: Racketeering Conspiracy

* * *

48. From in or about January 1985 up to and including the date of the filing of this Indictment, the defendants JOHN GOTTI, FRANK LOCASCIO, SALVATORE GRA-VANO and THOMAS GAMBINO, together with others, comprising the leadership of and being employed by and associated with the Gambino Family, conspired to conduct and participate in the conduct of the affairs of that enterprise through a pattern of racketeering activity by agreeing to commit and actually committing the acts of racketeering with which each such defendant is charged in Count One.

Racketeering Act Thirteen: Bribery of a Public Servant

49. In addition, JOHN GOTTI, FRANK LOCASCIO and SALVATORE GRAVANO conspired to conduct and participate in the conduct of the affairs of the enterprise by agreeing on or about January 17, 1990, to confer a benefit upon a public servant with the agreement and understanding that such public servant's opinion, judgment, action, decision and exercise of discretion as a public servant would thereby be influenced.

Count Three: Conspiracy to Murder— Robert DiBernardo

* * *

51. Between December 16, 1985 and June 5, 1986, JOHN GOTTI and SALVATORE GRAVANO, together with others, for the purpose of maintaining and increasing their positions in the Gambino Family, an enterprise engaged in racketeering activity, conspired to murder Robert DiBernardo.

[Counts Four through Twelve are as follows: Count Four, Murder—Robert DiBernardo; Count Five, Conspiracy to Murder—Liborio "Louie" Milito; Count Six, Murder—Liborio "Louie" Milito; Count Seven, Conspiracy to Murder—Louis DiBono; Count Eight, Murder—Louis DiBono; Count Nine, Conspiracy to Murder—Gaetano "Corky" Vastola; Count Ten, Illegal Gambling Business—New York; Count Eleven, Conspiracy to Obstruct Justice; Count Twelve, Obstruction of Justice—The Thomas Gambino Trial.]

Count Thirteen: Conspiracy to Defraud the United States

75. Between in or about January 1985 and the date of the filing of this Indictment, both dates being approximate and inclusive, within the Eastern District of New York and elsewhere, the defendants JOHN GOTTI and FRANK LOCASCIO, together with others, conspired to defraud the United States by impeding, impairing, obstructing and defeating the lawful functions of the Department of the Treasury in the ascertainment, computation and collection of income taxes from JOHN GOTTI.

76. As part of the conspiracy, and in order to further its objectives, the defendant JOHN GOTTI, with the assistance of his coconspirators, (a) took steps to conceal his true employment and source of income, that is, his position as Boss of the Gambino Family; (b) took steps to create the false impression that he was employed as a salesman for a construction company, a plumbing salesman and a salesman of zippers, hangers and other garment-related items; (c) took steps to create the false impression that an associate of the Gambino Family was employed as a salesman of zippers, hangers and other garment-related items; (d) conducted and arranged for the conduct of financial transactions in ways designed to conceal the true amount of his income; (e) received income from numerous sources in ways designed to conceal those sources of income; and (f) failed to file any income tax returns.

United States v. Salvatore Gravano,
Plea Agreement

Pursuant to Rule 11 of the Federal Rules of Criminal Procedure and the Sentencing Reform Act of 1984, notice is given to the Court that the United States Attorney's Office for the Eastern District of New York (the "Office") and the attorney for SALVATORE GRAVANO have engaged in discussions and agree to the following:

1. SALVATORE GRAVANO will waive indictment and plead guilty to a [RICO charge]. The charge to which GRAVANO agrees to plead guilty carries, among other sanctions, a maximum term of imprisonment of 20 years and a maximum fine of $250,000. The guilty plea will be in satisfaction of all criminal acts by SALVATORE GRAVANO that have been disclosed to the Office as of the date of this agreement.

2. The parties agree that the sentencing court will be informed of all criminal activity engaged in by SALVATORE GRAVANO, and that such information may be considered by the probation department in preparing the presentence report and the court in imposing sentence.

3. SALVATORE GRAVANO will cooperate fully with the Office, agents of the Federal Bureau of Investigation ("FBI"), and other law enforcement agencies, as the Office may require. This cooperation will include, but is not limited to, the following:

   a. SALVATORE GRAVANO agrees to be fully debriefed concerning his knowledge of, and participation in, any criminal activities about which the Office may inquire. This debriefing will be conducted by the Office, agents of the FBI, and other law enforcement agencies, as the Office may require. All documents that may be relevant to such activities and that are in the possession, custody or control of SALVATORE GRAVANO will be furnished to the Office;

   b. SALVATORE GRAVANO agrees to testify in any proceeding as requested by the Office, either in the Eastern District of New York or elsewhere. In this regard, the Office will make a good faith effort to complete GRAVANO's obligation to testify within two years of the date of this agreement. However, it is the intent of the parties that such obligation continues beyond that two-year period provided the government has acted in good faith in making its request;

   c. SALVATORE GRAVANO consents to reasonable adjournments of his sentence, as requested by this Office.

4. No information disclosed or testimony given by SALVATORE GRAVANO during the course of his cooperation will be used against him, except as provided in para-

graphs 2 and 6 of this agreement. The Office will, however, inform the sentencing court of the nature and extent of SALVATORE GRAVANO's conduct and activities with respect to this case and all other information in its possession relevant to sentencing.

5. The Office agrees that, except as provided in paragraphs 1, 2 and 6, no criminal charges will be brought against SALVATORE GRAVANO in the United States District Court for the Eastern District of New York for his heretofore disclosed participation in criminal activity. This agreement, however, covers only those criminal acts that have been disclosed to the Office as of the date of this agreement.

6. SALVATORE GRAVANO must at all times give complete, truthful and accurate information and testimony, and must not commit, or attempt to commit, any further crimes whatsoever. Should it be judged by the Office that SALVATORE GRAVANO has intentionally given false, misleading, or incomplete information or testimony, or has committed or attempted to commit any further crimes, or has otherwise violated any provision of this agreement, SALVATORE GRAVANO shall thereafter be subject to prosecution for any federal criminal violation of which the Office has knowledge, including, but not limited to, perjury and obstruction of justice.

7. If the Office determines that SALVATORE GRAVANO has cooperated fully, provided substantial assistance to law enforcement, and otherwise complied with the terms of this agreement, the Office will file a motion with the sentencing court, setting forth the nature and extent of his cooperation with the Office, including its investigative and prosecutive value, truthfulness, completeness and accuracy. Such a motion will permit the court, in its discretion, to impose a sentence below the applicable sentencing guidelines range. In this connection, it is understood that the Office's determination of whether SALVATORE GRAVANO has provided complete cooperation and substantial assistance, and the Office's assessment of the value, truthfulness, completeness, and accuracy of the cooperation, shall be binding upon him. The Office cannot and does not make a promise or representation as to what sentence will be imposed upon the aforementioned plea of guilty.

8. This agreement is subject to the approval of the Court. The rule provides that such approval may be given at the time SALVATORE GRAVANO enters his plea of guilty, and the Office agrees to recommend that the Court approve the agreement at that time.

9. If SALVATORE GRAVANO requests, the Office will make application and recommend that he and, if appropriate, other individuals be placed in the Witness Security Program operated by the United States Marshal Service.

10. This agreement is limited to the United States Attorney's Office for the Eastern District of New York, and it cannot bind other federal, state, or local prosecuting authorities. It is further understood that this plea agreement does not prohibit the United States, any agency thereof, or any third party from initiating or prosecuting any civil proceedings directly or indirectly involving SALVATORE GRAVANO, including, but not limited to, proceedings by the Internal Revenue Service relating to potential civil tax liability.

United States v. Gotti and Locascio, Attorney Disqualification Ruling by Judge Leo Glasser

(January 21, 1992)

GLASSER, District Judge:

The government has moved this court for an order disqualifying George Santangelo from representing any of the defendants in this case at trial. This motion, like the motion previously made to disqualify Gerald Shargel, Bruce Cutler and John Pollok, is based upon the assertion that counsel's continued participation would give rise to conflicts of interest which cannot be waived or remedied save by an order of disqualification. Defendants have cross-moved for an order disqualifying Assistant United States Attorney John Gleeson from prosecuting this case on behalf of the government.

I: The Government's Motion to Disqualify George Santangelo

The government predicates its motion on the assertion that Santangelo's "presence at counsel table would needlessly deprive the government of a fair trial, create a conflict of interest that cannot be waived or remedied by measures other than disqualification, and compromise the integrity of these proceedings by fostering an appearance of impropriety."

[1] A review of the government's proffer yields two bases upon which a motion for disqualification may be predicated: 1) that Santangelo is answerable to defendant John Gotti, the alleged leader of the Gambino Family—the "enterprise" on which counts 1 and 2 of the indictment are bottomed; and 2) that Santangelo's presence at this trial would offend DR 5-102 of the Model Code of Professional Responsibility.

A. Santangelo's Connection to Counts 1 and 2

The government contends that Santangelo is "house counsel to the Gambino Family." In addressing the motion, the court shall use the phrase "answerable to Gotti" rather than "house counsel." The difference is purely semantic: in either case, the pernicious effect upon the constitutional interest in the rendition of just criminal verdicts is the same, whether Santangelo is the recipient of "benefactor payments" (an allegation not vigorously advanced by the prosecution) or whether he simply answers to Gotti rather than to Locascio.

Evidence of Santangelo's subservience to Gotti would be relevant to establishing that Gotti is the head of an "enterprise" as that term is used in the RICO statute. The evidence the government proffers in support of its claim is the testimony it represents will be given by Salvatore Gravano as well as the tape recordings of conversations intercepted through authorized electronic surveillance.

Gravano has now chosen to cooperate with the prosecution. The government states that Gravano will testify that shortly after the defendants were arraigned, Gotti told Gravano that he (Gotti) would assign Santangelo to represent either Gravano or Locascio. Such an "assignment" of counsel by Gotti for his co-defendant would clearly be probative of the existence of the charged RICO enterprise.

That it mattered little which defendant Santangelo would represent—that, in effect, the clients were fungible—may be readily inferred by the jury from excerpts of intercepted conversations in which Gotti is heard to decree that lawyers (both his and others') work within certain parameters prescribed by him, and that their concern must be not only for their ostensible clients but for others in the Gambino Family as well. See, e.g., United States v. Gotti, 771 F.Supp. at 558. Gravano will further testify that Gotti's insistence that lawyers representing the Family march in lock-step contributed to his own decision to cooperate with the government. Evidence of Santangelo's eleventh-hour appearance may warrant the jury to believe that Gravano's testimony in this regard rings true.

The Intercepted Conversations

The government contends that there is other evidence from which a jury could readily conclude that a criminal association exists between Santangelo's clients and Gotti, and that Gotti is the final arbiter of Santangelo's decisions. Accompanying the government's motion is a transcript of a lawfully intercepted conversation from April 18, 1990 among Gotti, Bruce Cutler, and others. Having reviewed the tape of that conversation (and having compared it with the government's transcript), the court finds that the conversation pertains primarily to the then-pending civil RICO case United States v. Local 1804-1 referred to above. Gotti, a named defendant in that case, was represented by Cutler and the firm of Hoffman & Pollok. Santangelo represented Anthony Ciccone (whom the government describes as a Gambino Family captain), Anthony Pimpinella (characterized as a Gambino soldier), and John Potter, a union official.

The essence of the relevant portion of the conversation is Gotti's insistence upon knowing about, and ultimately approving of, all legal activity in the case not only on his own behalf, but also on behalf of others. Gotti ordains the response the attorneys must make to government assertions of the existence of a Mafia, a Cosa Nostra, or a Gambino Crime Family: there are to be no concessions, and there is to be no finger-pointing. Cutler acknowledges his compliance with Gotti's edicts in this regard, assuring Gotti that he met with the lawyers "three times to tell them your credo in life. . . . But I made them understand: no concessions, everything is denied, every-thing is fought down to the wire."

In an elaboration on his "credo," Gotti is heard to suggest to Cutler that "there ain't nothing" on the tapes as far as he is concerned, and "if there is, it's a mystery to me, I know nothing. . . . Maybe . . . talk to myself a little when I'm talking on that tape." After commenting unfavorably about a portion of a brief which he demands to have deleted, Gotti goes on to say:

Yeah, but you see, Bruce, these things I gotta see before we submit. How many times we gotta go through this . . . you know what I mean? How many times we gonna go through this? I don't want nothin' submitted. . . .

During a discussion in which Cutler attempts to explain the "legalese" of a particular brief, Gotti says: "But I don't want it. Since when have I agreed to that?" The conversation then proceeds as follows:

CUTLER: In other words, you and your friends are friends. It's not the Mafia, it's not the Gambino Family, it's not anything. That's what he means, it's not in your language, it's not written strong enough. I agree with it. I agree with you. I agree with you.
GOTTI: Okay, but here's what I'm saying.
CUTLER: It's not a concession.
GOTTI: Listen to me. Anything that's put in on my behalf, I wanna see it first, anyway. Who the fuck is he to take a liberty?

*   *   *

CUTLER: . . . what I told him in the meeting is, John, when you write this, if you ever say anything about anything like the Mafia, whatever the hell it is . . . you say "the government says it," not us say it.
GOTTI: And I say "No!" No matter what the fucking tape says, I didn't say anything.
CUTLER: I understand that.
GOTTI: That's what I wanna read!

Shortly thereafter, Gotti declares, "I don't want nothin' put in that they send out unless I love it and see it. I wanna see it. I don't give a fuck what anybody else feels." As the preceding excerpt indicates, Gotti insists on exerting equally absolute control over the submissions of attorneys representing not him but his associates:

GOTTI: I wanna, I wanna see that, —
CUTLER: From now on—
GOTTI: —not gonna be one word in that I don't see.
CUTLER: You got it, John.
GOTTI: You understand?
CUTLER: You got it, you got it.

GOTTI: And that goes for either George and them, you know what I mean. I'm involved in this. . . .

In discussing Gotti's obdurate insistence upon seeing all submissions, Cutler advises Gotti that he hasn't yet seen a particular brief by Santangelo. When Gotti upbraids Cutler for this oversight, the following exchange ensues:

CUTLER: . . . But with George, Johnny, it's different. With George Santangelo, I never even have to worry. I bet there's not even the slightest iota of a phrase like he says, you understand. With George, I mean, with John Pollok, I have to be more vigilant, and you're a thousand percent right. And I will. . . .

GOTTI: You tell them anything with my fucking meter—

CUTLER: I will.

GOTTI: —or anything that touches me even in perimeter, I wanna see it first.

＊   ＊   ＊

CUTLER: John, and I'm, and I'm not putting George in this category because George is not that way. But a majority of these lawyers, who you look at, are known as erudite, professorial, ah, egghead types. Will not put in the brief words to the effect "Go fuck yourself!" I know you can't do that. But they will not put in a brief "and we dispute the existence of the Mafia." I say it all the time. They won't write it down, they just won't write it down.

GOTTI: So don't let them do our work then. Don't do my fuckin' work!

Gotti's adamant stand on seeing everything that relates to him directly, or that is being done on his "meter," supports an inference that Gotti is the benefactor paying for the legal representation of others. Because it is fairly clear that the April 18 conversation relates to the civil RICO case in which Santangelo represented others, an inference that Gotti paid Santangelo's fee would advance the government's assertion that Santangelo is "house counsel" to the Gambino Family.

To the extent that a jury may conclude that Santangelo is "house counsel" to the Gambino Family and is answerable to Gotti, the proffered testimony of Gravano and the tape-recorded conversations are immediately probative of one of the elements necessary to the first two counts of the indictment in this case. Thus, Santangelo's relationship to Gotti and to Gotti's associates is properly the object of proof by the government in its case in chief. But, as with Cutler, Shargel, and Pollok, Santangelo cannot present himself as counsel for the defendants when his relationship to those defendants is itself an issue under the consideration of the jury. His presence at counsel table could readily serve as a signal to the jury that the court discounts the government's proof on this point—that the court does not believe this evidence. Moreover, Santangelo could not argue against the existence of the charged RICO enterprise without becoming an unsworn witness.

B. DR 5-102 of the Model Code
of Professional Responsibility

Disciplinary Rule 5-102(A) reads in pertinent part:

If, after undertaking employment in . . . pending litigation, a lawyer learns or it is obvious that he . . . ought to be called as a witness on behalf of his client, he shall withdraw from the conduct of the trial. . . .

It has often been noted that the Model Code of Professional Responsibility, although lacking the force of statute, provides guidance on the standard of conduct lawyers should observe.

In view of these clarion calls to professionalism and to the observance of ethical standards, and in light of the plain import of DR 5-102(A), Santangelo should not have undertaken to represent Locascio in this case when he became aware, whether at the outset or shortly thereafter, that he ought to be called as a witness on his client's behalf in response to the government proof regarding the existence of a RICO enterprise. Indeed, the fact that Santangelo may be called as a witness raises the selfsame issues that compelled the earlier disqualifications in this case.

PART III

7

A Post-1980 Bibliography of Organized Crime

Introduction

Part 3 includes four organized-crime bibliographies from 1980.* As we emphasized in the preface, scholarship on organized crime is difficult to carry out. Data are neither reliable nor readily available. There is no ongoing government data collection and no opportunity for participant observation. The explosion of government activity in the 1980s has generated an enormous amount of raw material that has scarcely been mined. It has also generated a steady stream of popular books, articles, and government hearings and reports.

The strike force cases section of this bibliography lists all of the indictments obtained by the fifteen federal strike forces between 1981 and 1989. The strike forces were disbanded in 1989, and their resources were merged into the various United States attorneys offices. We obtained the list of cases and attached synopses from the Department of Justice, Office of Racketeering. Since the list was prepared for the congressional hearings called to consider the disbanding of the strike forces, it is reasonable to conclude that the list is comprehensive. Unfortunately, the list does not

---

* Readers interested in works on organized crime published before 1980 are directed to two earlier bibliographies: Pamela Martin, *Organized Crime: A Bibliography* (Cornell Institute on Organized Crime, 1977); Eugene Doleschal, Anne Newton, and William Hickey, *A Guide to the Literature on Organized Crime: An Annotated Bibliography Covering the Years 1967–81* (National Council on Crime and Delinquency, 1981).

distinguish between Cosa Nostra and non–Cosa Nostra prosecutions; it also includes a number of prosecutions which we would not classify as organized crime. We have deleted some cases that obviously do not provide information about Cosa Nostra, but where we had any doubt, we included the case.

We have not attempted to compile a list of organized-crime cases prosecuted by the ninety-two United States attorneys offices up till 1989 or thereafter, when the strike forces were disbanded. During the years when the strike forces existed, they handled most of the important organized-crime cases in those cities and jurisdictions where they were located. But the United States attorneys' offices also handled some cases, especially the Southern District of New York (where after 1984 there was no strike force). There is no list of organized-crime cases prosecuted by these offices and no easy way to generate one. Furthermore, we have not attempted to compile a list of state and local prosecutions.

We constructed the articles section of the bibliography through searches of databases of law, sociology, and criminology journals. A large number of articles of varying quality appear in popular magazines and newspapers; we have chosen not to include them here, though particularly useful pieces are directly footnoted in the text.

Many of the books appearing in the bibliography were written by journalists for the popular market. We have decided to include all of the titles, as they provide an important resource and are typically the only readily available account of various events and personalities.

The list of government reports and hearings was drawn from the Congressional Information Service. Along with trial transcripts and legal documents, they provide the most useful and complete source of information on Cosa Nostra. We have included a few state government hearings and reports that have come to our attention, but we have not attempted to survey this genre systematically.

A. Organized Crime Strike Force Cases, 1981–1989

Boston Strike Force

United States v. Gennaro Anguilo, No. 83-235-N, D. Mass., 9/19/83.* Gennaro Anguilo and four others were convicted for six murders, two conspiracies to murder, loansharking, various illegal gambling businesses, interstate racketeering, obstruction of state law enforcement, and obstruction of justice.

United States v. John Gregory Ardito, No. 84-47, D. Conn., 8/30/84. Ardito was convicted of obstructing justice for planning to disrupt the trial of Francis "Fat Franny" Curcio.

United States v. Salvadore C. Basso, No. B-85-72, D. Conn., 12/12/85. All defen-

---

*Many of these prosecutions did not generate judicial opinions; they are identified here by indictment number. The first two digits indicate the year of the indictment; the remaining digits are the indictment number. We have not been able to determine the disposition of some of these indictments.

dants pled guilty in this RICO prosecution of the Connecticut branch of the Genovese family, for illegal gambling and unlawful collection of debts.

United States v. Frank Cotroni, No. N-83-47, D. Conn., 7/14/83. Cotroni and Lucchese family member Michael Corcione were indicted for heroin trafficking. Following a guilty plea, Corcione received a four-year prison sentence.

United States v. Francis Curcio, No. N-82-4, D. Conn., 1/13/82. Francis and Gus Curcio were convicted of loansharking.

United States v. Richard E. Gambale, No. 84-293, D. Mass., 9/18/84. Six defendants were convicted in a RICO prosecution charging loansharking, illegal gambling, a murder conspiracy, and obstruction of justice.

United States v. Frank T. Marrapese, No. 82-049B, D. R.I., 5/19/82. Marrapese pled guilty to a scheme involving fenced recliner chairs stolen in the Alexandria, Virginia, railroad yards.

United States v. Gerard Ouimette, No. 85-D14B, D. R.I., 2/20/85. Ouimette, leader of an independent organized-crime faction, was convicted for illegal gun dealing.

United States v. Amedeo Santaniello, No. 88-218, D. Mass., 8/3/88. Seven defendants pled guilty in this RICO prosecution of an illegal lottery in western Massachusetts.

United States v. Francesco J. Scibelli, No. 85-399, D. Mass., 10/29/85. All defendants pled guilty in this RICO prosecution of the Massachusetts branch of the Genovese family for various gambling offenses.

United States v. Anthony G. Rosetti, No. 86-2, D. Conn., 6/27/86. All defendants either pled guilty or were convicted in a RICO prosecution involving the fraudulent administration of the dental plans of most Teamster locals in Connecticut.

Brooklyn Strike Force

United States v. James Angellino, No. 86-00549, E.D.N.Y., 9/10/86. Angellino and Joseph Tomasello were convicted of dealing in highjacked television equipment.

United States v. Basil Robert Cervone, No. 87-579, E.D.N.Y., 8/18/87. Cervone and eight others were convicted in this RICO prosecution for labor bribery, bid rigging, and collusion in the award of masonry construction contracts in the New York City area.

United States v. Anthony Colombo, No. 85-00244, E.D.N.Y., 4/22/85. Twenty-three defendants pled guilty in this RICO prosecution of the Colombo family for their involvement in a pattern of activity, including murder, attempted murder, extortion, drug dealing, robberies, postal thefts, mail and wire fraud, and dealing in stolen goods.

United States v. Michael Franzese, No. 85-00755, E.D.N.Y., 12/19/85. Franzese and four others pled guilty in this RICO prosecution alleging the infiltration of legitimate business through fraudulent activities.

United States v. Joeseph N. Gallo, No. 86-452, E.D.N.Y., 6/19/86. All but two defendants were convicted in this RICO prosecution of the Gambino family for racketeering activities, including murder, extortion of local businesses, armed robbery, labor union payoffs, loansharking, illegal gambling, and an attempt to bribe federal officials.

United States v. Gennaro Langella, No. 84-408, E.D.N.Y., 9/7/84. Langella was convicted in this perjury and obstruction-of-justice case.

United States v. Philip Rastelli, No. 85-00345, E.D.N.Y., 6/10/85. All major defendants were convicted in this case for the domination of the moving and storage industry in the New York City area.

United States v. Salvatore Reale, No. 86-302, E.D.N.Y., 4/28/86. Salvatore Reale pled guilty to conspiracy to extort sums of money from a freight forwarding company at JFK Airport.

United States v. Salvatore Santoro, No. 85-00100, E.D.N.Y., 2/20/85. This RICO prosecution charged that Santoro, Paul Vario, and members of the Lucchese family dominated the air freight business at JFK Airport through labor payoffs and extortion.

United States v. Paul Vario, No. 83-289, E.D.N.Y., 6/22/83. Paul Vario was convicted of making false statements to federal prison and parole authorities and conspiracy to defraud the government.

Buffalo Strike Force

United States v. Angelo Amico, No. 87-177, W.D.N.Y., 10/1/87. Amico and four others were indicted on RICO charges for extortion of a "street tax" from illegal gambling operators, and operation of four such businesses themselves.

United States v. Angelo Amico, No. 87-178, W.D.N.Y., 10/1/87. Amico and one other were indicted for tax evasion.

United States v. Anthony Guarnieri, No. 87-157, W.D.N.Y., 8/27/87. "Guv" Guarnieri was indicted with Charles Sturniolo for dealing in silenced weapons.

United States v. Salvatore Napoli, No. 89-00108, W.D.N.Y., 6/23/89. Napoli and eleven others were indicted for their involvement in a cocaine distribution ring active in Buffalo, New York.

United States v. J. Michael Robilotto, No. 86-43, N.D.N.Y., 4/24/86. Three defendants were convicted for shaking down a Universal Studios crew filming *Ghost Story*.

United States v. Samuel J. Russotti, No. 82-156, W.D.N.Y., 11/8/82. The hierarchy of the Rochester crime family was convicted in this RICO case for murder, arson, extortion, and obstruction of justice.

United States v. Dominic Taddeo, No. 89-42, W.D.N.Y., 3/22/89. Taddeo and his brother Michael were indicted for bail jumping.

United States v. Dominic Taddeo, No. 89-59, W.D.N.Y., 4/19/89. In this case Taddeo was indicted for possession of a sawed-off shotgun and for being a felon in possession of firearms.

United States v. Thomas Taylor, No. 84-126, W.D.N.Y., 5/15/84. Taylor pled guilty in this prosecution for trafficking in cocaine.

Chicago Strike Force

United States v. Frank Peter Balistrieri, No. 81-CR-152, E.D. Wis., 10/1/81. Balistrieri and Steve DiSalvo were convicted in this gambling prosecution.

United States v. Frank Peter Balistrieri, No. 81-CR-153, E.D. Wis., 10/1/81. Balistrieri and his sons were convicted in this extortion prosecution.

United States v. Thomas Campione, No. 89-166, N.D. Ill., 2/23/89. Campione was indicted for running a bawdy house in Franklin Park, Illinois.

United States v. John Cappas, No. 88-91, N.D. Ill., 9/1/88. Cappas and two others were convicted while seventeen others pled guilty in this CCE prosecution of a drug ring.

United States v. Thomas Covello, Sr., No. 84-556, N.D. Ill., 7/18/84. Six defendants were convicted in this RICO/theft prosecution.

United States v. Joseph "Little Caesar" DiVarco, No. 83-955, N.D. Ill., 12/7/83. Peter Duncias was convicted of extortion while Divarco was acquitted.

United States v. Joseph DiVarco, No. 84-507, N.D. Ill., 6/27/84. DiVarco was convicted of gambling and wagering-tax evasion.

United States v. Allen Dorfman, No. 81-CR-269, N.D. Ill., 5/22/81. All defendants, including Dorfman and then Teamsters president Roy Lee Williams, were convicted of interstate bribery, mail fraud, and conspiracy.

United States v. Anthony Leone, No. 88-80, N.D. Ind., 8/19/88. In this RICO indictment, Leone and five others were indicted for running a numbers game in Gary, Indiana.

United States v. Frank Panno, No. 86-329, N.D. Ill., 4/3/86. Panno and one other defendant were convicted while the remaining defendants pled guilty in this prostitution outcall service case.

United States v. Michael Russo, No. 85-501, N.D. Ill., 7/9/87. Michael Russo and four others were convicted of running a bawdy house, Michael's Magic Touch in Lyons, Illinois.

United States v. Victor P. Spilotro, No. 86-331, N.D. Ill., 4/24/86. Victor Spilotro pled guilty to extortion charges, alleging attempts to collect "street taxes."

Cleveland Strike Force

United States v. Salvatore T. Busacca, No. 86-81, N.D. Ohio, 4/30/86. Busacca was convicted of racketeering and of looting of a union.

United States v. Salvatore T. Busacca, No. 88-283, N.D. Ohio, 12/5/88. Busacca and four others were indicted for diverting funds from Teamster Local 436 to pay for Busacca's legal defense.

United States v. William E. Dileno, No. 88-001, N.D. Ohio, 1/8/88. This was a RICO prosecution of a gambling and loansharking ring allegedly operating in the "Little Italy" section of Cleveland.

United States v. Joseph Charles Gallo, No. 82-119, N.D. Ohio, 7/6/82. All but one of seven defendants were convicted in this RICO prosecution of the "Westside" organization that was seeking to control all drug trading in Cleveland.

United States v. James Licavoli, No. CR-79-103, N.D. Ohio, 5/3/79. All defendants were convicted in this RICO prosecution of a conspiracy to murder Danny Green.

United States v. Jackie Presser, No. 86-114, N.D. Ohio, 5/16/86. Former Teamsters president Presser was charged along with two others of defrauding Teamsters Local 507 and Local 19 of the Bakery Workers Union. Presser died before trial. The remaining defendants were convicted.

United States v. Thomas J. Sinito, No. CR-81-58, N.D. Ohio, 4/10/81. Sinito was convicted of loansharking, RICO, and filing false tax returns.

United States v. Lenine Strollo, No. 88-118, N.D. Ohio, 4/20/88. This was a gambling and corruption prosecution of a Cleveland gambling ring allegedly operating with police protection.

Detroit Strike Force

United States v. Pietro Alfano, No. 84-2022B, E.D. Mich., 4/30/84. This was a drug prosecution of the midwestern leg of the Badalamenti prosecution. (See No. 84-236.)

United States v. Giacchino Gagliano, No. 80-80659, E.D. Mich., 4/30/81. Gagliano pled guilty in this DEA case, the first to involve Sicilian immigrants in massive heroin importation.

United States v. Vito Giacalone, No. 86-80418, E.D. Mich., 6/5/86. All defendants pled guilty in this illegal gambling prosecution against Vito Giacalone and thirteen others.

United States v. Raffaele Quasarano, No. 9-80644, E.D. Mich., 11/15/79. Quasarano and Peter Vitale pled guilty to this RICO prosecution for extortion.

Kansas City Strike Force

United States v. William D. Cammisano, Jr., No. 89-00085, W.D. Mo., 6/16/89. Cammisano was indicted for obstruction of justice and subornation of perjury for intimidating a witness.

United States v. Anthony Thomas Civella, No. 84-00032-5, W.D. Mo., 2/10/84. All defendants pled guilty to numerous racketeering activities.

United States v. Carl DeLuna, No. 81-00107, W.D. Mo., 11/5/81. DeLuna and Carl Civella were charged and convicted of conspiracy, interstate gambling, and transportation of stolen property.

United States v. Carl DeLuna, No. 83-00124, W.D. Mo., 9/30/83. All major defendants pled guilty or were convicted in this interstate RICO prosecution.

United States v. James S. Duardi, No. 85-00050, W.D., Mo., 3/28/85. Duardi pled guilty to tax evasion.

United States v. James S. Duardi, No. 85-00089, W.D. Mo., 5/21/85. Duardi pled guilty to loansharking.

United States v. Clarence M. Smaldone, No. 82-216, D. Colo., 9/24/82; *United States v. Eugene Smaldone*, No. 82-215, D. Colo., 9/23/82; *United States v. Paul C. Villano*, No. 82-217, D. Colo., 9/24/82. In this series of prosecutions (dealing with extortion, loansharking, and extortion, respectively), the entire leadership of the Denver family pled guilty.

United States v. Peter Joseph Tamburello, No. 83-00126, W.D. Mo., 9/30/83. Tamburello, Carl DeLuna, and Carl Civella pled guilty in this false tax return prosecution.

Las Vegas Strike Force

United States v. Anthony Spilotro, No. C-LV-83-115, D. Nev., 9/13/83. This RICO prosecution charged burglary and a robbery ring involving a total of eighteen defendants. Spilotro and his brother Michael were murdered on June 14, 1986. All remaining defendants pled guilty.

United States v. Dominic Spinale, No. 86-95, D. Nev., 7/15/86. Spinale was indicted for illegal gambling.

United States v. Trans-Sterling, Inc., No. 84-83, D. Nev., 1/10/84. All defendants were convicted in this case for forging documents showing a false delivery of chips to gaming tables.

Los Angeles Strike Force

United States v. Dominic Brooklier, No. 79-126-TH-A, C.D. Cal., 5/15/80. All defendants, including Brooklier, Samuel Sciortino, and Louis Dragna, were convicted in this RICO case for conducting extortion and murder for the Los Angeles family.

United States v. Carlos Marcello, No. 81-720, C.D. Cal., 7/23/81. Marcello and Sciortino were convicted of interstate bribery and obstruction of justice.

United States v. Russell J. Masetta, No. 87-425, C.D. Cal., 5/14/87. Both Masetta and Luigi Gelfuso pled guilty to accepting ten thousand dollars from GAR-Man productions in order to insure labor peace.

United States v. Peter John Milano, No. 87-439, C.D. Cal., 5/21/87. All defendants pled guilty in this RICO case charging twenty-four acts of cocaine dealing, extortion, loansharking, attempted murder, and obstruction of justice.

United States v. Vito Dominic Spillone, No. 84-693, C.D. Cal., 7/12/84. Spillone was convicted of RICO, loansharking, and firearms charges.

United States v. Michael Anthony Rizzitello, No. 87-459, C.D. Cal., 5/28/87. Rizzitello was acquitted for attempting to sell $1 million in stolen bonds issued by Montgomery County, Maryland.

Miami Strike Force

United States v. Frank Abbandando, No. 83-8044-C-ALH, S.D. Fla., 8/8/83. Abbadando pled guilty and Salvatore Reale was convicted in this RICO case involving the competition for control of the Palm Beach, Florida, rackets between the Gambino and Colombo families.

United States v. Anthony Accardo, No. 81-230-CR-ALH, S.D. Fla., 6/3/81. While Accardo was acquitted, all other defendants were convicted in this RICO case involving kickbacks to service providers to the Laborers Union leaders for welfare fund services.

United States v. Anthony Accetturo, No. 80-00331, S.D. Fla., 8/12/80. All defendants execpt Accetturo were convicted of interstate gambling, mail fraud, and conspiracy charges that involved fixing horse races at Calder Racetrack by using drugged horses.

United States v. Anthony Accetturo, No. 83-6084-CR-A H, S.D. Fla., 4/15/83. Accetturo was indicted for tax evasion.

United States v. Joseph Armone,No. 87-6249, S.D. Fla., 12/22/87. Twelve defendants were convicted in this RICO prosecution involving the Gambino family gambling and loansharking operation in Florida.

United States v. Vincent Ciccarelli, No. 87-56, M.D. Fla., 3/19/87. Ciccarelli pled guilty to RICO and tax charges involving the shipment of stolen automobile parts to Gibsonton, Florida.

United States v. Carmelo F. Cocchiaro, No. 87-6248, S.D. Fla., 12/27/87. Rosario Cocchiaro pled guilty to loansharking charges involving the Decavalcante family in this RICO prosecution.

United States v. Frank Anthony Cocchiaro, No. 81-482, S.D. Fla., 11/4/81. Cocchiaro was convicted of bankruptcy fraud.

United States v. Carl Louis Coppola, No. 86-185, N.D. Ga., 5/8/86. Coppola was convicted in this RICO and drug kingpin prosecution, whose charges included murder and robbery.

United States v. Joseph Covello, No. 87-6117, S.D. Fla., 6/10/87. Covello and Richard Del Gaudio were convicted of charges relating to sports bookmaking.

United States v. Robert Di Bernardo, No. 80-56-CR-EPSS12, S.D. Fla., 10/15/80. Di Bernardo was convicted in this pornography prosecution.

United States v. Anthony Guarnieri, No. 87-6105, S.D. Fla., 5/27/87. Guarnieri was convicted for infringing trademarks by selling counterfeit watches.

United States v. Anthony Guarnieri, No. 87-6106, S.D. Fla., 5/27/87. Guarnieri pled guilty to conspiracy to distribute marijuana.

United States v. Joseph Indelicato, No. 87-0383, S.D. Fla., 6/9/87. All six defendants were acquitted in this money-laundering case.

United States v. Charles Musillo, No. 89-6056, S.D. Fla., 3/19/89. Musillo and Anthony Induisi were indicted for the smuggling of drugs and the management of three illegal casinos.

United States v. Michael R. Napoli, No. 89-9, M.D. Fla., 1/26/89. Napoli was indicted for distributing one kilogram of cocaine per week from various bars he owned.

United States v. Harold Joseph Rosenthal, No. 84-14A, N.D. Ga., 1/19/84. Philip Bonadonna was convicted with Rosenthal in this case involving the importation of five tons of cocaine.

United States v. Dominic Santarelli, No. 84-854, S.D. Fla., 12/11/84. Santarelli was convicted of tax evasion and mail fraud.

United States v. Dominic Sanatarelli, No. 84-855, S.D. Fla., 12/11/84. Santarelli and Dante Grassi were convicted for extortion for the takeover of a tax shelter scheme.

United States v. Santo Trafficante, Jr., No. 83-27-C.T.15, S.D. Fla., 3/31/83. Most major defendants pled guilty in this RICO prosecution involving the partnership of the Trafficante family with the Bonanno and Lucchese families to organize the rackets of northwest Florida.

Newark Strike Force

United States v. John DiGilio, No. 86-340, D.N.J., 11/3/86. Most defendants either pled guilty or were convicted in this RICO prosecution of labor racketeers associated with the Genovese family.

United States v. Louis Anthony Manna, No. 88-239, D.N.J., 6/23/88. Manna and five Genovese family members were convicted of a plot to murder the boss of the Gambino family.

United States v. Milton Parness, No. 87-458, D.N.J., 12/17/87. Parness, Anthony "Fat Tony" Salerno, and others pled guilty to the extortionate takeover of a sand and gravel company.

United States v. Milton Parness, No. 88-368, D.N.J., 10/27/88. Parness, Salerno, and Matthew Ianniello were indicted for monopolizing a residential development center.

United States v. Salvatore Profaci, No. 84-21, D.N.J., 8/2/84. This prosecution charged Profaci with RICO and fraud in the operation of numerous companies. The jury acquitted on the RICO charge but convicted on mail fraud counts.

United States v. Michael Taccetta, No. 85-292, D.N.J., 8/19/85. All defendants were acquitted on mail fraud, gambling, and drug dealing charges in this RICO prosecution.

United States v. Michael Taccetta, No. 86-218, D.N.J., 6/11/86. Taccetta pled guilty to false tax return and conspiracy charges involving a bankruptcy scheme perpetrated against the Caramata Petroleum Company.

New Orleans Strike Force

United States v. Vincent Bruno, No. 85-451, E.D. La., 12/10/85. Bruno and "Junior" Provenzano were convicted of fraud.

United States v. Salvadore D'Angelo, No. 88-8, S.D. Tex., 4/6/88. D'Angelo, Salvadore Ardizzone, and their conspirators were convicted of mail fraud.

United States v. Salvadore D'Angelo, No. 88-176, S.D. Tex., 5/27/88. Both D'Angelo and Salvadore Ardizzone pled guilty to heroin-trafficking charges.

United States v. Carlos Marcello, No. 80-274, E.D. La., 6/17/80. Marcello was convicted in this RICO prosecution for bribery.

United States v. Joseph Robert Provenzano, No. 83-510-A, E.D. La., 11/15/83. Provenzano was convicted of obstruction of justice for assaulting a grand jury witness.

United States v. Joseph Robert Provenzano, No. 84-103, E.D. La., 3/20/84. Provenzano was convicted in this RICO prosecution involving arson fraud and interstate extortion.

New York Strike Force

United States v. Gaetano Badalamenti, No. 84-236, S.D.N.Y., 4/19/84. See chapter 4.

United States v. Paul Castellano, No. SS-84-CR-63-NTD, S.D.N.Y., 3/30/84. This was a RICO prosecution of the "crew" working directly for Castellano. Predicate acts included twenty-six murders, loansharking, perjury and witness bribery, drug trafficking, organized auto theft, and firearms offenses. Castellano was slain during the trial, which resulted in the conviction of six defendants.

United States v. James Coonan, No. 87-CR-249, S.D.N.Y., 3/26/87. Coonan and seven others were convicted in this RICO prosecution of the Irish organized-crime group called the "Westies." Charges included murder, kidnapping, loansharking, extortion, illegal gambling, counterfeiting, and fraud.

United States v. Federico Giovanelli, No. S-88-CR-954-CDM, S.D.N.Y., 2/8/87. Giovanelli and two others were convicted on RICO charges based on gambling, loansharking, and an assault upon two officers of the city's joint organized-crime strike force.

United States v. Matthew Ianniello, No. S-85-CR-116-EW, S.D.N.Y., 2/19/85. Ianniello and eight codefendants were convicted of RICO offenses for license and tax fraud and for tax evasion.

United States v. Carmine Persico, No. S-84-CR-809, S.D.N.Y., 10/24/84. The

Colombo family hierarchy, Persico, Gennaro Langella, and six others, were convicted in this RICO case of extortion, loansharking, bribery, and the infiltration of several unions.

United States v. Anthony Salerno, No. S-85-CR-139-RO, S.D.N.Y., 2/26/85. See chapter 3.

United States v. Anthony Salerno, No. 86-CR-245, S.D.N.Y., 3/21/86. Nine defendants were convicted in this RICO prosecution of the hierarchy of the Genovese family, which charged Salerno and others with bid rigging, bribery, extortion, sports wagering, and murder.

Philadelphia Strike Force

United States v. Cosmo Aiello, No. 84-00321, E.D. Pa., 7/30/84. Aiello pled guilty to conspiracy and mail fraud charges that involved the manufacture of vast numbers of sport shirts made to look like Izod La Coste "Alligator" shirts.

United States v. Leland Beloff, No. 86-453, E.D. Pa., 1/5/87. Beloff and Nicodemo Scarfo were convicted of extortion, including an attempted $1 million shakedown of major commercial developer Rouse and Associates.

United States v. Vito Buzzetta, No. 81-358, E.D. Pa., 12/9/81. All defendants were convicted in this heroin-distribution case, one of the first to involve persons with known Sicilian connections.

United States v. Nicholas Caramandi, No. 86-524, E.D. Pa., 12/23/86. Caramandi pled guilty to extortion and murder.

United States v. Thomas Del Giorno, No. 87-00001, E.D. Pa., 1/5/87. Del Giorno pled guilty to murder and four conspiracies to murder.

United States v. Raymond Martorano, No. 82-00011, E.D. Pa., 1/23/82. Martorano and two others were convicted on drug charges.

United States v. George Martorano, No. 83-00314, E.D. Pa., 8/19/83. Twelve of fourteen defendants were convicted, including Martorano, on charges of dealing in heroin, cocaine, marijuana, and quaaludes.

United States v. Augustine Mazzio, No. 80-291, E.D. Pa., 9/8/80. Mazzio was convicted of bribery.

United States v. Frank Narducci, No. 80-00213, E.D. Pa., 7/14/80. This RICO/gambling case, initiated through bribery offers, led to Narducci's conviction.

United States v. Nicodemo Scarfo, No. 87-00258, E.D. Pa., 6/17/87. Scarfo was indicted with twenty-eight other defendants on drug charges for attempting to monopolize Philadelphia's trade in amphetamines. He was acquitted but many other defendants were convicted.

United States v. Nicodemo Scarfo, No. 88-3, E.D. Pa., 1/11/88. Scarfo and eighteen others were convicted in this RICO case which detailed the Philadelphia family's involvement in drug, extortion, and gambling offenses and in fourteen murders and attempted murders.

United States v. Philip Testa, No. 81-00049, E.D. Pa., 2/19/81. This case was intended to encompass all of the hierarchy of the Philadelphia crime family. While Testa, Frank Narducci, and Angelo Bruno were slain before trial, other defendants were convicted.

San Francisco Strike Force

United States v. Joseph Bonanno, No. 79-01701-WAI-SJ, N.D. Cal., 4/26/79. Bonanno was convicted of obstruction of justice for an attempt to cover up ownership of private businesses.

United States v. Angelo Commito, No. 88-435, N.D. Cal., 9/20/88. Commito was indicted for paying kickbacks to union officials and corporate employees to induce them to sign up for his dental care plan for their members/employees.

United States v. Jerome Gatto, No. 82-111, E.D. Cal., 7/7/82. Gatto pled guilty and Bonanno was convicted of fraud.

United States v. Cologero Lomonaco, No. 88-763, N.D. Cal., 11/29/88. This was a drug prosecution of a Sicilian cocaine distribution network.

B. Articles, 1980–1993

Albanese, Jay S., *What Lockeed and La Cosa Nostra have in common: The effect of ideology on criminal justice policy.* Crime & Delinquency 28: 211–32 (April 1982).

———, *Government perceptions on organized crime: The presidential commissions, 1967 and 1987.* Federal Probation 52: 58–63 (March 1988).

Albini, J. L., *Donald Cressey's contributions to the study of organized crime.* Crime & Delinquency 34: 338–54 (July 1988).

Arlacchi, Pino, *The mafioso; from man of honour to entrepreneur.* New Left Reporter 53–72 (November/December 1980).

Baker, John S., *Nationalizing criminal law: Does organized crime make it necessary and proper?* Rutgers Law Journal 16: 495–588 (Spring/Summer 1985).

Bassiouni, M. Cherif, *Effective national and international action against organized crime and terrorist criminal activities.* Emory Law Review 4: 9–42 (Spring 1990).

Blake, W., *Role of the police administrator v. organized crime.* Police Chief 50: 60–63 (April 1983).

Blakey, G. Robert, *Law and the continuing enterprise: Perspectives on RICO.* Notre Dame Law Review 65: 873–1105 (1990).

Blakey, G. Robert, and B. Gettings, *RICO: Evening up the odds.* Trial 16: 58–60 (October 1980).

Blakey, G. Robert, and Greg A. Walker, *Emerging issues under the Colorado Organized Crime Control Act: Colorado's little RICO.* Colorado Lawyer 18: 2077–78ff. (November 1989).

Brady, James, *Arson, urban economy, and organized crime: The case of Boston*. Social Problems 31: 1–27 (October 1983).

Braga, Stephen L., *"Of all liars, the smoothest and most convincing is memory"*: A critique of the application of the Recalcitrant Witness statute to the nonrecalling witness. American Criminal Law Review 21: 425–44 (Spring 1984).

Catanzaro, R., *Enforcers, entrepreneurs, and survivors: How the Mafia has adapted to change*. British Journal of Sociology 36: 34–57 (March 1985).

Catino, Theresa M., *Italian and American cooperative efforts to reduce heroin trafficking: A role model for the United States and drug-supplying foreign nations*. Dickinson Journal of International Law 8: 415–40 (Spring 1990).

Cohen, Michael Paul, *The constitutional infirmity of RICO's forfeiture*. Washington and Lee Law Review 46: 937–59 (Fall 1989).

Constantine, Thomas A., *Organized crime: The New York State police response*. Police Chief 55: 36–37ff. (January 1988).

Daly, Richard M., *Fighting organized crime in Illinois: Tough sentencing is not enough*. Illinois Bar Journal 77: 638–41 (August 1989).

Daviss, B., and T. Hess, *Coke, cadillacs, and credibility: After a year of scandal, Colorado's elite Organized Crime Strike Force gets a chance to rebuild*. Police Magazine 6: 39–46ff. (March 1983).

Dellatre, E. J., *New faces of organized crime*. American Enterprise 1: 38–45 (May/June 1990).

Dempsey, R. R., *Integrated approach to organized crime*. Police Chief 53: 84–86 (March 1986).

———, *The integrated approach to combating organized crime*. Police Chief 54: 47–49 (April 1987).

Dintino, J. J., and Frederick T. Martens, *Process of elimination: Understanding organized-crime violence*. Federal Probation 45: 26–31 (June 1981).

Dombrink, John, and James W. Meeker, *Racketeering prosecution: The use and abuse of RICO*. Rutgers Law Journal 16: 633–54 (Spring/Summer 1985).

Edelman, B., *Shaking down Atlantic City*. Police Magazine 5: 40–46ff. (November 1982).

Feldman, Daniel L., *Principled compromise: The New York State Organized Crime Control Act*. Criminal Justice Ethics 6: 50–60 (Winter/Spring 1987).

———, *Individual rights and legal values in proceeds of crime legislation: A comparative approach*. Anglo-American Law Review 18: 261–88 (September/December 1989).

Fijnaut, C., *Organized crime: A comparison between the United States of America and Western Europe*. British Journal of Criminology 30: 321–40 (Summer 1990).

Fried, David J., *Rationalizing criminal forfeiture*. Journal of Criminal Law and Criminology 79: 328–436 (Summer 1988).

Frohnmayer, David B., Donald C. Arnold, and H. Robert Hamilton, *RICO: Oregon's message to organized crime*. Willamette Law Review 18: 1–22 (Winter 1982).

Gerber, Ethan Brett, "A RICO you can't refuse": New York's Organized Crime Control Act. Brooklyn Law Review 53: 979–1005 (Winter 1988).

Gibbons, John F., and Louis J. Weber, Labor law—section 7 of the National Labor Relations Act and New Jersey's Casino Control Act: Who will control organized crime in Atlantic City? Notre Dame Law Review 59: 817–39 (1984).

Goldberg, Michael, Cleaning labor's house: Institutional reform litigation in the labor movement. Duke Law Journal 1989: 903.

Goldsmith, Michael, The Criminal Supreme Court and Title III: Rewriting the law of electronic surveillance. Journal of Law and Criminology 74: 1 (1983).

———, Eavesdropping reform: The legality of roving surveillance. University of Illinois Law Review 1987: 401.

———, RICO and enterprise criminality: A response to Gerald E. Lynch. Columbia Law Review 87: 661–764 (May 1987). Columbia Law Review 88: 774–801 (May 1988).

Goldstock, Ronald, and Steven Channie, "Criminal" lawyers: The use of electronic surveillance and search warrants in the investigation and prosecution of attorneys suspected of criminal wrongdoing. University of Pennsylvania Law Review 136: 1855–77 (June 1988).

Gegios, Robert L., and Deborah M. Jervis, RICO and WOCCA. Wisconsin Lawyer 63: 18–22ff. (April 1990).

Giuliani, Rudolph W., Organizing law enforcement as well as organized crime. Public Administration Review 45: 712–17 (November 1985).

Haller, M. H., Illegal enterprise: A theoretical and historical interpretation. Criminology 28: 207–35 (May 1990).

Henry, J. S., How to make the mob miserable. Washington Monthly 12: 54–84 (June 1980).

Hermann, Donald H. J., Organized crime and white-collar crime: Prosecution of organized-crime infiltration of legitimate business. Rutgers Law Journal 16: 589–632 (Spring/Summer 1985).

Hettinger, Glen James, Due process in preliminary proceedings under RICO and CCE. Columbia Law Review 83: 2068–98 (December 1983).

Hewig, William III, Massachusetts law—relaxing the organized-crime requirement for electronic surveillance: A carte blanche for the "uninvited ear"?—Commonwealth v. Thorpe (424 N.E.2d 250 [Mass.]). Western New England Law Review 5: 725–61 (Spring 1983).

Hiddleston, Clark, Organized crime and labor union pension funds: Towards new criminal remedies using democratic organization theory. Criminal Justice Journal 7: 305–61 (Summer 1984).

Hughes, Graham, Agreements for co-operation in criminal cases. Vanderbilt Law Review 45: 1 (1992).

Ita, T. A., Criminal forfeiture of proceeds of racketeering activity under RICO. Journal of Criminal Law and Criminology 75: 893–939 (Fall 1984).

Jenkins, P., and G. Potter, *The politics and mythology of organized crime: A Philadelphia case study*. Journal of Criminal Justice 6: 473–84 (1987).

Kaplan, Stuart David, *The forfeiture of profits under the Racketeer Influenced and Corrupt Organizations Act (RICO)*. American University Law Review 33: 747–74 (Spring 1984).

Kelly, R. J., *Dirty dollars: Organized crime and its illicit partnership in the waste industry*. Criminal Justice Ethics 7: 47–68 (Winter/Spring 1988).

Kessler, Steven L., *And a little child shall lead them: New York's Organized Crime Control Act of 1986*. St. John's Law Review 64: 797–823 (Fall 1990).

King, M., *B.L.O.C.: Business Leaders against Organized Crime*. FBI Law Enforcement Bulletin 59: 21–23 (June 1990).

LaLumia, J., *Mafia as a political mentality*. Social Theory and Practice 7: 179–92 (Summer 1981).

Landon, R. W., *Penetrating Organized Crime*. Police Chief 54: 9 (February 1987).

Lawless, J. F., and L. R. Jacobs, *Criminal RICO: The gang's all here*. Trial 22: 40–45ff. (Spring 1986).

Levin, J. M., *Organized crime and insulated violence: Federal liability for illegal conduct in the Witness Protection Program*. Journal of Criminal Law and Criminology 76: 208–50 (Spring 1985).

LiPuma, E., *Capitalism and crimes of mythology: An interpretation of the Mafia mystique*. Journal of Ethnic Studies 17: 1–21 (Summer 1989).

Loewy, Arnold H., *A modest proposal for fighting organized crime: Stop taking the Fourth Amendment so seriously*. Rutgers Law Journal 16: 831–51 (Spring/Summer 1985).

Londa, Felice T., *Organized Crime—racketeering—RICO interpreted as requiring benefit to flow from illegal activity to its associated business—United States v. Webster, 639 F.2d 174*. Seton Hall Law Review 12: 116–35 (1981).

Lupsha, P. A., *Individual choice, material culture, and organized crime*. Criminology 19: 3–24 (May 1981).

Lynch, Gerald E., *RICO: The crime of being a criminal*. Columbia Law Review 87: 661–764 (May 1987); 87: 920-84 (June1987).

———, *A reply to Michael Goldsmith, 88 Columbia Law Review 774–801 (May 1988)*. Columbia Law Review 88: 802-7 (May 1988).

McIntire, Christopher, *RICO, reporter's privilege, and the Boston–College Point shaving scandal*. Loyola Entertainment Law Journal 5: 269–81.

McWeeney, Seqan M., *The Sicilian Mafia and its impact on the United States*. FBI Law Enforcement Bulletin 56: 1–10 (February 1987).

Maltz, M., *Toward defining organized crime*, in *The Politics and Economics of Organized Crime*, ed. Herbert E. Alexander and Gerald E. Caiden. Lexington, MA: Lexington Books, 1985.

Mangum, Garth L., *RICO versus Landrum-Griffen as weapons against union corruption: The Teamster*. Labor Law Journal 40: 94–104 (February 1989).

Martens, Frederick T., *The illusion of success: A case study in the infiltration of legitimate business.* Federal Probation 48: 40–45 (March 1984).

———, *African-American organized crime: An ignored phenomenon.* Federal Probation 54: 43–50 (December 1990).

Martens, Frederick T., and M. Cunningham-Niederer, *Media magic, Mafia mania.* Federal Probation 49: 60–68 (June 1985).

Martens, Frederick T., and Colleen Miller-Longfellow, *Shadows of substance: Organized crime reconsidered.* Federal Probation 46: 3–9 (December 1982).

Martens, Frederick T., and F. Pulley, *Cross-cultural reflections of organized crime.* Police Chief 50: 62–65 (April 1983).

Marshall, Leslie, *The right to democratic participation in labor unions and the use of the Hobbs Act to combat organized crime.* Fordham Urban Law Journal 17: 189–216 (July/August 1989).

Mass, Richard W., *Forfeiture of attorneys fees: Should defendants be allowed to retain the "Rolls Royce of attorneys" with the "fruits of the crime?"* Stanford Law Review 39: 663–87 (February 1987).

Mass, Stuart, *The dilemma of intimidated witnesses in federal organized-crime prosecutions: Choosing among the fear of reprisals, the contempt powers of the court, and the Witness Protection Program.* Fordham Law Review 50: 582–610 (March 1982).

Mastro, Randy M., Steven C. Bennett, and Mary P. Donlevy, *Private plaintiffs' use of equitable remedies under the RICO statute: A means to reform corrupted labor unions.* University of Michigan Journal of Law Reform 24: 571–646 (Spring/Summer 1991).

Mastrofski, Stephen, and Gary Potter, *Evaluating law enforcement efforts to control organized crime: The Pennsylvania Crime Commission as a case study.* Policy Studies Review 6: 160–70 (August 1986).

Meeker, James, and John Dombrink, *Criminal RICO and organized crime: An analysis of appellate litigation.* Criminal Law Bulletin 20: 309–20 (July/August 1984).

Minnis, James Clann, *Clarifying RICO's conspiracy provision: Personal commitment not required.* Tulane Law Review 62: 1399–417 (June 1988).

Modjeska, Lee, *The NLRB and the mob.* Labor Law Journal 37: 625–31 (September 1986).

North, D. V., *RICO: A theory of investigation.* Police Chief 55: 44–47 (January 1988).

O'Brien, Thomas, and Mary Jo Flaherty, *Regulation of the Atlantic City casino industry and attempts to control its infiltration by organized crime.* Rutgers Law Journal 16: 721–58 (Spring/Summer 1985).

O'Neill, Thomas, *Functions of the RICO enterprise concept.* Notre Dame Law Review 64: 646–721 (1989).

Orr, Maryann E., *The currency reporting laws and the war on organized crime.* Suffolk University Law Review 20: 1061–87 (Winter 1986).

Palm, Craig W., *RICO forfeiture and the Eighth Amendment: When is everything too much?* University of Pittsburgh Law Review 53: 1–95 (Fall 1991).

Palmer, R. Scott, and Barbara M. Linthicum, *The statewide prosecutor: A new weapon against organized crime.* Florida State University Law Review 13: 653–80 (Fall 1985).

Panel Discussion. *Contemporary issues in organized crime.* Police Chief 54: 44–48ff. (March 1987).

Panter, Danielle Ruth, *The changes accomplished by the labor racketeering amendments of the Comprehensive Crime Control Act of 1984.* Labor Law Journal 36: 744–61 (October 1985).

Plautz, Robert, *Little RICO: New York State's Organized Crime Control Act.* New York State Bar Journal 62: 20–25 (February 1990).

Pritchard, Eric J., *RICO and labor corruption: The propriety of court-imposed trusteeships.* Temple Law Review 62: 977–1012 (Fall 1989).

Reuter, Peter, *Police regulation of illegal gambling: Frustrations of symbolic enforcement.* Annals of the American Academy of Political and Social Science 474: 6–47 (July 1984).

Reuter, Peter, and Jonathan Rubinstein, *Illegal gambling and organized crime.* Society 20: 52–55 (July/August 1983).

Rochford, J. M., *Fight against organized crime: Whose responsibility?* Police Chief 50: 46–48 (June 1983).

Roukis, George S., and Bruce H. Charnov, *The RICO statute: Implications for organized labor.* Labor Law Journal 36: 281–91 (May 1985).

Saney, Parviz, *In praise of organized crime.* Rutgers Law Journal 16: 853–67 (Spring/Summer 1985).

Santino, Umberto, *The financial Mafia: The illegal accumulation of wealth and the financial industrial complex.* Contemporary Cases 12: 203–43 (Spring 1988).

Sassoon, D., *Italy: Busting the pizza connection.* Economist 293: 53–54 (6 October 1984).

Sessions, W. S., *Gang violence and organized crime.* Police Chief 57: 17 (November 1990).

Smith, D. C., Jr., *Paragon, pariahs, and pirates: A spectrum-based theory of enterprise.* Crime & Delinquency 26: 358–86 (July 1980).

Smith, Jeffrey M., and Thomas B. Metzloff, *RICO and the professionals.* Mercer Law Review 37: 627–46 (Winter 1986).

Symposium, *Organized crime.* Police Chief 48: 20–40 (November 1981).

Symposium, *Perspectives on organized crime.* Rutgers Law Journal 16: 439–989 (Spring/Summer 1985).

Symposium, *Reforming RICO: If, why, and how?* Vanderbilt Law Review 43: 621–1101 (April 1990).

Symposium, *The twentieth anniversary of the Racketeer Influenced and Corrupt Organizations Act (1970–1990).* St. John's Law Review 64: 701–951 (Fall 1990).

Szasz, A., *Corporations, organized crime, and the disposal of hazardous waste: an examination of the making of a criminogenic regulatory structure.* Criminology 24: 1–27 (Fall 1986).

Tarlow, Barry, *RICO revisited.* Georgia Law Review 17: 291–424 (Winter 1983).

Thomas, William V., *Organized crime: The American shakedown.* Editorial Research Reports 451–68 (19 June 1981).

Varsam, Nick H., *Assets held hostage: Pretrial restraint of third party property under criminal RICO.* Washington University Law Quarterly 67: 1187–217 (Winter 1989).

Wallentine, Kenneth R., *A leash upon labor: RICO trusteeships on labor unions.* Hofstra Labor Law Journal 7: 341–68 (Spring 1990).

Wynn, Simon, and Nancy Anderson, *Organized Crime, RICO, and the media: What we think we know.* Federal Probation 46: 9–14 (December 1982).

———, *Organized crime and insulated violence: Federal liability for illegal conduct in the Witness Protection Program.* Journal of Criminal Law and Criminology 76: 208–50 (Spring 1985).

C. Books, 1980–1993

Abadinsky, Howard. *The Mafia in America: An Oral History.* Westport, CT: Greenwood, 1981.

———. *The Criminal Elite: Professional and Organized Crime.* Westport, CT: Greenwood, 1983.

———. *Organized Crime.* 3d ed. Chicago: Nelson-Hall, 1990.

Albanese, Jay S. *Organized Crime in America,* 2d ed. Cincinnati, OH: Anderson, 1989.

Albini, Joseph L. *The American Mafia: Genesis of a Legend.* New York: Irvington, 1979.

———. *All-American Mafioso: The Johnny Roselli Story.* New York: Doubleday, 1991.

Alexander, Herbert E., and Gerald E. Caiden. *The Politics and Economics of Organized Crime.* Lexington, MA: Lexington Books, 1985.

Alexander, Shana. *The Pizza Connection: Lawyers, Money, Drugs, Mafia.* New York: Weidenfeld, 1988.

Anastasia, George. *Blood and Honor: Inside the Scarfo Mob—The Story of the Most Violent Mafia Family.* New York: Morrow, 1991.

Barthel, Joan. *Love and Honor: The True Story of a Mafia Daughter and an Undercover Cop.* New York: Morrow, 1989.

Block, Alan A. *Organizing Crime.* New York: Elsevier, 1981.

———. *East Side, West Side: Organized Crime in New York.* New Brunswick, NJ: Transaction, 1983.

———. *Poisoning for Profit: The Mafia and Toxic Waste in America.* New York: Morrow, 1985.

———. *The Business of Crime: A Documentary Study of Organized Crime in America*. Boulder, CO: Westview, 1991.

———. *Masters of Paradise: Organized Crime and the Internal Revenue Service*. New Brunswick, NJ: Transaction, 1991.

———. *Space, Time, and Organized Crime*. New Brunswick, NJ: Transaction, 1994.

Blum, Howard. *Gangland: How the FBI Broke Up the Mob*. New York: Simon and Schuster, 1993.

Blumenthal, Ralph. *Last Days of the Sicilians: At War with the Mafia: The FBI Assault on the Pizza Connection*. New York: Random House, 1988.

Bonanno, Joseph (with Sergio Lalli). *A Man of Honor: The Autobiography of Joseph Bonanno*. New York: Simon & Schuster, 1983.

Buckwalter, Jane R. *International Prespectives on Organized Crime*. Chicago: Office of International Crime and Justice, 1990.

Bynium, Timothy S., ed., *Organized Crime in America: Concepts and Controversies*. Monsey, NY: Criminal Justice Press, 1987.

Cantalupo, Joseph, and Tom Renner. *Body Mike: The Unsparing Exposé by the Mafia Insider Who Turned on the Mob*. New York: Random House, 1989.

Carmello, Charles. *La Matanza: The Sicilian Madness*. New York: Freundlich, 1986.

Cox, Donald. *Kingfish: Carlos Marcello and the Assassination of John F. Kennedy*. New York: Mcgraw Hill, 1989.

———. *Mafia Wipeout: How the Feds Put Away an Entire Mafia Family*. New York: Shapolsky, 1989.

Crowe, Kenneth C. *Collision: How the Rank and File Took Back the Teamsters*. New York: Scribners and Sons, 1993.

Cummings, John. *Goombata: The Improbable Rise and Fall of John Gotti and His Gang*. New York: Brown, 1990.

Davis, John H. *Mafia Kingfish: The Life and Crimes of Carlo Marcello*. New York: McGraw-Hill, 1989.

———. *Mafia Dynasty: The Rise and Fall of the Gambino Crime Family*. New York: HarperCollins, 1993.

Demaris, Ovid. *The Last Mafioso: The Treacherous World of Jimmy Frattiano*. New York: Bantam, 1985.

Dintino, Justin J., and Frederick T. Martens. *Police Intelligence Systems in Crime Control: Maintaining a Delicate Balance in a Liberal Democracy*. Springfield, IL: Thomas, 1983.

Edelhertz, Herbert. *The Containment of Organized Crime*. Lexington, MA: Lexington Books, 1984.

English, T. J. *The Westies*. New York: Putnam's, 1990.

Fieden, Douglas. *Sleeping the Good Sleep: The Life and Times of John Gotti*. New York: Random House, 1990.

Fijnaut, Cyril, and James B. Jacobs. *Organized Crime and Its Containment: A Transatlantic Initiative*. Boston: Kluwer Law and Taxation, 1991.

Fox, Stephen. *Blood and Power: Organized Crime in Twentieth-Century America*. New York: Morrow, 1989.

Friel, Frank, and John Guinther. *Breaking the Mob*. New York: McGraw-Hill, 1990.

Frost, Thomas. *Organized Crime in Chicago: Myth and Reality*. Chicago: Center for Urban Policy, Loyola University of Chicago, 1984.

Giancana, Sam, and Chuck Giancana. *Double Cross*. New York: Warner, 1992.

Hall, Richard. *Disorganized Crime*. New York: Special Books, 1987.

Herbert, Daniel L., and Howard Tritt. *Corporations of Corruption: A Systematic Study of Organized Crime*. Springfield, IL: Thomas, 1984.

Hofman, Paul. *That Fine Italian Hand*. New York: Holt, 1990.

Kelly, Robert J. *Organized Crime: A Global Perspective*. Totowa, NJ: Rowman & Littlefield, 1986.

Kirby, Cecil, and Thomas Renner. *Mafia Enforcer*. New York: Villard, 1987.

Lewis, Norman. *Honored Society (The Sicilian Mafia Observed)*. New York: Hippocrene, 1985.

Lyman, Michael D. *Gangland: Drug Trafficking by Organized Criminals*. Springfield, IL: Thomas, 1989.

Maltz, Michael D. *Measuring the Effectiveness of Organized Crime Control Efforts*. Chicago: Office of International Criminal Justice, 1990.

Mills, James. *The Underground Empire: Where Crime and Governments Embrace*. New York: Doubleday, 1986.

Moldea, Dan E. *Interference: How Organized Crime Influences Professional Football*. New York: Morrow, 1989.

Monkkonen, Eric H. *Prostitution, Drugs, Gambling, and Organized Crime*. Westport, CT: Meckler, 1991.

Morris, Norval and Gordon Hawkins. *The Honest Politician's Guide to Crime Control*. Chicago: University of Chicago Press, 1969.

Mustain, Gene, and Gerry Capeci. *Mob Star: The Story of John Gotti*. New York: Dell, 1989.

———. *Murder Machine*. New York: Penguin, 1992.

Neff, James. *Mobbed Up: Jackie Presser's High-Wire Life in the Teamsters, the Mafia, and the FBI*. New York: Atlantic Monthly Press, 1989.

New York State Organized Crime Task Force. *Corruption and Racketeering in the New York City Construction Industry: The Final Report*. New York: New York University Press, 1990.

O'Brien, Joseph F., and Andris Kurins. *Boss of Bosses: The Fall of the Godfather— The FBI and Paul Castellano*. New York: Simon & Schuster, 1991.

O'Neill, Gerard, and Dick Lehr. *The Underboss: The Rise and Fall of a Mafia Family*. New York: St. Martin, 1989.

Pace, Denny F., and Jimmie C. Styles. *Organized Crime: Concepts and Control*. New York: Prentice-Hall, 1982.

Peterson, Virgil. *The Mob: Two Hundred Years of Organized Crime in New York*. Ottawa, IL: Green-Hill, 1983.

Pileggi, Nicholas, and Henry Hill. *Wiseguy: Life in a Mafia Family.* New York: Simon & Schuster, 1985.

Pistone, Joseph D., and Richard Woodley. *Donnie Brasco: My Undercover Life in the Mafia.* New York: New American Library, 1987.

Reuter, Peter. *The Organization of Illegal Markets: An Exploratory Study.* Washington, DC: Rand, 1980.

———. *Racketeering in Legitimate Industries.* Washington, DC: Rand, 1987.

Rhodes, Robert P. *Organized Crime: Crime Control vs. Civil Liberties.* New York: Random House, 1984.

Rivele, Stephen J., and Joe Salerno. *The Plumber: The True Story of How One Good Man Helped Destroy the Entire Philadelphia Mafia.* Vinton, VA: Knightsbridge, 1990.

Roemer, William F., Jr. *War of the Godfathers: The Bloody Confrontation between the Chicago and New York Families for Control of Las Vegas.* New York: D I Fine, 1990.

Rudolph, Robert. *The Boys from New Jersey.* New York: Morrow, 1992.

Sifakis, Carl. *The Mafia Encyclopedia.* New York: Facts on File, 1988.

Smith, Dwight C. *The Mafia Mystique.* New York: Basic Books, 1975.

Sterling, Claire. *Octopus: The Long Reach of the International Sicilian Mafia.* New York: Norton, 1990.

Taylor, Nick. *Sins of the Father: A Family Escapes Its Mafia Past.* New York: Simon and Schuster, 1989.

Walch, George. *Public Enemies: The Mayor, the Mob, and the Crime That Was.* New York: Norton, 1980.

D. Government Hearings and Reports, 1980–1993

Kaboolian, Linda. Teamsters Local 560: A Case Study of the Court Imposed RICO Trusteeship, unpublished report, Harvard University, John F. Kennedy School of Government, June 1992.

Lacey, Frederick. The Independent Administrator's Memorandum on the Handling and Disposition of Disciplinary Matters—Report to Judge Edelstein, unpublished report, October 7, 1992.

National Institute of Law Enforcement and Criminal Justice (Robert Blakey, Ronald Goldstock, Charles Rogovin). *Rackets Bureaus: Investigation and Prosecution of Organized Crime.* Washington, DC: U.S. Department of Justice, 1978.

National Institute of Justice (Peter Reuter). *Racketeering in Legitimate Industries: Two Case Studies.* Washington, DC: National Institute of Justice, January 1983.

New Jersey Committee on Investigation. *Report and Recommendations on Organized Crime Infiltration of Dental Care Plan Organizations.* Trenton, NJ: New Jersey Committee on Investigation, 1981.

———. *Organized Crime in Boxing: Final Boxing Report.* Trenton, NJ: New Jersey Committee on Investigation, 1986.

New York State Organized Crime Task Force. *Corruption and Racketeering in the New York City Construction Industry: The Interim Report.* Ithaca, NY: Cornell Industrial and Labor Relations Press, 1988.

New York State Organized Crime Task Force. *Corruption and Racketeering in the New York City Construction Industry: The Final Report.* New York: New York University Press, 1990.

Pennsylvania Crime Commission. *Organized Crime in Pennsylvania: A Decade of Change: 1990 Report.* Conshohocken, PA: Pennsylvania Crime Commission, 1990.

President's Commission on Organized Crime. *The Cash Connection: Organized Crime, Financial Institutions, and Money Laundering.* Washington, DC: President's Commission on Organized Crime, 1984.

————. *Materials on Ethical Issues for Lawyers Involved with Organized-Crime Cases.* Washington, DC: President's Commission on Organized Crime, 1984.

————. *Organized Crime and Labor-Management Racketeering in the United States.* Washington, DC: President's Commission on Organized Crime, 1985.

————. *America's Habit: Drug Abuse, Drug Trafficking, and Organized Crime.* Washington, DC: President's Commission on Organized Crime, 1986.

————. *The Edge: Organized Crime, Business, and Labor Unions.* Washington, DC: President's Commission on Organized Crime, 1986.

————. *The Impact: Organized Crime Today.* Washington, DC: President's Commission on Organized Crime, 1986.

United States Congress. Senate Committee on Governmental Affairs. *Organized Crime and the Use of Violence.* 96th Cong., 2d Sess., May 1980.

————. Senate Committee on Governmental Affairs. Senate Committee on Foreign Relations. *Sicilian Connection: Southwest Asian Heroin en Route to U.S.* 96th Cong., 2d Sess., Sept. 1980.

————. Senate Committee on Governmental Affairs. *Witness Security Program: Hearings.* 96th Cong., 2d Sess., Dec. 15, 16, 17, 1980.

————. House Committee on Interstate and Foreign Commerce. *Organized Crime and Hazardous Waste Disposal: Hearing.* 96th Cong., 2d Sess., Dec. 16, 1980.

————. Senate Committee on Governmental Affairs. *Oversight Inquiry on the Department of Labor's Investigation of the Teamsters Central States Pension Fund: Report.* 97th Cong., 1st Sess., May 20, 1981.

————. Senate Committee on Governmental Affairs. *Oversight Inquiry of the Department of Labor's Investigation of the Teamsters Central States Pension Fund.* 97th Cong., 1st Sess., Aug. 3, 1981.

————. Senate Committee on Governmental Affairs. *Witness Security Program: Report.* 97th Cong., 1st Sess., Dec. 14, 1981.

————. Senate Committee on Labor and Human Resources. *Labor Management Racketeering Act of 1982: Report.* 97th Cong., 2d Sess., July 19, 1982.

————. Senate Committee on the Judiciary. *Comprehensive Criminal Forfeiture Act of 1982: Report.* 97th Cong., 2d Sess., Aug 10, 1982.

———. House Committee on Energy and Commerce. *Organized-Crime Links to the Waste Disposal Industry: Report.* 97th Cong., 2d Sess., December 1982.

———. *Labor Management Racketeering Act of 1983: Report.* 98th Cong., 1st Sess., May 11, 1983.

———. Senate Committee on Labor and Human Resources. *Oversight of the Teamsters' Union, 1983: Hearing.* 98th Cong., 1st Sess., June 7, 1983.

———. Senate Judiciary Committee. *Comprehensive Crime Control Act of 1983: Report.* 98th Cong., 1st Sess., Sept. 14, 1983.

———. Senate Committee on Governmental Affairs. *Waterfront Corruption: Report.* 98th Cong., 2d Sess., March 27, 1984.

———. House Committee on the Judiciary. *Organized Crime Commission Subpoena Power: Report.* 98th Cong., 2d Sess., May 7, 1984.

———. House Judiciary Committee. *U.S. Marshals Service and Witness Security Reform Act of 1984: Report.* 98th Cong., 2d Sess., May 15, 1984.

———. Senate Judiciary Committee. *Organized-Crime Commission Subpoena Power: Report.* 98th Cong., 2d Sess., June 4, 1984.

———. Senate Committee on Governmental Affairs. *Profile of Organized Crime: Mid-Atlantic Region: Report.* 98th Cong., 2d Sess., July 17, 1984.

———. Senate Committee on Governmental Affairs. *Profile of Organized Crime: Great Lakes Region: Report.* 98th Cong., 2d Sess., Oct. 3, 1984.

———. Senate Judiciary Committee. *Money Laundering Crimes Act of 1986: Report.* 99th Cong., 2d Sess., Sept. 3, 1986.

———. House of Representatives. Committee on Government Operations. *Abusive Labor Practices Used by Organized Crime in the Construction Industry in New York City: Statement of David C. Williams.* Washington, DC: GAO., 1988.

———. Senate Committee on Governmental Affairs. *Organized Crime: Twenty-Five Years after Valachi: Hearings.* 100th Cong., 2d Sess., April 11, 15, 21, 22, 29, 1988.

———. Senate Judiciary Committee. *Amending the Racketeer Influenced and Corrupt Organizations Act: Report.* 100th Cong., 2d Sess., August 8, 1988.

———. House Committee on the Judiciary. *Oversight Hearing on Organized Crime Strike Forces.* 101st Cong., 1st Sess., June 20, 1989.

———. House Committee on the Judiciary. *RICO Reform Act of 1989.* 101st Cong., 1st Sess., May 4, June 15, July 20, 1989.

———. House of Representatives. Committee on Foreign Affairs. *International Drug Money Laundering: Issues and Options for Congress.* Washington, DC: GPO, 1990.

———. Senate Judiciary Committee. *Amending the Racketeer Influenced and Corrupt Organizations Act: Report.* 101st Cong., 2d Sess., April 24, 1990.

———. Senate Committee on Governmental Affairs. *Federal Government's Use of the RICO Statute and Other Efforts against Organized Crime: Report.* 101st Cong., 2d Sess., Aug. 1, 1990.

———. House Committee on the Judiciary. *RICO Amendments Act of 1990: Report.* 101st Cong., 2d Sess., Oct. 27, 1990.

———. Joint Hearing. *Status of the Organized Crime Strike Forces: On the Attorney General's Plan to Abolish the Justice Department's Organized Crime Strike Forces.* Washington, DC: Department of Justice, 1990.

———. Senate Committee on Governmental Affairs. *Asian Organized Crime: A Hearing before the Permanent Subcommittee on Investigations of the Committee on Governmental Affairs.* Washington, DC: GPO, Oct. 3, Nov. 5–6, 1991.

———. House Committee on the Judiciary. *RICO Amendments Act of 1991: Report.* 102d Cong., 1st Sess., Nov. 13, 1991.

United States Department of Justice. *The Organized Crime Drug Enforcement Task Force Program: Annual Report.* Washington, DC: Department of Justice, 1984.

———. *Major Issues in Organized Crime Control: Symposium Proceedings.* Washington, DC: Department of Justice, Sept. 25–26, 1987.

———. *The Organized Crime Drug Enforcement Task Force Program: Guidelines.* Washington, DC: Department of Justice, 1990.

———. Criminal Division (David B. Smith, Edward C. Weiner). *Criminal Forfeitures under the RICO and Continuing Criminal Enterprise Statutes: (Title 18 United States Code, Sections 1961–1968 and Title 21 United States Code, Section 848).* Washington, DC: Department of Justice, 1980.

———. (Alexander S. White). *RICO: A Manual for Federal Prosecutors.* Washington, DC: Criminal Division, Department of Justice, 1985.

United States General Accounting Office. *War on Organized Crime Faltering: Federal Strike Forces Not Getting the Job Done.* Washington, DC: GAO, 1976.

———. *Stronger Federal Effort Needed in Fight against Organized Crime.* Washington, DC: GAO, 1981.

———. *Organized Crime Drug Enforcement Task Forces: Status and Observations: Report to the Honorable Joseph R. Biden, Jr.* Gaithersburg, MD: GAO, 1983.

———. *Investigations of Major Drug Trafficking Organizations.* Washington, DC: GAO, 1984.

———. *Witness Security Program.* Washington, DC: GAO, 1984 (microform).

———. *Organized Crime Figures and Major Drug Traffickers: Parole Decisions and Sentences Served: A Report.* Washington, DC: GAO, 1985.

———. *Sentences and Fines for Organized Crime Figures and Major Drug Traffickers.* Washington, DC: GAO, 1985.

———. *Criminal Fines: Imposed and Collected as a Result of Investigations of the Organized Crime Drug Enforcement Task Force Program: A Fact Sheet for the Honorable Paul Laxalt, Chairman, Subcommittee on Criminal Law, Senate Judiciary Committee.* Washington, DC: GAO, 1986.

———. *Criminal Penalties Resulting from the Organized Crime Drug Enforcement Task Forces: A Briefing Report to the Chairman, Subcommittee on Criminal Law, Senate Judiciary Committee.* Washington, DC: GAO, 1986.

———. *Drug Investigations: Organized Crime Drug Enforcement Task Force Program: A Coordinating Mechanism: A Briefing Report to the Honorable Joseph R. Biden, Jr.* Washington, DC: GAO, 1986.

———. *Drug Investigations: Organized Crime Drug Enforcement Task Force Program's Accomplishments: A Briefing Report to the Chairman, Senate Judiciary Committee.* Washington, DC: GAO, 1987.

———. *Tax Administration: Investigating Illegal Income—Success Uncertain, Improvements Needed: A Report to the Joint Committee on Taxation.* Washington, DC: GAO, 1988.

———. *Nontraditional Organized Crime: Law Enforcement Officials' Perspectives on Five Criminal Groups: A Report to the Chairman, Permanent Subcommittee on Investigations, Committee on Governmental Affairs.* Washington, DC: GAO, 1989.

———. *Organized Crime: Issues Concerning Strike Forces: A Report to the Chairman, Permanent Subcommittee on Investigations, Committee on Governmental Affairs, Senate.* Washington, DC: GAO, 1989.

United States Law Enforcement Assistance Administration. *Curbing Organized Crime.* Washington, DC: Department of Justice, 1977.

Waterfront Commission of New York Harbor. *Annual Report.* New York: Waterfront Commission of New York Harbor, 1980–81.

Index

RENNER LEARNING RESOURCE CENTER
ELGIN COMMUNITY COLLEGE
ELGIN, ILLINOIS 60123